THE WAY MY FATHER

The story of an Australian life

THE WAY MY FATHER TELLS IT

The story of an Australian life

TIM BOWDEN

Published by ABC Enterprises for the
AUSTRALIAN BROADCASTING CORPORATION
20 Atchison Street (Box 8888) Crows Nest NSW 2065

First published September 1989 in hardback
Reprinted October 1989
This paperback edition first published June 1990

National Library of Australia
Cataloguing-in-Publication entry
Bowden, Tim, 1937–
The way my father tells it: the story of an Austalian life.
ISBN 0 7333 0010 3.
1. Bowden, John, 1906– . 2. Australia—History—20th century. 3. Australia— Social conditions—20th century. I. Bowden, John, 1906– . II. Title.
994.06

Edited by Nina Riemer
Designed by Helen Semmler
Set in 11/13 pt Baskerville by Caxtons Pty Ltd, South Australia
Printed in Australia by Globe Press, Victoria
5.1-1699

For Peg

ACKNOWLEDGMENTS

It is no easy task to reminisce, alone, into a tape recorder. Yet that is how John Bowden dictated almost all of his own story, with some minimal prompting from me in Sydney. He began taping in February 1983 and always responded cheerfully to requests for elaboration on incidents in his long and varied life.

Happily this has been a family affair, with help from various Bowdens. My brothers Philip and Nicholas and my sister Lisa reminded John of some of his vintage anecdotes that might otherwise have escaped the tape. Fran Bowden made her research on the Bowden family tree available to me, and Peggy Playford (nee Bowden) was generous with the results of her investigation of Edward Garth and Suzannah Goff's time on Norfolk Island. My cousin Jonathan Bowden spent many hours painting John's portrait, and has taken a keen interest in the progress of the book.

Nina Riemer's enthusiasm ensured the project moved from a collection of family papers to a published book. Hank Nelson, as always, was generous with ideas during the gathering of material, and read and commented on the manuscript in its formative stages. Helen Semmler designed the book with elegance and flair, and a melting heart for John's dogs, and Fleur Bishop and 'Willie' Wilson effectively created the first chapter by opening the doors of *Hazeldene* to John and me on that sunny winter's morning in 1987. Jeff Boyes researched the archives of the Hutchins School to great effect, and Major Tony Gill (of 1 Watercraft Workshop, Sydney) researched the arcane army phraseology behind the acronym for the amphibious World War Two DUKW. Nora Bonney typed the transcript from John's original tapes with her customary meticulous attention to scholarly detail. Julie Anne Ford—can she be thanked enough?—had one of her notorious intuitive flashes and spotted the title. I apologise if I have left anyone uncredited.

And Ros—once again—endured her husband having a protracted affair with his word processor.

CONTENTS

INTRODUCTION

Years ago, I read a book about how to be an author. One chapter was headed 'The Importance of an Unhappy Childhood'. I have not had one. I am now over fifty years of age, and still enjoy a close friendship with my father John Bowden—it has always been so. At the time of writing he is eighty-two.

This book really came about by accident. I work with the ABC Radio's Social History Unit. Early in 1983, conscious of the fact that I knew very little of the history of my own family, I asked my father to record what he could remember about his early family life. John Bowden, born in 1906, was the youngest of a family of six children. There were practical difficulties. He lived in Hobart, I was in Sydney. I sent him a list of general questions and topics, and he taped his replies in a series of monologues. Before my mother died in 1982, our two families used to correspond by cassette tape—sometimes recorded informally at the dinner table while we just chatted about the latest goings on—so he was not unused to talking into a tape recorder.

As the cassettes came in and were transcribed, I was delighted with their narrative flow and descriptive detail. I had asked him to describe what it was like growing up in the Hobart of 1910 to 1920. Be basic, I wrote to him—talk about the food you ate, the family house, *Hazeldene*, your relationships with other members of the family, the services that came to the house, the people who visited, the entertainments, the holidays. I began to wonder whether the information on the tapes transcended family interest and might be the basis for a book. But I was far too close to the material to judge. I imposed yet again on Nina Riemer, a senior editor with ABC Enterprises, who had supported my first attempt at writing a book, *Changi Photographer.* (That book was based on the reminiscences of George Aspinall, interviewed as part of an oral history project on Australian prisoners of war of the Japanese during World War Two.) With Nina's encouragement I began to assemble the raw material for this book.

But a book about John Bowden is more than a window into the first half of this century. It chronicles a great love affair—his courtship and marriage with Peggy Lovett in Launceston, Tasmania, the forced separation of the war years and their devoted partnership reinforced during the long period of my mother's struggle with rheumatoid arthritis, that cruellest of diseases where the body's defence mechanisms fight against themselves, inflaming and breaking down every moving joint.

I once asked my father whether—if he had been able—he would have chosen a different career. His elder brother won scholarships, went to Cambridge University, became a Fellow of the Royal Society, and headed the Research Laboratory for the Physics and Chemistry of Solids at the Cavendish. Dr Philip Bowden was a friend and confidant of the late CP Snow, and the model for the caring and ethical scientist, Francis Getliffe, in Snow's novels. But by contrast, and for reasons detailed in this book, my father had to leave school at fifteen to be apprenticed as a motor mechanic.

He thought about my question for a moment or two, and said: 'I think I would have made a good negotiator. I'm not sure in what particular field, but I do think I have something to offer in getting two opposing sides to agree on the common ground they do have as a pre-requisite to reaching some kind of agreement.' He undoubtedly has that rare skill and is often asked for advice by those far outside his immediate family circle. The high quality of his innate good sense and belief in the power of reasonableness in human affairs have been tapped by me all my life. I still seek his counsel.

In this book John Bowden tells his story in his own words, and I have helped shape his narrative. Only here can I say how much I admire him, how grateful I am for the quality of family life he and

Peg provided me and my brothers and sister—a secure but high cholesterol launching pad in the era of clotted cream, sponge cakes, steamed puddings and roast dinners. To have him as a friend and confidant for more than half a century is an immense bonus.

Godammit, how can I be a proper writer without the angst of a deprived upbringing? Perhaps that is why I have embraced the field of oral history, to explore other people's experiences in their own words.

John Bowden will now tell his own story.

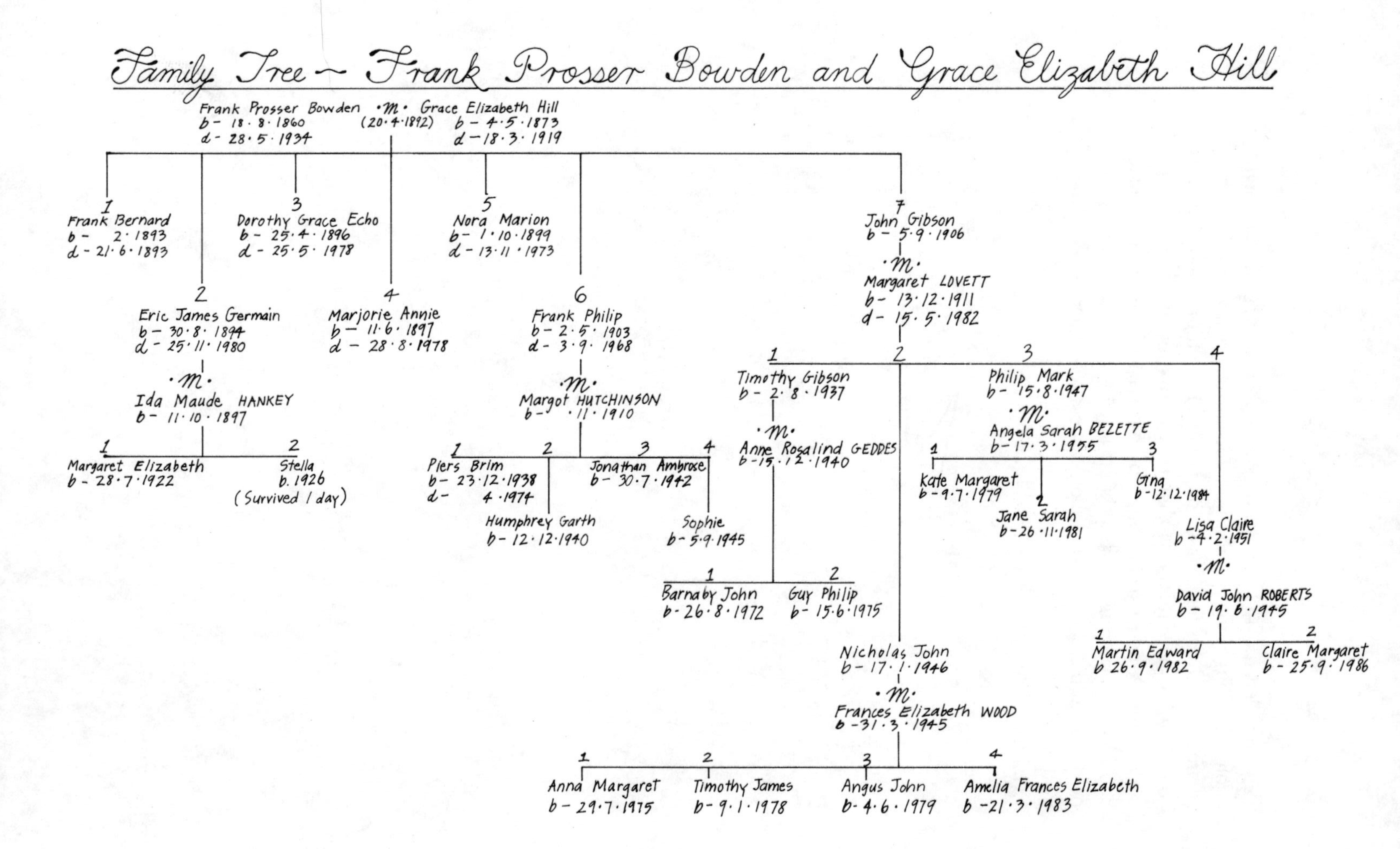
Family Tree ~ Frank Prosser Bowden and Grace Elizabeth Hill
Frank Prosser Bowden ·m· Grace Elizabeth Hill
b - 18·8·1860 (20·4·1892) b - 4·5·1873
d - 28·5·1934 d - 18·3·1919
1 Frank Bernard b - 2·1893 d - 21·6·1893
2 Eric James Germain b - 30·8·1894 d - 25·11·1980
·m·
Ida Maude HANKEY b - 11·10·1897
1 Margaret Elizabeth b - 28·7·1922
2 Stella b. 1926 (Survived 1 day)
3 Dorothy Grace Echo b - 25·4·1896 d - 25·5·1978
4 Marjorie Annie b - 11·6·1897 d - 28·8·1978
5 Nora Marion b - 1·10·1899 d - 13·11·1973
6 Frank Philip b - 2·5·1903 d - 3·9·1968
·m·
Margot HUTCHINSON b - ·11·1910
1 Piers Brim b - 23·12·1938 d - 4·1974
2 Humphrey Garth b - 12·12·1940
3 Jonathan Ambrose b - 30·7·1942
4 Sophie b - 5·9·1945
7 John Gibson b - 5·9·1906
·m·
Margaret LOVETT b - 13·12·1911 d - 15·5·1982
1 Timothy Gibson b - 2·8·1937
·m·
Anne Rosalind GEDDES b - 15·12·1940
1 Barnaby John b - 26·8·1972
2 Guy Philip b - 15·6·1975
2 Nicholas John b - 17·1·1946
·m·
Frances Elizabeth WOOD b - 31·3·1945
1 Anna Margaret b - 29·7·1975
2 Timothy James b - 9·1·1978
3 Angus John b - 4·6·1979
4 Amelia Frances Elizabeth b - 21·3·1983
3 Philip Mark b - 15·8·1947
·m·
Angela Sarah BEZETTE b - 17·3·1955
1 Kate Margaret b - 9·7·1979
2 Jane Sarah b - 26·11·1981
3 Gina b - 12·12·1984
4 Lisa Claire b - 4·2·1951
·m·
David John ROBERTS b - 19·6·1945
1 Martin Edward b 26·9·1982
2 Claire Margaret b - 25·9·1986

Chapter One

A TIME WARP

I didn't know what to expect, really, when my eldest son Tim suggested we drive to North Hobart to have a look at *Hazeldene*, the old Bowden family home, but it turned out to be a delightful experience.

I was in my eighty-first year. It was July 1987 and I had moved away from *Hazeldene* for the last time sixty years before. Our idea was just to walk around and have a look at it from the outside and, if possible, go into the garden or surrounding area to see the old Summerhouse my father and my two other brothers slept in—to get the general feel of the place. It was curious to go up Jordan Hill Road again, on the slopes of Mount Stuart. It is still the same old road, rather narrow and bendy, and now only considered safe for one-way traffic. In my days the horse-drawn cabs and milk carts had no problem with two-way operation.

I was the youngest of six children and enjoyed an excellent relationship with my father Frank Bowden who was very much the strong paternal figure. It gave me a certain amount of satisfaction to be accompanied by my own eldest son on that clear, sunny Tasmanian winter's day.

It's quite extraordinary, really, that the old weatherboard house *Hazeldene* is still there, literally as I remember leaving it more than half a century ago. I don't think it has even been painted since then.

Not wanting to disturb whoever might be living there, we took some photographs from the footpath, looking down the hill past the

Hazeldene—*exactly as I remember it sixty years ago.*

Even the Bowden paddock was still there.

side of the house—overlooking the old square Summerhouse—to the steep acre paddock where Mother grazed her cow and kept fowls. I noticed the original three big pear trees were there, doubtless still producing vast quantities of crisp and juicy Napoleon pears.

But it isn't polite to peer at someone else's house so ardently, and we climbed up the three brick steps to the verandah—the original wooden letters spelling out *Hazeldene* were clinging precariously to the peeling weatherboards—and knocked on the front door to explain our interest. The young people living inside were quite genuinely delighted that I had come to see the house. They had often wondered who had lived there in the past, as they considered it an unusual house in many ways. Just inside the door there was a noticeboard headed 'The Hazeldene Hilton' with photographs and memorabilia of the people who had roomed there in recent years.

Two of the young women, Fleur Bishop and 'Willie' Wilson, invited us in for a cup of coffee and some very fine *Hazeldene* poppy seed cake. Now, it was indeed a strange feeling for me to be there. I don't know whether I transmitted the fact that I was a little moved—I rather hope I didn't. But the first room just inside the door to the left was the old main living room, which we used to call the dining room, with its original fireplace and same old bow window overlooking the Derwent Bowling Green and also the Summerhouse.

Incidentally, the reason why *Hazeldene* is frozen in time is that the man who rents the house doesn't consider it a business proposition to renovate and the next major attention paid to it will probably be by a bulldozer. So the house was a nice little bit of personal history sitting there to be looked at. The only alteration—a very good one—was to knock down the wall of what was Mother's bedroom, to enlarge the tiny kitchen. So we had our cup of coffee and ate our poppy seed cake in Mother's bedroom.

The house was rather small, and my first memories are of sleeping in a Summerhouse in the garden with my father and two elder brothers. Further on, in my late teens, the Old Man managed to build some extra rooms at the back of the house and, after coffee and poppy seed cake, I walked through to his bedroom. I didn't comment at the time, but the Old Man died in that bedroom and he died as he lived. The Old Man's death was a happy business.

I don't mean that from a family point of view. We were aghast with grief, of course, and heavily stricken when Father died because he was much loved. When he retired from his job as Manager for Telephones and Telegraphs at the Hobart Post Office he took a part-time job as a chairman of the Benevolent Society. He became ill with pneumonia and I think he walked home from the city because he didn't believe in trams very much, but the walk home didn't help his pneumonia and he died very quickly within three or four days. He became delirious towards the end and he was saying cheerful things in his delirium—reciting bits of verse and lines from plays he'd been in. So that's why I say his death was a cheerful one. It was as though he was his old self—and that all came back when I stood once again in his bedroom on that July day more than sixty years on.

My own bedroom never looked very big when I was in it, but it looked even smaller now. Outside, the old square Summerhouse had been shifted a bit further down the hill from where I remember it, but it was surprisingly little changed. It had paling walls which did not reach the roof. The gap used to be filled by canvas blinds but I noticed the space had been filled with some sort of galvanised iron which doesn't sound very attractive and it wasn't, really; it was just rather remarkable that the Summerhouse was there at all.

Apart from knocking down the wall of Mother's bedroom there had been no significant alterations to the house except a much needed repair of the balcony outside the kitchen door which, in my youth, opened out over a sheer four metre drop to the ground below. There were now steps which led down to the laundry under the house.

I had vivid memories of the laundry, which was unchanged, with its brick square and the copper, although the Huon pine wash troughs had gone. I associate this laundry—an awful place I now realise—with my mother. She would labour there under the house stoking the fire and prodding the washing with her copper stick, coping with the washing for a family of eight—and with great good humour and patience, too. Mother was a very beautiful woman and a very nice woman and my memories of her are very fond. But she died when I was about twelve, and while I was eating the poppy seed cake in what had been her bedroom, I remembered the days of her nervous pack-up. She used to ask me if I would sleep in her

The shingles and the topsails had gone, but the old Summerhouse was otherwise unchanged.

room with her, which I did. I think now that had Mother had access to the psychiatric and medical advances of today, she could have had some successful treatment. But she just went into a decline, bless her heart.

Next to the laundry, under the house, was a second room known as 'the workshop' where my eldest brother Eric used to have his tools, which we younger members of the family used to take out into the garden and lose. He was naturally annoyed about this, but very good about it, really. He never stopped us using them. I would have. We built all kinds of things in there, even a hot air balloon. We had seen the design in a *Boys Own Paper* or some such. It showed you how to cut the paper out and paste it up into this big balloon. It finished up two metres high and more than a metre in diameter. The idea was that you heated the air in it, and it rose up to the skies.

We thought it would be a good idea if we tried it out in the workshop first, and let it go up to the ceiling. Well, the directions said to use some very fine form of tissue paper, which we didn't have, so we used newspaper. This made the balloon rather heavy and when we lit a primus stove and put it underneath it, it wouldn't lift. So we pumped the primus further and finally lit a petrol blow-lamp which we put there as well. Suddenly, to our horror, there was a WHOOMP and up she went—all that nice hot newspaper in a great sheet of flame.

There we were, underneath a wooden house with a wooden floor, surrounded by the usual bric-a-brac that collects in workshops. How we got it out I'll never know, but we beat at it and got buckets and threw water on it—but that was the end of our hot-air balloon. I hadn't thought of this until I stood in the workshop again.

Fleur Bishop and 'Willie' Wilson said that the house had a very happy feeling and atmosphere, and they had often wondered about its past. They said others had felt the same thing. Their interest in what it was like in my day was absolutely genuine and it gave me an absurd amount of pleasure to know that *Hazeldene* not only seemed to generate good cheer, but that such an agreeable collection of young people were enjoying life under its roof.

Anyway, the time came for us to go and we went out on the old front verandah, down the same old steps I had been down so often, and it was there that I looked around for the neighbours' houses which were all full of memories, too. The one opposite, on the higher side of Jordan Hill Road, was where the Kalbfells used to live. Jack Kalbfell was exactly my age and my bosom pal; he died quite young, of a heart attack. I used to go and stay the night at his place from time to time and, as a matter of fact, he showed me how to masturbate. I think I was a fairly apt pupil, but it is quite true that my first orgasm—artificially produced—took place on the Kalbfell's balcony.

But there were other things to remember. Just a couple of doors up the street were the Longs—well, just Mrs Long in my day. I think she had been deserted by her husband. There are stronger memories of her two sons, both of whom went to World War One. Tas came back with a bullet through his lung and the other son, Les, returned with one leg. I remember his long convalescent period with the leg. All that seemed to be quite taken for granted. The Hibberds lived next door to them and they had a son who came back with a kind of nervous twitch—people used to call it shell-shock. All those men were very pale with a tired look in their eyes.

I didn't mention it to the people we were saying goodbye to because I thought it might sound boring, but the neighbourhood, as well as the house, evoked strong memories. Anyway, it was remarkable to find *Hazeldene* in some curious time warp, and I suppose in the not so very distant future someone is going to come along with a bulldozer and heavy machinery and build something in its place.

However, I am the last of my family with memories of *Hazeldene* and once they are recorded that is something that can't be destroyed.

Chapter Two

HAZELDENE

My first memory was nearly my last.

I must have been about four and, because of antrum trouble, I always seemed to have a snotty nose. To combat this I had a Gibson's oatmeal bag pinned to my tunic. As people walked past me they would pick up the bag, wipe my nose and let the bag drop again.

One day during 1910 I was in our living room with Jack Kalbfell and we were playing with the fire in the grate. We were alone in the room—that's why we were playing with the fire, no doubt—and when I leaned too far over the coals, this wretched oatmeal bag caught alight. Well, I did what kids usually do, let out a yell and headed for the nearest grown-up. The fire was beaten out with someone's hand but it could have been very serious.

My next clear memory is of my seventh birthday. I had wanted a tricycle very badly and I was given one as a present. I remember standing in the living room of *Hazeldene* when the door opened and my brother Philip, then aged ten, rode in with this bike. He had a kind of silly look on his face—I can see it now—when he rode in. He was wearing a grey outfit where the trousers buttoned onto the outside of the shirt. That was a fairly standard rig of the day for small boys. I think Mother, poor Mother, made them. I also remember that he continued riding this bike even though it was mine! I was relegated to standing on the back axle while he sat on the saddle and rode it. The time came, however, when he thought it was not the done thing to ride my bike, and I was able to enjoy it undisturbed.

Looking back, I had a pleasant childhood. I have really been fortunate in that respect. Our house *Hazeldene* was on a steep block and was quite inadequate, really, for the size of the family. But my father, Frank Bowden, had this capacity for making things do. And it was to that house that I was taken after my birth in Hobart, Tasmania, on September 5, 1906.

The house had only two bedrooms: Mother had one, and the other was shared by my three sisters, Dorothy, Marjorie and Nora. I think things used to get pretty tense in there from time to time, but they got along well enough, I suppose, under the circumstances.

To house the rest of the family including himself, my brothers Eric and Philip and me, the Old Man had bought a kind of shed or pavilion at some disposal sale. I think it had been used in an exhibition somewhere. We called it the Summerhouse. It was about five metres square, and it had paling sides which came up about half-way to the timber roof. The space between the palings and the shingle roof was filled in with canvas. Two of the sides could be raised and lowered by a system of pulleys. The Old Man always referred to these canvas screens as the topsails. 'John, would you hoist the topsails?', or, 'Drop the topsails'. The Summerhouse was quite close to the house in the top part of our quite large garden, under a big pine tree. It had an earth floor, just roughly excavated with the dry cracked earth you only get inside a building which has no floor. It was eventually floored when I was much older.

The Old Man, God bless him, always slept on a camp stretcher. He didn't like beds. I think it was a reflection of his love of camping out in the bush. I can hear it creaking now as he turned over. He used to snore like buggery and fart a lot, yes, indeed he did. I mustn't give the impression that he was an eccentric, or a kind of disgusting old man, he wasn't. He was a marvellous bloke, a highly sensitive, gentle man, of rather portly build and medium height with a distinguished air. He had a trimmed, pointed beard and a neat moustache. His straight hair was parted on one side and, as befitted an executive in the civil service, he was always smartly dressed in three piece suits with collar and tie. Relaxed dress did not really exist in those days. But he did have an unconventional

From left: My mother Grace nursing Marjorie, the Old Man with Dorothy and my elder brother Eric, circa 1900.

approach to sleeping. He didn't like sheets or blankets, and for as long as I can remember he slept under a possum skin rug on his canvas camp stretcher.

I had a bed in one corner: Philip, Eric and the Old Man slept in the other corners—four beds in all. It was very nice, really. You went out into the garden to piddle. No one seemed to worry much about that sort of thing in those days. As a matter of fact, the door didn't have a handle, and someone had drilled a hole in it. Philip and I as kids thought it was designed to pee through. Mind you, we never did. We had no sheets, just blankets. Lighting was by oil lamp, although we did get the electricity connected in later years.

The Old Man had a standard evening routine. Before he left the house at about 10 pm or 11 pm, he would remove his collar and pour himself a pretty generous whisky. He would drink that while he sat in his chair and relaxed a bit, and then pour another one which he took to bed with him. He would lie in bed under his possum skin rug, read, smoke his pipe and finish his nightcap whisky. By the time we boys went to sleep, he had finished his whisky, turned out the lamp and prepared for sleep himself. And he sure slept—thunderous snores and farts seemed to shake the Summerhouse walls.

I still remember the various traumas of youth with troubles at school and that kind of thing, and waking in distress at night. I would go to the Old Man and get into his bed, under this lovely warm possum rug smelling of tobacco and with the security and comfort of his nice beard. He stopped farting while you were in bed with him. And he would talk about your problem whatever it was with the greatest of ease. That was a very good part of life.

Father used to keep a chamber pot under his bed and he had a very good scheme where he just lifted it into bed and used it. At 8 am my eldest sister, Dottie, used to come down with a cup of tea in one hand and slop bucket in the other. She'd give the Old Man his cup of tea and empty the slops and off she'd go. It didn't seem odd behaviour in those days. I suppose it went on everywhere.

I still look back on wet nights in that Summerhouse, the lovely sound of rain on the shingles and, when the wind hit the big pine tree, large drops splashing down. With the topsails up the rain couldn't come in and it was always dead dry, comfortable and very cosy. I look back on it with great pleasure, perhaps more so than if I had slept in an ordinary room in a house, although I used to envy kids who did.

Hazeldene had two bedrooms, a living room and a sitting room. You always had to have a sitting room in those days. That was kept for furniture which was used on state occasions, but no one ever went into it. It wasn't a very attractive room. The living room had a big bow window looking down over our paddock and over the town. The fireplace had an iron grate in it and we used to burn coke in the winter. There was a big dining room table and our family life went on in that room. The sitting room was used as an emergency bedroom if anyone got ill or needed treatment. At one stage Eric and I were in it with pneumonia. He was a teenager and I was about four. Then Philip and I were in there during the 1919 Spanish Flu epidemic. That was a bad time. I can also remember sleeping in the sitting room when Eric came back from the Royal Flying Corps in World War One. He came back a little earlier on compassionate grounds because Mother had just died.

The kitchen was a very small room. It had a sink on one wall and a table on the opposite side. Beside the table was the door that actually opened out on nothing. There had once been a balcony, but it had rotted away and nothing was ever done about it. The kitchen door was never locked and if anyone was unwise enough to step through, it would have been rather like the episode in RL Stevenson's book *Kidnapped* when a flash of lightning showed Davie Balfour there were no stairs outside the tower door and another step would have caused him to fall to certain death from the House of Shaws. I remember this balcony situation caused me great shame when I went to school, that we had a house with something like this stuck on it and no one ever did anything about it. I felt sure all the other boys I went to school with had lovely houses with perfect balconies! The Old Man was always talking about having the balcony done up but it was never repaired.

There was a beautiful old fuel stove built into one wall of the kitchen with an oven beneath. I forget who had to light it. It wasn't the Old Man. He somehow managed to keep himself exempt from that sort of thing. I do know there was one occasion when he came home on pay day with his modest roll of money and, as a joke, tossed the notes on top of the stove saying, 'I don't want this, let's get rid of it'. Unfortunately one of the round covers was off and the money skidded along and dropped in amongst the coals. Grace Ward, the family help (she was the one who had beaten out the flames when my oatmeal bag caught fire), somehow or other retrieved it, singed but safe. God knows what would have happened to the family's well-being for the week if that had gone.

When Mother cooked a roast in this oven, she had a special spoon that she used to burn sugar in for the gravy. The sugar would fizz up and turn to caramel to darken and flavour the gravy.

The washing up was always quite a procedure. For some reason it wasn't done in the sink which was only used for drawing water. The washing up was done on the kitchen table in a big tin dish and with an oval tin tray. My eldest sister Dorothy used to wash up mostly, and Marjorie and Nora would do the drying. There were many discussions over that washing up dish. Dottie tended to be rather tough in her attitudes to topics and people and Marge was a bit unbending. Poor Nora had bloody hell all her life from Dot and I can remember as a kid listening to the rows and other people's problems getting a fair belting over that washing up dish. However I think I have a tendency to make my sisters sound not so good. They did generate quite a bit of friction between themselves, but they were very good to me. There was a great deal of kindness, and also humour.

The only heating in the house—apart from the fuel stove in the kitchen—was a grate in the living room. We usually burnt coke which we used to get from the Hobart Gas Company. That made lovely fires and I think coke was relatively cheap. In the days before electricity that was the only room that was heated. The bedrooms were cold.

The lighting at *Hazeldene* as I first remember it was by oil lamps. They were rather nice lamps with a glass tube up the middle and a round bowl to hold the kerosene. We ran short of them at one stage—I suppose they must have been knocked about or damaged. Mother said, 'Frank, we must do something about the lamps'. But nothing happened for some time, so she went to the shop and bought half a dozen lamps. There always seemed to be a bit of credit available, which was surprising considering we didn't have much money. As it happened, the Old Man got a twinge of conscience on the same day and ordered another half dozen lamps. Goods were delivered then and they all arrived on the same day. We children thought this was a great joke, so we put the whole dozen on the table and lit them—which meant that none of them could be returned. But from then on we had lots and lots of lamps.

Before he went away to World War One my brother Eric built an acetylene outfit like a miniature gasometer. He made it from two carbide tins. The big ones were about the size of an oil drum, and the second drum just fitted inside it. The bottom one—the big one—was half filled up with water, and the other was turned upside down into it so that the trapped air inside stopped it being submerged. Then he made an ingenious gadget using another tin on top of the floating drum which dropped carbide through into the water. This fizzed up and the ensuing gas lifted the top drum higher in the water to create the pressure.

There was another device which stopped the carbide being added to the water once the upper drum rose to a certain predetermined height. It was automatic and Eric ran it all through the house with lead pipes so we had acetylene gas in every room. This was quite an advantage over people who only had kerosene lamps. On occasions the gas lamps would go dim and I would be sent outside to give the carbide container a tap from the outside because sometimes the outlet would get blocked up. Eric's system lit the house for many years very successfully and was only discarded when the Hydro Electric Commission dammed the Great Lake and introduced a hydro-electric system to Hobart around 1916.

Before hydro electricity, some houses were on town gas and so was the street lighting. A man used to come around and pull a little ring at dusk and the gas light would come on. We didn't have electricity connected right away as my brother Eric's ingenious home-made acetylene gas system still did the job. It was a matter of cost, of course. I remember a neighbour had the electricity connected, and there was a certain amount of envy because they used to leave their lights on in front of their house in the evening to show off. We noticed, in our mean way, that that stopped as soon as they got their first bill!

The bathroom had a terrible old tin bath over which was a cold shower. There was a chip bath-heater which used to be lit for the ceremonial bath on Saturday night. I can't remember using the cold shower very much, but there was a wash basin and the main ablution was just washing yourself in cold water and being told to go back and wipe behind your ears a bit better. There was only one tap on the basin.

Hazeldene was sewered quite early in my life—the lavatory was outside in the woodshed about ten yards from the house—and there was always that journey, wet or fine, dark or light. There was a candle there and a box of matches. As a ten-year-old I remember getting a bit of stringy bark from the woodshed, rubbing it up and rolling it in a piece of torn-up newspaper—toilet paper—and sitting there having a quiet smoke at the same time.

One of the most distinctive features of *Hazeldene* was an acre paddock attached to the house. It sloped down steeply at the back with a bit of a hump before it dropped away. There was enough almost level land to make a cricket pitch. We built sledges there on wooden rails, cricket nets and stockades where we would theoretically have battles with the lads who lived around us. Dried cow dung was the principal ammunition. My elder brother Philip used to take part in all this, of course, but even at an early age he had an aura of leadership about him, and organised our neighbourhood group. The only boy who challenged it was Jack Hawson, the son of a war widow who lived in a house that bordered on to the bottom of the paddock. Every now and then Jack Hawson would challenge Phil—as we called him in those days—and they would physically fight. It would always end by Jack Hawson, who was a cumbersome heavily-built boy, taking off down the steep slope of the paddock and tumbling over the fence into the safety of his own back yard. He had a technique of getting over the paling fence by hitting it—bang—and ricochetting over the top. I think Jack Hawson went through life like that. But Philip stayed our leader.

I do recall one personal triumph over Philip when he was about twelve and I was nine. We were having a game of 'hunters'. Everyone but Philip was armed with a thing called a mud-pelter which was a most primitive weapon. It was just a nice dob of juicy clay or mud, moulded into a ball and stuck on the end of a twig or piece of apple pruning. You went 'swish' and with luck could throw it quite a long way, or no distance at all. It either went a long way or hit the ground at your feet. Philip was armed with an air rifle. Most of the games were generally designed to Philip's advantage and, in this case, he was hunting three or four of us, armed only with mud-pelters, around the *Hazeldene* garden. We were hiding in the bushes and he was stalking us.

I might add that the bloody air gun hurt like hell when you got hit with it and it was also bloody dangerous if you got hit in the eye. Anyway, I came creeping around the corner of the house in the best Indian style with a big dollop of clay on the end of my mud-pelter only, to my horror, to see Phil standing right in front of me with the air gun and a leery look on his face, in the act of drawing a bead on me! In a frenzy of fear and desperation, I made a wild swish with the mud-pelter. Well, God was with me because the mud ball flew off just at the right angle and the right velocity, and hit him, *splat*, fair in the mouth. It sealed his lips together. I can see it now. His hands went up in the air, the gun dropped and he gave vent to loud boo hoo hoos—in fact, he had to pull the lump of clay from his lips so he could cry properly. Even now I am still full of wonderment and satisfaction for the way God guided that bloody pellet.

The Bowden paddock was a great thing in our lives and in the neighbourhood generally. Mother converted a section of it into a farm. She was originally a country girl from Port Cygnet to the south of Hobart and we were an animal loving family. It stemmed more from Mother. The Old Man was always kind to animals, but didn't have the kind of dedication that we all had and Mother certainly had. We had a cow which she looked after and milked regularly and we had fowls, too, but I don't think they were a terribly successful venture. Poultry farmers generally keep fowls for a year and then kill and eat them, while getting another lot in. Mother was too tender hearted to go through with this. She knew them all by name. There was one old grey Andalusian I can remember, a pretty old chook, which never went in the fowl house. She had special privileges. Once, as a kid, I tried to put her in the fowl house but I remember Mother saying, 'Just leave her alone son. She doesn't go in the fowl house, she lives outside'.

The fowls used to range around the paddock during the daytime but, at night, all of them apart from the grey Andalusian used to have to be shut up safely in four little hen houses to protect them from marauding dogs. At about nine every night, and later in the summer months, the cry would always be, 'Jack or Phil . . . have you shut the fowls in?' And we would have to go down and shut the bloody fowl house doors.

Phil and I decided to do something about this. I suppose I'd have been about ten and Phil thirteen. Our eldest brother, Eric, was an engineer with the Post Office and he had certain electrical knowledge which used to rub off on us. We used to build things in his little workshop and we knew that if you gathered a number of old, spent dry cell batteries, punched holes in their metal sides with a nail and immersed them in an ammonium chloride solution called salammoniac, they would rejuvenate. If you stood a number of cells in this salammoniac bath and connected them in series, you could build up a reasonably working voltage.

To get something to close the doors of the chook houses automatically, we had to design a system of weights and pulleys so that the

Mother was a country girl and loved our pet cow, Kerp.

doors were under tension and had to be propped open. If the props were taken away they would swing shut. Well, from then on it was simple. We had, again thanks to Eric, quite strong electromagnets that I think had come out of old telephones. We arranged some big metal hinges to hook over the tops of the chook house doors to keep them open and we up-ended the magnets just above them. Fortunately we had plenty of wire from old telephone cables: Eric was a boundless source of such goodies for us kids.

We ran this wire down to the fowl houses and put a big old porcelain bell-press switch just inside the door of the kitchen onto the balcony that wasn't there. What happened then was a source of wonderment to everybody. When it came time to shut the fowls in after dark, someone pressed the button and, some 50 or 60 yards away, four fowl house doors went 'clang' shut. It was quite impressive now I come to think about it. One of my contemporaries, Bert Dechaineux, used to think it was some form of magic.

Mother was very fond of cats and had two: Buster, an old tom, was a fair old bugger—he would haul off and rip pieces out of you at the drop of a hat; Snowy was a nice cat, a gelding we adopted out of the bush. He was a great destroyer of mice and rats. We had dogs, too. The first was Nelson, a collie, but not the sort of long-haired, long-nosed idiotic creatures you see today. He had some spaniel in him, I think. Nelson had rather a noble head and he was a good dog. He belonged to Eric and I remember it was a great grief to Mother when old Nelson died during World War One just before Eric came home.

We were a fairly healthy family, but I do recall some of the home remedies of the day that Mother used to have available at *Hazeldene*. It wasn't quite the castor oil era, although I do remember having a dose called 'Tasteless Castor Oil' on a number of occasions. I remember another substance in a bottle called Scotts Emulsion which was probably quite good because it was made from cod liver oil, but it tasted absolutely vile. You can imagine how delicately they made cod liver oil in those days. It was a white liquid and we were given that for colds and our 'weak chests' as they were called. Mother also used to make a cough mixture which had all kinds of nice things in it. It had a liquorice base and a thing called ipicacuanha wine, whatever that was, and honey. The liquorice used to be bought from the chemist in the form of a log which you chipped. Very potent stuff was Mother's mixture and I dare say it was pretty good. It was the standard cure for coughs and colds and that sort of thing and was probably as good as anything else like that you can get these days. If you felt a bit down or below par, Dr Morse's Indian Root Pills were supposed to buck you up, and their advertisements featured prominently on the sides of building and shop fronts.

We used to have what we called bilious attacks, when the whites of your eyes turned slightly yellow and you were physically sick. Thinking back, I wonder if these periods of sickness were really classic bilious attacks or were caused by the fatty foods which were a big part of our daily diet. Fats were not considered bad for you. Bilious attacks were countered by a homeopathic medicine called Nux Vomica—literally 'vomit nut', I suppose—from the chemist. It was a clear liquid in a very small corked bottle and Father used to measure several drops into a glass of water. It had a slightly bitter flavour which seemed to counteract the nausea and reputedly came from the 'Amazon Valley in South America'. Since then I have discovered that Nux Vomica is in fact a powerful drug containing strychnine, poisonous to both human beings and animals—unless used in minute quantities. In larger doses it causes convulsions and death!

The food at *Hazeldene* was good. Father had got on in life a little bit and was earning, I think, about £500 a year. As a family of eight we weren't well to do, but we were comfortable and well fed. Mother was an excellent cook of the period. There were roasts and stews, or casseroles, and vegetables like potatoes and greens. Cabbage was cooked ad infinitum. Occasionally—much to my horror because I hated them in those days—the Old Man would come home with a couple of crayfish. That was a black day for me. I was known to appear at table with a mint leaf in each nostril for protection.

We ate our main meal at night and sat down as a family of eight. Father carved. He used to have a ritual saying as he sharpened the carving knife on the steel: 'Sharp enough to kill a cat and skin a rat and take fourteen spots off the inside eyeball of the *ornithorhynchus anatinus*'. Which, of course, is a platypus. While Father carved, Marge served the vegetables. She sat on his right and I sat on her right.

Being the youngest of six children I was the last served. The Old Man had to carve eight servings before I got anything. I must say he was pretty good, indeed generous. Occasionally I used to get a bit anxious, but Marge was very good to me. She always stacked a few vegetables away to one side. We had a private joke about keeping enough for her and me. Whether she actually kept enough for herself I don't know but I always got a reasonable share. Not the best cuts of course. I used to say I was eighteen before I realised there was any part of the rabbit but the neck and the ribs. However, there was plenty of good food available. How the Old Man managed it, I'll never know.

We usually had second helpings of potatoes and gravy, which were plentiful. The Old Man had his standard jokes: 'I've never succeeded in stopping Jack in one yet', when I asked for my second helping. After the main course we had our pudding. The Old Man was a great believer in puddings. They were mostly steamed. The wheatmeal pudding was his absolute favourite, sometimes with cream and sugar on it. Mother cooked the pudding in a cloth or basin, and it was carved in slices. There was usually a nice sweet white sauce to go with it or a custard.

Because we had our own cow there were big wide dishes for scalding milk. Of course there were no refrigerators, just a mesh-covered safe in a cool spot. In that safe there was always a big bowl of clotted cream—beautiful golden cream. But we only ate it on rare occasions because it was wanted for the butter. Mother used to churn her own butter in two splendid wooden churns. Although it was beautiful butter, it meant that the cream was sacrosanct and not served with our puddings. I think that is why we had the white sauce. But occasionally the fuel stove would be a bit too hot while Mother was scalding the milk and it 'caught' as she put it. The cream would have a slightly burnt flavour which would have affected the taste of the butter. Then we had clotted cream on the table. If ever cream appeared on the table someone would say, 'Well what's the matter with it this time?'

Every meal was formal to a degree, except for breakfast which was porridge and hot buttered toast. Dottie used to make the porridge after soaking the oatmeal overnight. But Dottie had one terrible habit: when there was a little porridge left over from the previous day, she would put it back in the bowl to be added to the brew for the next day. I used to say time and time again, 'Don't add that to the porridge, it spoils it'. I might add she didn't eat the bloody stuff herself. She would say, 'It makes it better', or say she didn't do it. She never said she would stop adding it, and she never did.

So, at breakfast you got your plate of porridge and your piece of toast and you carried it into the living room with the big table and sat down to eat. The Old Man used to play his cards very shrewdly. He would read his paper in the Summerhouse, drink the cup of tea that Dottie brought him to his bed—the camp stretcher with the possum skin rug—rise about 8 am and come up to the house. The facilities for showering and bathing were limited in those days, as I've mentioned, so he would arrive in the living room dressed except for his collar which he had left on the mantlepiece when he had his whisky the night before. By this time Mother or Dottie would have cooked his breakfast. He was not a porridge man, he always had toast, eggs and bacon. Incidentally, he always gave us a little bit of his bacon to put on our slices of toast. This must have been a considerable sacrifice because he didn't have much bacon. It was more a ritual than anything else.

There were occasions, however, on which other members of the family had eggs and bacon, and they were if you were going to sit for an examination or face up to something unusual in the day. There was a book written about World War Two entitled *Two Eggs On My Plate* in which the first sign to a pilot that he had been selected for a special mission was to find two fried eggs staring at him from his breakfast plate. It was a bit like that. I can remember going on an excursion to Launceston in the north of Tasmania to watch a school football match. I was only a small child at the time and I had eggs and bacon then. And again when I sat for my Junior Public Examination.

We took our lunches to school. Usually sandwiches of one sort or another, sometimes nice, sometimes uninteresting. Nora was the lunch-cutter as I remember.

We drank tea after our evening meal which I didn't like much, while the Old Man read to us. We used to sit around the table until quite late, having started dinner at 6 pm. It would usually be a short story, perhaps an R L Stevenson or a W W Jacobs. The typical W W Jacobs short story began, 'Speaking of women, said the Night Watchman . . .' There was one book about a bloke called Nobby Clark, who was one of two soldiers in the permanent army at Aldershot in England. Funny stuff; at least we thought it was.

The greatest hit was Brer Rabbit, because we had the full collected works of J C Harris who wrote the Uncle Remus stories set in the American Deep South. It is a pity they have racist overtones because they are good stories and gave us tremendous pleasure. In fact, a lot of our humour was based on Brer Rabbit and it entered our conversation a great deal. When Brer Rabbit would outwit Brer Fox, the Negro lingo of Uncle Remus would say something like, 'Den Brer Rabbit'd burst out in er laff, en ole Brer Fox, he'd git a spell er de dry grins'. So 'a spell of de dry grins' would stay in our language for a while. The Old Man was extremely adept at taking on the manner and accent of old Uncle Remus and read the stories with great understanding and skill. We just loved it and asked him to read them over and over. We laughed at the same things and liked the same stories.

Later, when we got older and members of the family had to go out at night to do other things, the Old Man rather deplored the fact that we weren't reading the stories like we used to and that there wasn't the time to do it any more.

Chapter Three

'A WILD RABBYO'

Most of our supplies were brought to the house by tradesmen rather than by us going to shops. The baker would come with his horse and cart. He was something of a philosopher but rather a gloomy one. He used to talk to Mother by the hour about how bad things were, and I can remember as a kid standing beside her while the baker talked. He was a sad little figure saying, 'Things will never be what they were . . . getting worse every day', and Mother would agree heartily in the manner of the housewife of the day.

The butcher's name was Willing—indeed every butcher in Hobart seemed to be called Willing. Just after I was married, my wife Peg and I used to deal with Willings in Liverpool Street, Hobart. But in my boyhood it was Willings in North Hobart that traded in our area. Gerald Willing, the youngest son, used to ride around on a horse and get the orders. The next day he would return with a huge basket resting on his knees, which looked most unsafe. He would yell out 'Butcher-O' or something like that, and we used to run out to get the meat. It was handed to us open, between bits of white paper. The basket had a cloth over it.

One day poor Gerald's horse threw him just outside *Hazeldene*, meat and all. I can remember he wept—he was only a young kid—and we went out and helped him pick his meat from the dusty road and put it back in the basket and got him back on his horse.

The delivery of vegetables was particularly interesting. Down below us where the Derwent Bowling Green is now there was a

Chinaman's garden. He used to come around almost every day with two beautiful big round wicker baskets on a yoke over his shoulder. The vegetables were superb: great bunches of onions, carrots and greens and prices so low he almost gave them away. He was called Charlie, of course, and he was very nice to me. He always used to give me a carrot, a small but delicious young carrot. Poor Charlie, he was an amiable fellow but he could hardly speak English and the local lads used to kick his baskets over. They set fire to his house twice. It is very sad when you reflect on it: this bloke producing these beautiful vegetables and being bullied by the local people. I have no doubt he didn't get much help from anybody. He lived on his own too. The Chinese in the suburbs got a raw deal in those days.

The rubbish men came with a horse and cart. Our rubbish tins were unspeakable by present day standards. Everything was just slurped into a galvanised iron tin, slops, muck, kitchen scraps—nothing was wrapped. Of course, there were no plastic bags but nothing was wrapped in paper parcels either and the liquids were allowed to go in. The rubbish men would pull up their horse and cart outside and come in with an oval metal bath with a handle on each end, and they would pick up your rubbish tin and up-end it into the bath. If they thought your bin was a bit heavy they'd copy the modern day habit of tipping a bit out as they went, just to show you. They would then waddle out, two of them, one on each handle of the bath and slosh it all into the cart. It wasn't very hygienic.

The rabbito was a man named Mr Hardings. We called him the rabbyo, actually, because as he drove up in his open horse and cart, he called out a distinctive cry, 'A wild rabbyo . . . a rabby' and worked a yodel into it which was most effective. Mr Hardings wore a wide brimmed hat and a blue suit complete with collar and tie. The rabbits were hung singly and in pairs over the tailgate and sides of his box cart. He was always very nice to us kids—he nicknamed me 'Rabbity Jack' for some reason—and we used to ride on his cart. His yodelling cry would bring Mother and other neighbours out to do some trade. I'm not sure how well he did out of the bunny business, but he certainly did sell a lot of rabbits. As I recall he charged fourpence each or sixpence a pair. He'd expertly skin the rabbits while you waited and pass you the carcase by the fur still left on the back feet.

The postman walked around the streets with a big heavy bag on his back and a very fine sou'wester outfit for wet days. You weren't required to have letter boxes then—I'm talking of around 1915—and the postman brought your letters to the front door. If you weren't home he pushed them under the door. I seem to remember there were two deliveries a day.

I was always being sent down to the corner store to buy a pound of sugar, or half a pound of butter. People bought things as they went along. There was no domestic refrigeration, just a Coolgardie safe cooled by damp hessian, or a meat safe. Our corner store was run by a Mr Woods. He was a white-whiskered mean old son-of-a-bitch. He had a lean, underfed looking lad called, inevitably, 'Splinter'. He gave no credit and gave nothing away. Not only that, he had a bad habit of telling you how much money he was losing on everything he sold you. This used to irritate Father immensely. He was a very tolerant fellow, but this really got under his skin.

Father went in one day to buy a plug of tobacco which he would cut with a penknife, rub between his hands, and so feed his pipe. Old Woodsy flung a plug of tobacco down on the counter and said in his usual miserable way, 'I lose fourpence on that'. The Old Man—it was most unlike him—said, 'Well, I'm going somewhere where they only lose tuppence'.

We didn't move around much in those days. If you wanted to go somewhere you usually walked. Where *Hazeldene* was situated was a steady downhill run into the centre of Hobart and you could walk from home to the Post Office where Father was the Manager for Telephones and Telegraphs. I walked to school and if we went to the pictures at night the whole family walked there and home afterwards which was very pleasant. The Old Man encouraged us to walk.

Sometimes we took trams. My sister Nora was very generous to Philip and me as kids. Her first job was at the Army Barracks as a typist. There was a tram we called the West Hobart tram that ran around Lansdowne Crescent and finished up at the top of Newdegate Street. We were literally in between two tram routes, because you could also walk down Newdegate Street to Elizabeth Street and catch a tram into town that way. Nora went to the Barracks on the West Hobart tram and, being the nice generous

Cars were only for special occasions.

girl she was, occasionally bought us a book of tram tickets which were much treasured. They were red, tear-out tickets in a little book and what a luxury they were because not only could you ride to school on the West Hobart tram, but we used to go with Nora, too. It was very companionable and pleasant.

We had double-decker trams in Hobart on the main lines. They were nice old things but they used to rock like mad and occasionally rocked off the tramlines. They were the main transport around the town.

Sometimes Father had to travel to Launceston on Masonic business and that was quite an event. It started off by a horse-drawn cab arriving at the door. We kids always had the cab ride down to the station to see Father off on the train. We had to walk home afterwards, of course. The horse-drawn cabs were used instead of taxis and had a low-slung body cradled between very high wheels with nice springing. The driver sat up on a high bit in front and the cabs were drawn by two horses. They were very luxurious to ride in. More wealthy people used them all the time, but if our family were going on a holiday and had to go to the railway station the Old Man usually shouted us a cab as part of the holiday. I can still remember the lovely feeling of getting into those cabs. They were very quiet, the only sound being the clip clop of the horses.

One popular excursion was to hire a brake from Austin's Livery Stables for a drive half-way up Mount Wellington to the Springs. I once went with Father, Mother and Philip for a Saturday afternoon drive and one of the horses was very fractious. He went up all right, but when we came down from the Springs I don't know whether he had something that was hurting him or just wanted to get home, but I know it was touch and go at times. The driver was superb the way he handled him but I know Mother heaved a sigh of relief the moment we stepped out back at the stables. It was quite an experience though, being driven up to the Springs with a pair of horses and an experienced driver.

Mr Austin also had some land on the slopes of Mount Wellington and was clearing it to put an orchard in. Phil and I used to go up with him sometimes to his bush hut near the clearing. He had horses and dogs but I don't know who fed them when he wasn't there. Phil once asked him who did feed his dogs. Austin was a religious crank and he said, 'Oh well, God looks after everybody, and sometimes a cow dies'. We quoted this for a long while. He also told me at one stage that he didn't run his livery business, that God ran it. And Phil said in an aside, 'Well God's pretty stingy with the chaff'.

Before the days of social welfare, small places like Hobart had various eccentrics existing as best they could. An old bloke we knew as Cranky Jimmy lived in a slab timber hut on the slopes of Knocklofty, not far from *Hazeldene*. He was a bit simple, and I seem to remember he had a cleft palate. Cranky Jimmy eked out some sort of a living cutting clothes props from the bush, and selling them around the streets of North Hobart.

Father and a friend of his, Tas Long, used to go for walks in the bush at the weekends. It started to rain heavily on one occasion, and they sheltered in Cranky Jimmy's hut. There wasn't much shelter as it happened, because the rain poured in through a large hole in the roof. The Old Man casually asked Jimmy why he hadn't fixed the leak.

'When it's raining, it's too wet to go up there—and when it's fine, it doesn't matter'!

Not a bad philosophy of life when you come to think about it.

There weren't many cars about in my early years in Hobart, although the wealthier people had them. When I was about ten I can remember going to Swansea on the East Coast for a holiday. We went in an old Berliet which was a vehicle with rows of seats in it and a canvas hood that pulled over the top. Its straps went down to the front of the bonnet. Not far out of Hobart the East Coast Highway crosses two causeways over the shallow estuary of Pittwater and there was a loud bang as a tyre punctured. I can remember the driver saying, 'Well, there's the first'. He changed the tyre and we went on. This was during World War One and the bus was absolutely overcrowded. There were two soldiers on board, and they sat happily on the big flowing mudguards for the entire journey. It was all very cheerful.

At Swansea our host was a man called Morris who ran the general store. He had a T Model Ford and he used to drive us to the Swan River for bream fishing. There was no bitumen and all the roads were unsealed. They were dusty but, curiously enough, quite smooth. Corrugations were something brought about by pneumatic tyres, I think, and the springing of the modern car. The main roads were quite well constructed, but were quickly ruined by more modern cars. They got bad by the late 1920s. I remember when parlour coaches were introduced on the Hobart to Launceston run. They were Fageols and were very fine looking buses, but they corrugated the highway. It was terrible—two- to three-inch deep corrugations all the way. If you were driving a motor car you just bounced from one side of the road to the other.

Sunday was a very important day in our lives. Father was the choir master at Holy Trinity Church and a lay reader. Mother sang in the choir and so did Philip and I as boy sopranos. Incidentally, the Old Man couldn't read music but he had an excellent ear and could follow a score instinctively so it was not as big a problem for

The older women dressed in black, to the left of this family group, are old Aunty Lizzie Chaplin and Aunt Annie Fryer who worried so much about our social status.

him as it might have been had he not been so naturally musical. Each Sunday we would go to church in the morning, sing in the choir and come home for midday dinner. I'm referring to the period from 1910 onward. Somehow Mother organised the midday dinner. I am sure my sisters helped as they didn't go to church very often. I don't know why they weren't in the choir also.

Sunday dinner was a big deal, with roast beef or a leg of lamb, and there were at least two or three regular visitors. One was Ida Morris, the organist at Holy Trinity Church, who used to walk home with us after the service. She was a spinster lady who lived alone. She played without any musical expression at all, but she had the invaluable attribute of being able to sight-read any music that was put in front of her. No problem at all. I remember one occasion at choir practice when we decided to try Haydn's Gloria from the Twelfth Mass—I've never heard it since—and old Ida propped up the music in front of her. You heard all the stops and things, plop, plop, plop, coming out, then away she went, pedals thumping and heaving. She played it according to the book and, indeed, we sang it.

Another regular visitor was a maiden lady of considerable age, Elizabeth Chaplin. We called her Aunty Lizzie but she was not a relation. She wasn't very literate and I don't know what the connection was with our family. My sister Dorothy did a great deal for her and would visit her dingy little room in North Hobart if she got ill or needed help in any way. Elderly single women could lead very miserable lives in those days. Both Ida Morris and Aunty Lizzie lived alone in rooms they rented for about five shillings a week, and somehow managed to get by. I'm sure the Sunday lunches at *Hazeldene* were very important to them, and my parents realised that.

Elizabeth Chaplin was considerably older than Ida Morris. She wore one of those Queen Victoria-style toques—a kind of black bonnet, sequinned and tied under the chin with a black bow—with a veil that came down over her face. They were old women's hats, therefore when you put one on, you were an old woman. It was a rather becoming thing in a way. It opened up in the front, rather like a halo.

I can see Aunty Lizzie now. I suppose she must have been in her seventies. She looked awfully old to me. She used to totter up the steep hill, up Jordan Hill Road, and sit on the slatted verandah seat before lunch. The Old Man would go out the front door and say, 'Lizzie, how about a little drop of . . .', and she would say, 'Oh thank you Frank', and he would pour her a whisky. She would roll up the veil clear of her nose and mouth and drink her whisky while she recovered her strength. She was a nice old thing but I don't think she amounted to much judging by her limited conversation, although if things weren't all she thought they ought to be with the dinner, she let you know!

I can remember Mother saying nervously one day, 'Frank, I'm afraid this beef is rather tough'. Old Lizzie looked up from her knife and fork, poked a bit round her plate and said, 'Bit of old bullock, if you ask me'. That was remembered in the family for a long while.

After Sunday lunch the Old Man turned on cider. I hated the bloody stuff and I hate it now. I used to get a little in the bottom of a glass. It was the real dinky-di fizzy Mercury cider. Then we would sit down at the table over a cup of tea and he would read to us from well loved books.

There was also a woman who came to *Hazeldene* a great deal in my early childhood. Her name was Grace Ward and for the life of me I can't remember whether she lived in the house or whether she just came every day. God knows where she slept if she did stay with us. She must have been in her thirties or forties. I was only a small boy and everybody seemed old, but she was not unattractive. She was a kind of housekeeper who used to help Mother; I think she sang for her supper, as it were. Grace was a disciplinarian with us kids and I remember being in awe of her. I was never in awe of Mother; we respected and loved her, but with Grace you watched your step a bit.

An old bloke named Cyril Harbottle used to come to the house to visit. He was my godfather and I still have a silver serviette ring with my initials, J B, that he gave me at my christening. He was a kindly, gentle fellow and he died when I was about ten years old. I think he was my first bereavement.

One day I was talking to Mother in the wash house underneath our house. There were several rooms there, one of which was floored and used as a workshop, and the wash house, like the Summerhouse, was unfloored and was used as a laundry. There was a bricked-up copper with a fire underneath and wash troughs. I remember Mother was washing—God, she must have had some washing to do—and I was holding the old white cat and asking her what it meant that Cyril had 'died'.

She said, 'Jack, you'll never see Cyril again', and she explained death to me. I can remember feeling very sad and I've no doubt I forgot it soon afterwards, but I'm sure we missed him. Cyril Harbottle was a tailor by trade and used to make us all sorts of beautiful toys. He made one animal like a big seal. It sat on a trolley with little wooden wheels and you could ride around the room on it. It was beautifully made but we took this talent for granted, I'm sure. One toy was an Aunt Sally that you threw things at and, if you hit it, it swung right over. Cyril was a nice man. I think he hovered around Grace Ward but she would have none of him. He was just a sad, affectionate man around the place. I know Mother was very fond of him. I think he was a fairly ineffectual fellow.

Then there was Percy. Now, I can't get away from the fact that he was called Percy Grainger! I don't want to downgrade the real Percy Grainger, but his namesake looked as though he could have written some of Grainger's more florid music like 'Molly On The

Shore'. He was a flamboyant character with curly hair and I seem to picture him in spangled trousers like a Cockney, although that was probably not so. He used to come to the house and to the summer camps we had on top of nearby Mount Stuart.

I don't think Mother altogether approved of Percy. The attraction was the organist, Ida Morris. I think of her as being old, but she could have been in her late twenties or early thirties. Percy used to do a dance which Mother disapproved of very much and which was called the Rooster Dance. He used to do it for Ida Morris's benefit. As he did it, Ida would throw her hands in the air and say things like, 'Oh Percy stop it, you'll be the death of me'. I don't recall what became of Percy, but he was one of the more colourful characters to come to *Hazeldene* in those early days.

One very popular visitor was a man called Bradshaw Major. He was a professional pianist of considerable ability who used to teach the piano and who played in orchestras. One of his biggest jobs was musical director of Alan Wilkie's travelling Shakespearian company, where he not only conducted the orchestra, but also composed a good deal of the music used in the productions. He was a close friend of my parents and, of course, whenever he came to the house he played. Everybody did in those days. We weren't all gummed up with television, and people performed in any way they could. Perhaps we were simpler souls then.

Brad was a pretty heavy handed pianist and on one occasion he was belting out Schubert's March Militaire when three hammers broke off and flew right out into the middle of the room just like in a comic film. Poor old Brad was most embarrassed and got up, grabbed the hammers and tried to hide them. We all laughed, and so did he—but his laughter had a slightly hollow ring. The next day a piano tuner called to replace the hammers.

Later on I can remember him talking to Father about a young girl he and others who were members of various musical organisations had discovered. He wanted the Old Man to subscribe to a fund to send this little girl overseas for advanced musical training as a pianist. She was about fourteen at the time and her name was Eileen Joyce. I believe they did help to finance her overseas tuition and she became a very well known pianist.

Bradshaw Major was a German and he had some difficulty volunteering for World War One. He was a bit long in the tooth as well, but he stuck to it and eventually managed to get into the Pioneers where you did fatigue duties like cleaning up muck and tidying up things. He did go to France and was full of interesting stories about the war. You can imagine how popular he was with the troops whenever there was a piano available. In fact, the war changed Brad's approach to music. He used to be very stiff and classical about his approach, but after the war he'd roll anything off like 'Tipperary' and all the songs he played for the troops.

On one occasion he was scrubbing out a hall to be used for a piano recital in which one of the items was to be a duet—music for four hands. One of the celebrity pianists turned up to practise but his partner didn't. It's not impossible, being France, he might have been killed! Anyway, Brad, who was swabbing the floor with an old mop, suggested to the virtuoso pianist that he might like him to play through the piece with him.

The virtuoso thought he was joking, of course, but Brad persisted and offered to help him practise. Somewhat incredulously the Great Man sat down at the keyboard with Brad, discussed what he wanted, produced his music and away they went—right through non-stop. When they finished, the virtuoso is supposed to have said, 'My God, I hope my partner doesn't turn up because you're a much better pianist than he is'. That was the kind of story that used to unfold about old Brad.

Unfortunately he had a row with Alan Wilkie, the director of the touring Shakespearian company, and left. Brad was rather a touchy fellow. Afterwards he discovered he had signed a document that ensured all the music he had composed for the productions remained the property of Alan Wilkie. He was very sad and bitter about that.

Our neighbours were a mixed bunch as most people's neighbours are. Directly opposite us in Jordan Hill Road were the Hibberds. I mention them because they adopted a girl called Claire who became a great family friend. It was a curious kind of adoption, done well before proper procedures were established. The tragic thing is that no one ever told Claire she was adopted, although I knew she was when we played together as seven-year-old kids. She only found out after her husband died in his sixties. By then it

Claire Hibberd and I often used to play together.

was too late to find out anything much about her origins. My sister Marjorie remembered that Claire was handed over at the bottom of the gangway of the boat that brought her to Hobart from Sydney, but that's all that is known. Claire always felt she was different from the rest of the Hibberds.

The Kalbfell family also lived across the road. Their son Jack, my childhood buddy, was a friend for most of our lives. I mention him because of a coincidence, really. He eventually bought or rented the house exactly opposite the house I built, after I married, in Maning Avenue, Sandy Bay.

Then there were the Chandlers. Phemie Chandler was a great friend of my sisters. Her name was Euphemia Selena Chandler and her parents were horticulturalists. They didn't call them that in those days, but they had to do with nurseries and producing plants. Phemie married a chap named Ted Hopkins who later managed Sydney's Luna Park for many years. But the point of the story is Ted's father Tommy Hopkins, who was quite a character. Tommy was a professional musician who gathered together a small orchestra and used to play at the picture theatres during the silent movies. He played the cornet.

Once seen Tommy was not quickly forgotten. He didn't have a hair on his head and affected the most awful and obvious red wig.

I remember he had an old motor boat which we christened 'The Coffin' because it was completely enclosed and the only way you could get your head out into the fresh air was to stick it through a hatch. It was like a floating box. Tommy used to put a hat on, and tie hat and wig in place with a handkerchief right around it and under his chin against the inevitable Hobart summer sea breeze.

There are many stories about Tommy Hopkins. He suffered from gout and I fail to see any humour in this because I have it myself! Anyway, his orchestra was playing away one day for a Charlie Chaplin film, and Tommy had his gouty foot bandaged and propped up on a little stool. It so happened that a comedy sketch in the film centred on a man in a wheelchair with a gouty foot. When Charlie Chaplin, or whichever comic it was, stamped on the foot of the unfortunate man in the wheelchair it was too much for Tommy Hopkins. His cornet sort of split the air, he let out a roar of sympathetic agony and was most upset about the whole thing.

Tommy had a bit of a booze problem and one time he was warming up for a really good session with some of the lads of the town when a friend who could see what was about to happen went up to him and said, 'Tommy, no more. Don't drink that one, you've had enough.' Of course, Tommy said, 'Oh come on, what nonsense, we're just having a good time'. The friend was getting very worried because once Tommy got going there was no stopping him. He tried all the persuasion he could and got nowhere. Finally he said, 'Tommy, if you have that drink, I'll go straight away and tell Frank Bowden'.

Tommy put his glass down instantly and said, 'For Christ's sake old man, no no, don't do that. I won't drink it. Come on, take me home.' The Old Man never knew why he had that effect on Tommy Hopkins because he was certainly no wowser himself.

On one occasion Tommy had worked out a score for a particular film in which the flute player had a twenty bar rest. When the interval came the owner of the cinema said to Tommy, 'Why wasn't that bloke playing his flute just then?' Tommy said, 'Oh he had a long twenty bar rest. He isn't supposed to play his flute during that. It wasn't in the music.' The owner said, 'Well get some music that makes them play all the time. I'm not paying these blokes to sit on their arses and do nothing!'

One of Father's greatest friends, Lucien Dechaineux, used to come to *Hazeldene* a great deal. He was a Belgian, and principal of the Hobart Technical College. As well as running the college he was the head artist in the Art Department. He taught not only technical drawing but art and sculpture and all the crafts like enamelware. Just one of those jobs would have been enough for any other man, but Lucien ran the lot. One of his ex-pupils told me he remembered on many occasions Lucien would be in the middle of a lecture when someone would come in and tell him that he was wanted on the phone on some administrative matter.

His close friendship with Father is reflected by the number of his paintings that were in the house. Although he lived most of his long life in Tasmania he never lost his heavy French accent. Lucien's son, Emil, joined the navy as a midshipman or naval cadet and went to Jervis Bay. He used to come home for the holidays. Emil Dechaineux was the captain of HMAS *Australia* in World War Two, and was killed on the bridge by a Japanese kamikaze attack in October 1944. He became a very sophisticated young man during his cadetship and always used to have a large number of packets of State Express cigarettes. We all smoked them. I don't know how old I was but I used to smoke them also. Smoking was the thing of the day. It was not a matter of 'if' you smoked. When you turned sixteen you discussed with your father what brand of cigarettes or pipe tobacco you would use.

I had been smoking on and off for years as a teenager, ranging from stringy bark rolled up in newspaper to tobacco when I could get it. At this time I did something which was pretty awful. It didn't worry me at the time and still doesn't, really, but I have never told anybody about it.

When Mother was in hospital very ill, I went to see her after school, and on one occasion she gave me a shilling. I took the shilling and put it in my little drawer at home and kept it. After she died you'd have thought I'd have treasured this and had a hole drilled in it and hung it around my neck. I wish I had kept it actually. Do you know what I did? Jack Kalbfell, my friend opposite, had discovered a place where you could buy cherry wood pipes for a shilling, and he had bought one. We used to get tea leaves out of the caddy and smoke them, sharing the one pipe. He pointed out that I should have a pipe of my own, and I said, 'Oh yes, I've got a shilling'. And that's what I did with Mother's shilling. I bought myself a little cherry wood pipe and a tobacco pouch. I was twelve at the time.

We used to go down the paddock, literally behind the toilet, and smoke tea leaves which made us feel a bit queer. Years later a medical friend of mine, David Waterworth, told me that there is a toxic effect created by burning tea and inhaling the smoke which can be quite serious. Still, we did, and here we are.

Chapter Four

CHOPPINGS

My travel horizons were considerably widened when I was about twelve by inheriting my brother Phil's pushbike. It had three gears and was a superior bike. I rode quite long distances on it. About this time, 1919, I used to visit a family called Chopping, who had a farm at Woodbridge south of Hobart, during school holidays. Trading steamers and sailing ketches plied the waters around the coast, particularly between Hobart and the Channel region, down to places like Woodbridge, Kettering and Margate. At the end of one holiday I rode my bike down to the jetty to wait for the steamer *Dover* that would take me back to Hobart.

As I reached the end of the jetty a sailing ketch, *May Queen*, was leaving with a load of apples to go to town. I called out, 'Can I have a ride?' The skipper said, 'Yes son, hop on. You can bring your bike'. There was a lovely sea breeze and this superb old ship with two masts and big topsails took off for Hobart. As we sailed past Kettering another similar ketch was coming down and signalled him to sail close. Much to my dismay the other skipper said we had to turn around and go back to pick up a big load of timber from Southport to take somewhere else.

My skipper said, 'Oh Christ, son, what about you? If I land you at Kettering can you ride back to town?' I said of course I could. Kettering is only a short distance from Woodbridge—I hadn't gained much. So he did, and he must have cursed me because it took an hour or so to sail in and drop me off on the jetty with my bike. I was really only a bloody nuisance to him but, bless his heart, he put his hand in his pocket and gave me eight two-shilling pieces. Now, that was a lot of money and I remonstrated with him, but he said, 'No take it son, you might need it'. His name was Mackay and he was a nice fellow. He needn't have done that.

River steamers also plied the Channel district. They used to call at all the ports, Kettering, Woodbridge, Flowerpot, Gordon and so on, and around Blubber Head into Port Esperance. They used to go up the Huon, almost right up to Huonville sometimes, carting apples. There were the *Dover*, the *Cartela*, the *Togo* and the *Excella*. And then there were the beautiful ketches like the *Heather Belle*, *Mystery*, *Lenna* and *May Queen*. There was one steamer called the *Huon* when I was a lad. She was coming up to Hobart once with a load of fruit—she had too much cargo I've no doubt—and it was blowing a hard westerly. The wind and swell got her and she capsized. Three or four people drowned, I think, including the captain. It was quite a sad story. Oddly enough the capsize occurred almost in the identical place where my mother's father, Walter Hill, was drowned when a yacht he was on capsized off Woodbridge.

My association with the Chopping family was an important part of my schooldays and, indeed, my life. The connection was made through my sisters Marjorie and Nora. They were at business college with Dorothy Chopping, and invited her home to *Hazeldene*. She had a great sense of humour and got on well with our lot. She invited me to stay with them on their farm at Woodbridge for the mid-winter holidays.

Her father's name was Isaac H Chopping. He was an interesting old man. I don't know whether he was West Indian or Aboriginal. He was black, had a pointed beard and was a man of considerable education and culture. He was also as tough as old boots, but he was elderly and running the property was getting too much for him.

His son, Lin, had left the Royal Australian Navy and come home to settle on the property to run it and help the old man out. I guess this was around 1919, just after World War One. Lin was also an interesting character. He had bright ginger hair, he was tough, too—he had a scar on his nose where he'd had it nearly cut off in a brawl when a man took to him with a knife. He'd been a stoker in the Merchant Service in World War One, and later in the Navy. a real 'drag the door open, slam the coal in' stoker. I remember he told me about one wonderful ship he worked on. When you went into the stokehold, he said, you saw furnace doors being opened and coal shovelled in as far as the eye could see. The ship was the *Aquitania*. Oddly enough, that was the ship I went to the Middle East on when I joined the Army.

I was told later that when Dorothy Chopping told Lin that she had invited me down as a kid to have a holiday with them, he said: 'What the bloody hell did you do that for? There's nothing for him to do here.' Anyway, I went down by the river steamer *Dover* to Woodbridge and landed at the jetty to be met by the dray, and when I got up to the farm about 3 pm Lin was ploughing. They were breaking new ground to put an orchard in—they were expanding the orchards in those days. Lin was ploughing with a three-horse team and a big mouldboard plough. There were two big handles for the driver to hang on to while he steered behind three big draught horses, one walking the furrow.

When I arrived on the scene he was having great trouble with his horses and things weren't going well. I just stood there and watched. Lin nodded to me and said hello in a friendly way, obviously wondering what the hell he was going to do with this kid as he wrestled with the horses. Finally he said to me in desperation, 'Can you steer a horse?'

I said, 'Not much, but I'll give it a go'. Lin passed me the reins and I thought I was made. Somehow I managed to steer the plough reasonably straight in the furrow, and I kept the horses slow as he asked. We worked till dark, as you did in those days, and then I helped to disconnect the team and take them to the stable, watered them, rubbed them down and got the feed out. I thought this was just marvellous, and it was a fortunate start.

At the end of that first day and after we had got the horses back to the stable, Lin hoisted me up on the back of Nugget, an old black draught, and said, 'Take him down to the waterhole for a drink'. There was a gate on the way to the dam, and I said, 'How will I manage the gate?'

'Oh, Nugget'll show you', said Lin. Nugget was anxious to get to the water and set off with a quick walk down the lane towards the gate. When he got to it he just swung around sideways and put me in a position where my knee was near the latch. I lifted the latch, and then he turned half left and put his great big chest against the gate and pushed it open. Without me doing or saying anything he then turned around, put his chest against it again and heaved it shut, immediately swinging round to put me where I could reach the latch again. We then went down to the water and I experienced the peculiar feeling of sitting on a big draught animal while he was drinking. There is a 'thoomp, thoomp, thoomp' sound, and you can actually feel his sides swelling out. On the way back he did the gate routine in reverse. Lin had told me Nugget would show me how to manage the gate and he did.

The three draught horses all had very different personalities. Nugget was the oldest horse—I think the Choppings had used him to clear their original orchards. He was a black, ugly old bugger with a bent roundish nose. He was cunning and would pretend he was savage. He'd never really bite you, but you'd look around and see a great row of yellow teeth going 'clonk' three inches from the end of your nose. It was somewhat disquieting. When you were leading him by the bridle these great teeth would be going chomp, chomp, chomp, at your hand but, again, not quite reaching it. Colin, the big grey, was the converse of Nugget, a hardworking, gentle and rather nervous horse. He loved to work, and would pull his heart out. Nugget's attitude was why work if Colin will?

The farm was on a hill and all the goods and equipment for the property came by ferry boat, the *Dover* or *Cartela*, to the Woodbridge jetty, to be picked up by the dray.If it was a heavy load, there'd be two horses, not in tandem, but one in front of the other. Nugget would be between the shafts and the beautiful big grey Colin would be the lead horse on traces connected to the shafts. There was a steep pinch as you came up to the gate of the farm. You'd be coming up with a big load and Colin would have his great chest squared and his toes digging in as he pulled. Old Nugget would be pretending he was doing that, but if you walked over and dragged at his trace, it would bend in your hand. All he was doing was keeping the shafts up off the ground, the old bugger. You'd give him a boot in the backside or yell at him, and he'd pull slowly and then slack off again.

The third horse, Polly, was a smaller, rather nervous animal. One day, not long after I had learned to control the plough, Colin was working so hard and pulling so hard that his collar worked up on his neck and temporarily closed off his windpipe. He actually fainted—momentarily—staggered, and fell against Polly. Polly was very frightened of him and reared up. The next minute I—a twelve-year-old boy—found myself with my team of horses swung right around and dancing on top of the mouldboard plough. It was very risky. Lin came to help me and we got it all untangled. I remember Lin saying to me, 'Did you notice Nugget never moved, he just stood still. If he'd acted up, too, we'd probably have had broken legs'. That was another side to Nugget's character.

I remember one story about old Nugget. We were ploughing and had stopped for morning tea. The horses were tethered just outside the kitchen. The Choppings had some relatives called the Hurts also staying at the farm at the time, and they had a three-year-old boy called Rayburn. Lin was sitting at the kitchen table looking out the window while he drank his tea, and he suddenly said, 'Look . . . for Christ's sake!'

Outside, young Rayburn had walked over to Nugget's back leg, and had thrown his little chubby arms around it and was pulling and stroking on those long hairs that grow at the back of a horse's hoof. As Lin went out the door, old Nugget's ears were flicking back, but he stood absolutely still. He only had to lift his foot up and put it down, and Rayburn could have been killed, or at least seriously injured.

Lin said in a quiet voice, 'Rayburn, come here, I've got a biscuit for you'. The kid let go and walked over to him. But the old bugger, this bad tempered horse who could have kicked the kid into oblivion, hadn't moved.

That first session of ploughing went on for a week. I learned that a horse had to have a full hour for breakfast before ploughing started at about 6.30 am. That meant breakfast for humans and horses at 5.30—and getting out of bed on a freezing morning even earlier, and walking up through the orchard to the stable in the dark where the three horses would by lying down.

You had to get them up if they were lying down—they were very like human beings. Colin was always anxious to start, he'd leap to his feet when you walked into his stall, and Polly would also get up.

But Nugget—he wasn't going to be disturbed by any small boy. I'd have to do all kinds of acts to get him up. I'd kick him and jump on him and so on, and he would kind of pull the bedclothes over his head and go back to sleep. Finally he'd reluctantly stand up, and then he'd lean on you—it was a very narrow stall—squeeze you against the side of the stall, or stand on your foot. It was rather a helpless feeling. Somehow I'd extract myself and put a dipper of chaff in each of their feeding troughs and go back to the farmhouse for my own breakfast. Oh, he was a bugger—but you couldn't help liking him in his way. Nugget was the best of the plough horses without a doubt.

You can imagine a Tasmanian winter's morning in a farm kitchen. There was a big open fireplace with a great iron grid over it. There was no stove, just the grid, with a big pot of porridge on it. That was always followed by toast and dripping. Mrs Chopping used to go to a lot of trouble with the dripping. I still look back on toast and dripping with a certain nostalgia. I suppose we would be horrified to give it to kids now, but in those circumstances, my God, it was beautiful.

Then we would go to the horses and begin the day's work. If you were driving a plough team and you wanted to turn to the right, you said, 'Gee . . . gee-back', and believe it or not, whether you pulled the reins or not, this great mass of animals would turn to the right. To go left, you'd say, 'Coom 'ere'. If you wanted them to turn right and keep going around to come back in their tracks, all you said was, 'Gee . . . whooback . . . gee', and they would describe a complete turn and come back and face you, patiently and beautifully. And if you wanted them to turn left and come right around, the command was, 'Coom 'ere . . . whoa' and they would obey.

By the end of that first holiday they were treating me like a proper farm boy. One day a calf got out and disappeared up the road which goes over the mountains to Cygnet. Lin said, 'You like riding a horse, saddle up Bob and go and see if you can find it'. It was a cold day and rather wet as Bob, one of the general riding horses on the farm, and I took off up into the hills. I remember admiring the view back over the D'Entrecasteaux Channel as we climbed higher. Fortunately, I spotted the calf on the other side of a big wooden farm gate made from split palings and heavy eucalypt uprights. It was a heavy gate for a twelve-year-old to manage as I soon found

Bob, harnessed to the trap—the Choppings' regular transport around the district.

out when I tied old Bob—or young Bob I should say—up to the fence and undid the clip on this massive gate. But it was only leaning against the post, and I pulled it over on top of myself and down I went into the scrub. There I was, pinned under the great weight of the gate, with Bob munching grass happily a few yards away. Somehow I managed to wangle myself out from underneath and get the calf through, and even put the gate back, although it weighed a bloody ton. I got the calf home and all was well.

We ploughed and cleared land during those winter holidays. I got blisters on my hands and I was filthy dirty. I didn't have much in the way of clothes, certainly not the right clothes. Then it was back to school waiting eagerly for the next holidays to come in the spring. I think they were called the Michaelmas Holidays. I went down to Woodbridge again and the work was different. With spring coming the spraying program would start. I just absolutely bloody well loved it.

Lin Chopping was an ideal fellow for a boy to worship. He used to tell me naval stories, never about himself much. He described once being on a merchant ship in a hurricane when all the stokers were ill. The movement of the ship was so violent you were lucky not to be thrown against the hot furnace door while you were working. The cry came down from the bridge, 'More steam, more steam'. Lin said that the other stokers were 'just yellow' and went to their bunks. That left him six furnaces to stoke. He said he managed to do it, and every now and then he would rush out to where these other buggers were—they slept pretty close to their work—and drag a man out of his bunk and abuse him. But the water was getting over the plates on the floor underneath the furnaces which meant that if it got any higher it would douse the fires and they were a gone ship. He told me that as a matter-of-fact story while we were ploughing one day.

Another story I remember concerned the normal routine of a ship, when every now and then the Chief Engineer would come poking his nose into the furnace room on an inspection. Lin said they had a very good way of putting a stop to that: they used to break out a bloody great shovel full of coals on the floor outside the furnace and piss on it. The draught carried the urine-laden steam straight along the passage to the door where the Chief Engineer used to come in. He just clasped his hands to his throat and ran out the door choking, and wouldn't come back.

I think working down at Woodbridge on the Choppings' farm was one of the most valuable things I've ever done. Working with Lin was a great pleasure. He worked hard, was a patient man and was very good to me. So, indeed, was old Isaac Chopping but working with him was not pleasant. Lin used to say to me, 'You are going to work with the Old Man today. Don't get worried if he roars at you because he will'. And he used to. I can hear him now. 'Now Jack use your brains', sort of thing. 'Put the chocks in *this* way, not *that* way', and so on. But he was a kind man in his way. Apparently when he worked with people he behaved like this, but he showed me how to do all sorts of things.

The Choppings were fairly go-ahead farmers for their day. It worried them that a lot of apples used to go to waste every year. The mothy ones were thrown out after picking and left to rot under the trees. They were never pikers for trying new things and they decided to go into pigs in a big way, and feed the pigs with the apples that would normally have gone to waste.

One of my jobs was to cook these bloody apples in a great big old boiler and mix them with pollard and feed the mixture to the pigs. But the pigs had to be 'after hours' work, they weren't allowed to affect the orchard. So you finished your work there and then went and fed forty or fifty pigs in sties. But it wasn't a success. The apples scoured them and the Choppings spent more on pollard than they ever got back on bacon or pork.

But they were always forward looking. Fertilisers weren't as available as we know them today and I have no doubt what was available would have been very expensive. One year they tried an experiment and gave a fisherman a contract to land fish—barracouta or shark—on the Woodbridge jetty to be used as fertiliser. They used to catch them not far from Woodbridge.

Everything was landed on the Woodbridge jetty, freighted down by the river steamers and ketches. The Choppings' farm was up a hill, which could be a bit of a problem. We used to take the dray down to the jetty, pulled by old Nugget and Colin, cart the fish up through the orchard and follow a plough drawing a furrow. We would come behind with pitchforks and throw two couta to each tree on the way up the gap between two trees. Then the plough would come behind and throw another furrow over the fish. Then at the top you would turn to the other side of the row and do the same thing.

Now this was all right with nice silvery fresh couta going into the ground, and was not at all unpleasant. But every now and then the fisherman would really get ahead of us and start stockpiling bloody fish. It was believed that the fish must not get fly-blown because they would be eaten by maggots and not rot, and lose their value as fertiliser. So when we couldn't keep up with the fresh fish we would dig holes with a horse pulling a scoop, dump a couple of drayloads of couta and shark, then drag soil back over the top of them until we caught up. When you were ready, this mass of fish was uncovered—and by then it was soft and *rotten*!

The working rig of the day was a kind of overall made from a chaff bag with a hole cut for your head and two holes in the sides for your arms. When those fish went rotten, you'd start to fork one out of the dray and just get it over your head when it would drop off the fork and fall caressingly around your neck. I had it happen many times, particularly the shark. That smelt the worst. But we got them in the ground.

I don't know how successful it was. It was an expensive way of doing it although I think old Mr Chopping told me it worked out at about a farthing a fish. I often think of that these days when I go down to the Hobart wharves to buy a fish. They were beautiful

Lin Chopping and Spike—my first dog.

when they were fresh. Isaac Chopping built a smoke house and smoked quite a lot of them.

Apple growing was a very labour intensive industry. Most of the land had to be cleared of timber and ploughed with a hand plough. After the trees were established, all the fruit had to be hand picked for export to England. Then the apples had to be graded for size and quality. The apple they were picking and exporting at the time I was there was a bright green apple called a French Crab—a singularly unfortunate name, but there we are. There was a hand-operated grader into which the apples were poured and then passed through the appropriately sized hole into a bin. There each apple had to be individually wrapped in tissue paper and placed in a hardwood case which was then nailed up and stencilled. One stencil said IHC—which meant Isaac H Chopping—and the other was FC for French Crabs. Then the size was printed on—2¼, meaning two and a quarter inches in diameter. The cases were then loaded onto the dray and carted down the steep hill to the Woodbridge Jetty to be picked up by the *Dover* for transhipping to the big cargo ships that swung at anchor in that splendid Derwent estuary during the early autumn.

I have no doubt the operation of the Choppings' orchard was on the border-line of profitability and many of the properties were subsidised or actually owned by Henry Jones & Co, well known jam, tomato sauce and tinned fruit manufacturers in Tasmania. During one of my holiday visits there was quite a stir in the family over the impending visit of the great Sir Henry Jones himself, managing director of the whole company, who was coming to inspect the Woodbridge operation. He was invited to tea, and the best linen, snow white damask tablecloth and napkins were on show. I found myself sitting next to Sir Henry at the table and my contribution was to spill the beetroot juice on this white damask tablecloth. I can still see the look on Mrs Chopping's face. I don't blame her. But I was very nervous and that made me more so.

Then the family cat came in and it put its front feet up on Sir Henry's knee and made noises that were obviously translatable as, 'Give me a bit of that beautiful beef you're eating'. I thought I'd retrieve the situation, and hopefully my own reputation which was pretty low at that point, and I grabbed it by the tail to remove it. The cat yowled and screeched and dug its claws into Sir Henry's trousers as though it was going to be hauled away to be drowned or something. Oh dear.

Lin Chopping gave me Spike, my first dog. He was Lin's own dog, a big old fox terrier. It was extremely kind of him because Spike and I were never separated when I was down at the farm. Much to my surprise, when I was due to go back to school Lin came to me and said in his quiet way, 'Would you like to take Spike with you?' It was the ultimate kindness, because Lin was very fond of Spike. When I arrived back home from Woodbridge on the boat, my sister Dorothy said, 'What's he doing here?'

I said, 'He's mine, he's mine, he's mine! His name's Spike Bowden now, not Spike Chopping!' I was never allowed to forget this.

Spike quickly became part of the Bowden household at *Hazeldene*. He was a bigger dog than the modern fox terrier and he was a tremendous fighter. His particular enemy was a wire-haired fox terrier called Snowy that lived up the road. It probably had something to do with being king of the street. They used to fight and fight and fight—and they were terrible fights, silent bone-crunching affairs and you couldn't separate them. But they fought so often that a kind of truce was worked out. If they met in the street, the dog nearest to his own house would run inside the fence and bark, and the other would stay on the street side. If there was an open gateway they'd just pretend it wasn't there and run across it.

There were certain rituals Spike loved to observe. One frequent visitor to *Hazeldene* was a distant relative, Athole Pilgrim. She carried a large handbag and always had a piece of cake wrapped up which she would produce from this bag with some ceremony and give to Spike. He'd take the parcel in his mouth, go away and unwrap it. One day she came during some kind of family emergency without Spike's parcel. She put her bag in the bedroom and later in the day found that Spike had been in and carefully lifted everything out of it looking for his parcel! Nothing had been damaged in any way. Athole was so contrite she immediately raided one of our cake tins and put the parcel in the bag for old Spike to find.

He was such an impressive dog that a man called Creese came to me one day and said he had a fox terrier bitch on heat he wanted to mate with Spike. I was promised a modest fee to augment my pocket money. It had to be the same day, so I got on my bicycle, called Spike to follow and rode quite some distance to the suburb of Lenah Valley directly beneath Mount Wellington.

Spike and the bitch were introduced and the bitch did all those nice little fawning things that bitches do on heat. She sort of squirmed all around him and pushed her backside up against him and so on. And the old sod stood there and wouldn't have a bar of her. After a while he just walked over and stood by me, much as to say, 'When are we going?'

Both Creese and I were very disappointed and made arrangements to try again the following day. But next morning our phone rang quite early and it was Creese. 'Oh, by the way', he said, 'there's no need to bring your dog Spike over; he just came back on his own when there was nobody about and presented himself and mated comfortably with my bitch and then went home again!' So I got my half crown anyway. Spike obviously believed that such private affairs should not take place in front of his master.

Life at Woodbridge with the Choppings was so good I told the Old Man I wanted to be an orchardist and I asked Lin if I could be. He said yes, but to talk it over with my father.

'If you want to leave school at the end of the year and come here

The Old Man always had a distinguished air about him.

I'll give you five shillings a week and your keep and teach you the business.'

I told Father, who very wisely didn't say, 'You can't be an orchardist'. Instead he said, 'Why don't you go down for your long school holidays and give it a go'. So I did, and nothing in particular happened. I went home after the holidays and said to the Old Man, 'I don't want to be an orchardist', and the matter was dropped.

Chapter Five

THE BEST BEHAVED CHOIR BOY

Although we lived in a fairly poor neighbourhood, we considered ourselves in the upper middle class, I suppose. The Old Man had an executive position as Manager for Telegraphs and Telephones, and having the area's only telephone gave us a bit of an edge. One of our regular visitors, Aunt Annie Fryer, who came to the house as a sort of unpaid governess and to teach Dot music, felt it was her job in life to make sure the Bowdens had a sense of position and dignity.

Annie Fryer was one of those forgotten girls of a big, so-called important family—the Tranthem-Fryers. Her brother was a notable artist and sculptor who used to run the Blind and Deaf Institute in Melbourne. Aunt Annie was a stately sort of old duck with grey hair, big bosoms and the pulled-in waist of the day. She had pince-nez glasses with the little cord pinned to her chest. She may even have slept at *Hazeldene* from time to time. I remember walking into her room once and seeing her boobs, and she wasn't at all concerned about it, so I must have been pretty young. She was a nice old thing, but she had firm ideas on our social standing and position in the community.

She was no relation to us, we just called her 'aunt'. Nora was having some trouble at school at one stage with some girls called Brownell who were being a bit condescending towards her. Aunt Annie bristled and said, 'Nora—what's this, what's this? When you go to school tomorrow you go up to those Brownell girls and pull yourself up to your full height and say: "*My* father is a civil servant, *your* father is a tradesman!"'

Frank Bowden in full rig as the Grand Master of his Masonic Lodge.

The 'tradesman', by the way, owned the Brownell's business which was worth a million, but that was Aunt Annie's outlook on life and she infused it pretty heavily into the family. I had some pretty shitty jobs early in my time. The Old Man had started work at Walch's stationers as a paper boy, and he thought it would be a good idea if I did the same thing. There was talk of a job at Walch's and I remember Nora saying to me: 'Well, if you go to Walch's and you're washing the windows in the morning when I go past, don't expect me to speak to you'. That was Aunt Annie's influence.

I didn't get that job, but when I did start as an apprentice with an engineering firm, I arrived at work thinking that at least as an engineer I wouldn't have to clean windows. I hadn't been there long and was doing jobs like cleaning up the yard when the boss said, 'There's a bucket over there, go and clean the windows'. And I remember doing it, thinking how awful it would be if Nora passed, or someone that I knew. Well, if you gave me that bucket now and asked me to clean windows anywhere, I'd do it without batting an eyelid. But at the time—oh dear, I burned with shame and degradation.

Father was held in very high esteem. He was a man of considerable dignity and had a good job with a large office in the Post Office. He shared that office with a male secretary called Harry Needham. One night Father came home, and while we were sitting around the table having a meal he said, 'Harry Needham was taken to hospital yesterday with appendicitis. He was operated on today. And what do you think they found in his appendix?' And the whole family rose up and said, '*Father*—not at the table!' My ears were sticking out a mile, and I'd have loved to know what they found in Harry Needham's appendix but the matter was dropped. Every now and then it would occur to me, but I'd forget to ask the Old Man so I still don't know what they found in Harry Needham's appendix. It has been one of the great frustrations of my life.

Father was prominent in the Orpheus Club and a Mason of considerable note and popularity. Eventually he became Grand Master for Tasmania. This required dedication, a great capacity to learn things off by heart and a certain sincerity. It also required a great capacity to get on with people because selection was by boards and so on. The Old Man was a singularly successful Grand Master, so much so that when there were big Lodge gatherings in other parts of Tasmania, he would invariably be voted as a speaker and he had a great capacity for speaking well, humorously and to the point. He was particularly noted for his performance of The Captain in *HMAS Pinafore*.

Religion was pretty important to me up to my early teens, and perhaps a bit after. The Old Man's connections with the Church of England were very strong and I thought a lot of the church activity was good, particularly the choir. I liked singing and the Old Man was a benign choir master. Choir practice was on Wednesday

Philip and I both enjoyed singing as choir boys, but did not stay with the church.

nights. Philip and I used to walk from *Hazeldene* to Holy Trinity Church, one on each side of the Old Man, holding his arms. On the way home after choir practice he would invariably pull up in a 'surprise' sort of way and buy us some oranges or bananas or some little treat that was not in the house at the time.

Church services on Sundays at Holy Trinity I remember as pleasant occasions. I liked the music, although the bloody sermons were a pain in the arse. They seemed to go on for ever. There were certain distractions you could have as a choir boy like writing rude notes to each other and passing them along. Then they offered a prize for the best behaved choir boy for a year. A year mind you! The prize was ten shillings, which was wealth.

I thought, 'My God, I'll get that'. We had to be judged by the women of the choir because they sat in a position where they could watch us very closely. And for a whole bloody year I was a little prig. I used to sit there with a sanctimonious expression on my face, my hands crossed in front of me. I didn't pass any notes or slam hymn books shut during the sermon. I sang beautifully, and did everything a choir boy should do.

The women of the choir unanimously voted me the winner. But—and I only learnt this later—because Father was the choir master he said, 'Oh you can't give it to my son, give it to the next bloke'. God, I was livid over that. A whole year of my life wasted!

I have another, more pleasant, memory of the days when church was an important part of our lives. Father would sometimes hire a cottage at Lindisfarne, on the eastern shore of the Derwent, for the summer holidays. It's just a dormitory suburb of Hobart now, but in those days it was a self-contained community and a wonderful place for holidays. There was good fishing, and we kids would meet the lads of the village and go for swims on the beaches. Our holiday cottage was right on a little beach of its own up towards Rose Bay, and the whole family would move over for the summer break—cow and all. I recall one Christmas Day which began with a journey across the Derwent in my brother Eric's motor boat. We puttered across the river on this fine, glistening morning, tied up at the Cattle Jetty and walked up to Holy Trinity Church where we went through the very pleasant Christmas morning service with its cheerful music and plenty of double *ff*s so the choir could sing nice and loudly while old Ida Morris thumped away there in the organ loft. The church was specially decorated and everyone was dressed up for the occasion. Then we walked back to the Cattle Jetty, got in the boat and motored back across the river for our Christmas dinner.

As lay reader and choir master Father used to choose the hymns and generally rally round and help the parson in charge. He became very well known and popular in church circles, particularly with the clergy. There is a position called the Diocesan Registrar, and whenever the registrar was sick, or away, the Old Man would step in and do the job for him. This might even have been during his holidays, but he did it cheerfully because that's the sort of man he was.

After Father retired from the Post Office, the Diocesan Registrar's job became vacant and he applied for it. It had to be voted on at a meeting and the people concerned were so sure he was going to get it that they didn't go to the meeting to vote. Meanwhile, an Archdeacon who wanted *his* candidate in the job, rounded up enough votes and Father missed out. When they found the new bloke couldn't do the job, they asked the Old Man if he would go and teach him the job. All this without salary, of course. The only salary was paid to the useless Diocesan Registrar. The Old Man agreed without any bile to do it and remarked mildly that he had a hard job to teach him.

That made the family very bitter about the church and the way Father had been treated. By then I was a teenager and my religious views had changed completely. So had Philip's. He would eventually become a world renowned physicist at the Cavendish Laboratory in Cambridge and a Fellow of the Royal Society, and he always had an independent outlook. Some years earlier, on our way to church one Sunday morning, Philip declared that not only would he refuse to take Communion, but he wouldn't recite the Creed, 'I believe in God the Father Almighty, maker of Heaven and Earth. And in Jesus Christ, His only Son, who was conceived by the Holy Ghost, and born of the Virgin Mary . . .'

Father didn't say anything, but the girls got busy and said, 'You're not being fair to the Old Man, this'll break his heart' and so on. Anyway Philip stuck to his point and didn't say the Creed, or take Communion. He sat in his seat while we all went up, and that was that. I gave it up, too, not long after that. I didn't ape my brother, it just happened that way. When I was a little boy and we slept in the Summerhouse I used to kneel beside my bed every night, clasp my hands and recite:

Gentle Jesus, meek and mild,
Look upon a little Child;
Pity my simplicity
And suffer me to come to thee.

It didn't have any meaning for me, it was like cleaning my teeth or having a pee. My brother Philip used to pray, too, and Father used to kneel down beside his camp stretcher with the possum skin rug and mumble some kind of prayer which went on a bit longer. Later on I remember watching Philip sitting in Holy Trinity Church and realising that he was not singing the Creed. There was no conversation about it between us later, but I just started thinking about the words which I sang automatically and thought to myself, 'That's bloody nonsense. I don't believe in all this'. Eventually I did not go to Communion either, I just couldn't do it. And here I am now, just a bloody old heathen—evil and predestined for burning flames and all that goes with it. But it was the Creed—that great statement of all you believed and disbelieved—that caused me to question the whole religious edifice.

I should say that Father was not heavy about religion. He was mainly connected with the nice side of it, the music. He sometimes read the lessons, too. There are nice things to read from the Bible, and he read them well. He didn't preach sermons. It meant a lot to him and there was nothing he liked more than walking up to the altar rail with a great row of Bowden children behind him. But he never raised a word of objection when it didn't happen. I continued singing in the choir because I liked singing. As a matter of fact, I'd love to sing in the choir again, with harmony, the basses behind and old Ida Morris thumping and pumping away at the organ.

Dot always maintained her religious connections and lived for many years in the household of Bishop and Mrs Blackwood, in Sale, Victoria. Nora and Marge wouldn't have a bar of it and I escaped religion mainly because we were allowed to think for ourselves on that and everything else.

Aunt Annie's views on social standing affected both Marjorie and Nora when they had to find work. They felt they had to establish themselves in some position where they were not going to be put upon, and where they would be treated with great dignity. Marge eventually joined the staff of the Electrolytic Zinc Company in Hobart and worked as the general secretary of the Research Department where she typed all the scientific reports and enjoyed considerable esteem among the staff. Nora also finished up at the Zinc Company but, before that, she was not so lucky. After her first job at the Barracks, she went to the law firm of Dobson, Mitchell and Allport as secretary to an old prick called Cecil Allport. He was the older Allport in the show, and he had a son called Henry. Cecil was a bad tempered old bugger and he gave Nora bloody hell, even though she did her job very well. Eventually she worked for Henry who was even worse. He had designs on her, and nearly drove her mad.

At this time two Miss Butlers were running a restaurant in town, with some classical name. They ran it with great dignity and very little service. Old Cecil Allport used to go to their establishment for his morning tea. He was a testy fellow, and one morning his tea was a bit late or cold or something and he told the Misses Butler what he thought about it in no uncertain terms. They bristled, flushed red to their aristocratic necks and pointed out to Cecil Allport that his presence in their restaurant was no longer required, and what was more, they didn't want him ever to come back again!

After they kicked him out, he went back to his office fuming. The old Tasmanian families of Butlers and Allports had been at loggerheads for years. Nora heard him mutter, 'Butler . . . once a Butler you behave like a Butler!'

Philip and I were sent to Hutchins School and felt we were not quite on the right side of the tracks, as Hutchins was basically fed by the Sandy Bay families who considered themselves upper class. The other kids talked about their houses and yachts and what their fathers did, and we felt a little bit down the social scale.

Most of our leisure time was spent at home. Gramophones were the great thing, but we didn't have one. We had a piano, though, which my eldest sister Dottie used to play. There were bloody awful musical evenings when distant relatives and friends would come to *Hazeldene* with their little yellow bags with rolls of music in them, and sing songs like 'Trees' and 'You Along 'a Me'.

As a kid, I thought these evenings went on and on. We were taken out sometimes to similar sessions at other people's houses. An awful boredom used to descend on me, I can feel it now. Our neighbours, the Kalbfells, had a Magic Lantern, and we used to go there and watch that at times with great interest.

When broadcasting began we had crystal sets and headphones, but the first radio at *Hazeldene* was a French set called a Chapin. Using it was a very complicated procedure. It had three dials, and you turned two of them until you got a carrier whistle. You then had to tune the carrier out with the third dial, and then you heard the music. We had the Chapin for a long time.

The big event of the year was our annual holiday camp on top of Mount Stuart which was quite close to where we lived. It is more of a flat-topped hill than a mountain, but the approaches to it are quite steep. There was a stone house called *Eskdalemuir* which is still there—with a big garden and fruit trees.

A Mr Strathearne lived there. I think he may have been the Council Clerk for the suburb of Glenorchy. He was a big dour Scot with a white beard, and he shared the house (under what conditions we never quite knew) with two women called Jenny and Jonna Holmes. To me they were very old ladies but I suppose they were in their thirties or forties. Behind his big garden was a paling fence, and on the other side of that was the bush. There was also a garden shed with onions hanging up in the rafters and rats galore running round. The garden was managed and run by a man called Howard. His name was probably Bill Howard, but in those days you called gardeners by their surnames and he was 'Howard' even to us kids.

I don't know how the original thing started, but the Old Man got permission from Strathearne to take us camping there for Christmas and the school summer holidays. The shed was an important part of the site, because it had a tank full of mosquito-larvae infested water and we could take shelter there in extremely bad weather. The Old Man used to hire tents for the occasion, and we would pitch them in the bush at the rear of Strathearne's house.

Lucien Dechaineux painted a watercolour of one of our Mount Stuart camps which shows the layout, and the family engaged in holiday activities. I am pictured as a toddler, carrying some sticks over to the fire.

Getting up there was quite a business. The Old Man hired two carts, called floats, from Mathers the removalists. They were beautiful vehicles, with one axle and a pair of wheels, pulled by a single horse. If you lifted the shafts a bit, the rear part came down very close to the ground so that men could slide heavy weights on without having to lift them up into the cart. The two carts would come up the hill to 26 Jordan Hill Road. Mathers were always instructed to send drivers who were kind to their horses. Mother was fanatically fond of animals and although she was a timid woman, generally speaking, I have known her go out into the street and really take someone to pieces if she thought they were being cruel to their horses. I don't think she was always right about this, because horses coming up a steep hill often played up a bit, or tried to loaf, but woe betide any driver that beat his horse in Mother's sight. On one such occasion a driver said to her, 'Go home woman and look after your kids and leave me to me horses'.

It was amazing what was loaded into those one-horse carts to take us up to the camp. The carts had to go down Jordan Hill Road first, because they couldn't turn up Lochner Street. When they reached the main road, they would turn left and head up Mount Stuart Road. The hills were steep and, after all the gear was delivered, there was always a bottle of beer for each of the drivers. I remember this vividly, because many years later when we'd stopped camping and had taken the cottage at Lindisfarne, the same carts would be used to take our stuff down to the wharf to be loaded on the old ferry, the *Kangaroo*. One of the drivers who remembered our camp said to me, 'I don't see your mother about'. I said, 'No, she died'. He said, 'She didn't . . . Gawd strike me pink. Gee, no wonder I didn't get me bottle of beer.' He wasn't being selfish. It's funny how things like that stick in your mind.

The first camp started when I was about two and a bit years old, so my memories begin around 1912 and 1913. There was a set spot for each tent—one each for the boys, girls, the men, and a provision tent. The provision tent had a beautiful smell—mainly of limejuice, because that was the cordial of the day. Philip and I used to sleep in the boys' tent with Emil Dechaineux. In Lucien Dechaineux's painting there are two boys sitting in a hammock, Philip and Emil. There was no dining tent. We did all our eating outside and there were big long trestle tables which were also hired.

The Christmas camps became an institution in our family. They were just wonderful and the area offered so much to us kids. There was a pond with reeds around it. We played rounders almost every night. We threw quoits—big rubber quoits that I've never seen before or since—rather like the ones used for deck games on ships. There was a big swing and Eric, who was about fifteen or sixteen at the time, cut the top off a straight gum tree and with a coach bolt secured a cast iron wheel on top to which was tied a big thick rope with a knot in the end. We used to call it the Maypole. You grabbed

The annual Mount Stuart camp was a great event in our lives but my memories of this one are limited. I am the babe in arms in the background.

hold of it and ran, and swung yourself out and around.

The Old Man used to come up each night from work and stay the night. He liked to walk to *Hazeldene* from the Post Office and then on up to the camp. Mother used to come up every day with baskets of food and other necessary things, but never stayed the night. It wasn't quite her thing, although she loved the day part of it. Well, I thought she did. Maybe she was just being nice.

Cooking was done over an open fire with a couple of bits of iron across it, and this was backed right up against an enormous gorse patch. Why the hell a fire never went through it, I'll never know. We used to have occasional fires break out elsewhere which were beaten out. People seemed to be less strict about bushfires then. As a kid I was allowed to light gorse bushes. I was taught how to pick little isolated ones and watch them burn.

Old Ida Morris came up every day to do the cooking. God knows how she got her great bulk up the hill on a hot summer's day. We

Old ladies seemed to work hard at looking like old ladies in those days. Jonna and Jenny Holmes shared the house with Mr Strathearne near our camp.

used to eat a lot of tinned red salmon—I used to like that. Stewed cherry plums from Mr Strathearne's garden were popular and on occasions there would be a platter of fruit prepared by the Misses Holmes—cherries and gooseberries—laid out on a rhubarb leaf. The Misses Holmes were very good to us kids and we were 'given' an apricot tree and an apple tree in the garden for the duration of the camps.

No matter how bad the weather, and although we were only ten minutes from *Hazeldene*, we never went home. That became an unwritten law of the camp. In any case, we loved a bit of bad weather with the sound of the rain rattling on the canvas. The Old Man made us trench our tents and pitch them properly, but sometimes an easterly would really set in with a solid week's rain. There was still no question of going home: we moved into the Strathearne's shed with its smell of slightly rotten onions. That smell brings back nostalgic memories to me even now. We used to put our mattresses on the floor, light a kerosene stove and lie there snugly watching the rats run around the rafters while the rain splattered on the roof and the wind howled. When the weather eased we'd go and pick the tents up off the ground, pitch them again and dry things out.

Sunday was the ceremonial visiting day. I can remember up to fifteen people sitting around the trestle table. God knows how Mother and Ida Morris fed them all. At night old Strath often came over with his gramophone which we'd set up in the light of a hurricane lantern. He'd play Peter Dawson, Harry Lauder singing 'I Love A Lassie' and 'Roaming In The Gloaming', and other wonderful songs like 'Wait Till The Clouds Roll By Jenny'.

Sometimes music was provided by two men who worked at the Post Office, Ned Hannaford and Fred Miller. They were cornet players and on a set night each year they would come to have an evening meal at the camp with us. They would play cornet solos and duets, and I can still hear the beautiful sound of two cornets being played in harmony echoing into the night air. Fred's cornet was a treble and Ned's an alto. (In later years Fred Miller told me he played 'The Holy City' standing on the walls of Jerusalem in the moonlight during World War One. I think he said it was Armistice night. His audience was a bunch of shickered Australian diggers who were plying him with the local wine. On the last note he fell unconscious into the arms of his mates!)

The Mount Stuart camps went on for ten, possibly eleven, years. Of course, Hobart was spreading a bit and the Old Man very wisely saw that things couldn't go on indefinitely. I think he had a talk to old Strath, who was going to sell or was getting out—maybe he was going to die. In any case, the day came when the Old Man announced there would be no more camps.

My sisters wept and I remember trying to persuade him that they had to go on. But he didn't budge, of course. It was the end of an era.

Chapter Six

ORIGINS

I was twelve years old when Mother died. I tend to think of her as I last remember her, a slim, grey-haired, rather unhappy woman. But I have a photo of her at the age of nineteen when she was married, and she was extremely beautiful—a slimly built girl with delicate, fine-boned features. She dressed with great taste and care and, before she became ill, had a warm personality and a great sense of humour. Mother was very good to me, and being the youngest of her six children I think I became more important to her in the days when she was ill. What she died of I don't know, but I can remember a period of about two years during World War One when her illness clouded the life at 26 Jordan Road, Hobart. She became ill with what were called 'bad turns'. Looking back now, I suppose it could have been about the time of her menopause.

There was no shortage of medical care, such as it was. But I don't think the treatment of her case was very sophisticated although doctors were constantly involved. Mother became more and more ill and she would have bad turns and go grey. I often wonder whether they weren't mixed up with some form of thyroid deficiency, but that's only a guess. Anyway, the doctors did tell my father and my eldest sister Dorothy that they had to be tough with her. 'Don't let her get down like this', kind of thing. I have no doubt that this was quite wrong.

The result was she used to cling to me and depend on me. I remember her saying, 'They don't think much of me'. There was

Mother as a young bride

a long period when I actually used to sleep with her because she was scared.

I don't recall that Father and Mother ever actually slept together in a shared bedroom, although I was the youngest child and the household arrangements may have been different in earlier years. Mother's relationship with my father was very good, but what chances they had of a reasonable sex life is a bit of a mystery. Of course, that wasn't regarded as important in those days. As I have described, Father used to sleep with his three sons in the Summer-house, and my mother and my three sisters were in the house. I'm sure my parents did manage a satisfactory sex life, despite not

Grace and her mother, and Frank as a boy. Even children had to stand stock still in photographic studios, with an iron clamp on their necks while they clung to a chair for support.

sleeping together, by taking advantage of odd times—my sister Marjorie was embarrassed several times in her life by bursting in on things when the door was supposed to be locked. However, during Mother's illness I moved in to the house to be with her and comfort her.

Eventually the doctors were at a loss to know what to do and, as they often did in those days, they said a good rest in hospital would do Mother good. She went into the Stowell Hospital in Hampden Road, Battery Point, but she just seemed to go downhill.

On a hot windy March night several days after she went to hospital, I was sent down to deliver something to Mr D'Emden, the Postmaster General, at his private home. I went on my billycart down Jordan Hill Road, down Newdegate Street to Federal Street. But I met Mr D'Emden coming out his gate. He said, 'Give me your billycart, son, and go home. Your family wants you'. I was a bit mystified, but I did as he told me, and as I got to the bottom of our street I met the entire family walking down. My brother Philip handed me my cap and no one told me anything. We got in the tram and went up to the Stowell Hospital.

The memories of that night are still very vivid. We all went into a private bedroom on the ground floor, and Father went to Mother while we stayed in that room. An old family friend, Archdeacon

Mother, shortly before her death. I remember that confused and worried look very well.

Atkinson, was there. I suppose the Old Man must have known things were pretty bad to ask him to come to the hospital. It was all a bit traumatic for a kid. There was no adjustment for age which was understandable, I suppose. After a time Father came back into the room where we all were and told us that Mother had died. We were all terribly shaken, and I remember Archdeacon Atkinson trying to comfort Father. I was very upset, of course, and I can remember being horrified that the Old Man wept. I had never heard a grown man weep before. I had a sort of feeling that he shouldn't have done that, poor bloke.

We stayed at the hospital for quite a long while until we all recovered sufficiently to go home on the tram. It was all bewildering and very terrible. And when we got home it all started. There was a funeral service and burial, of course, and it was all very big. The service went on for ever and there were sermons and eulogies to Mother which were no great comfort to a boy of twelve. We all went from the church to the graveside and home to reality at *Hazeldene*.

After the funeral the house was filled with people who came and

My three sisters. From left, Marjorie, Nora and Dorothy

went, came and went. There were buckets of cakes made. It seemed to go on for days. I must have been a bit of a 'wreck of the *Hesperus*' because a nice neighbour, Mrs Austin, gathered me in and said, 'Look I want some work done. I've got some pears I want picking. Come home and do it.' She didn't say, 'Will you come home and do it?' just, 'Come and do it'.

I went with her, and within half an hour I was up a pear tree picking pears and life seemed to be a lot better.

It was taken for granted that my eldest sister Dorothy would take over the running of the family, which she did with great competence. She was twenty-two years old. It was a hell of a situation to be handed to her on a plate, but it was just taken for granted that she would handle it—and handle it she did. She cooked for us, she ironed and was the housewife. My two sisters were working at office jobs, and Dottie was at home.

She was very good to Philip and me, particularly Philip—she used to regard me as something of a figure of fun—but there was a constant battle with her sisters. Marjorie refused to be dominated. She had the capacity to stand up to Dot and the rows were pretty considerable. Unfortunately Dottie used to dominate Nora very heavily.

I suppose it emphasises the value of recording family history when I say I know almost nothing about the families of my mother and father. Eric and Dot did some research with the Archives Section of the State Library of Tasmania, and my niece Peggy Playford (Eric's daughter) visited Norfolk Island in March 1986 where she looked up details of Edward Garth, a First Fleet convict to whom I am related on my mother's side. My comments are based on their research.

When my eldest son Tim visited England in 1960, he passed through Plymouth and noted that there were pages and pages of Bowdens in the telephone book there. It seems that Joseph Bowden, a native of Plymouth, arrived in Hobart Town with his wife in the ship *Adrian* on May 12, 1824. This ship, which also brought Lieutenant Governor Arthur to Tasmania, had sailed from London on December 9, 1823 touching at Madeira and the Cape of Good Hope.

As his name does not appear in the passenger list, it is presumed (by the State Archives) that Joseph Bowden was one of the 'several others who had either come out in the service of His Honour Lieutenant Governor Arthur, or as servants to the passengers'. By 1829, when Joseph Bowden applied for a grant of land, he was already a man of property in Hobart with assets worth £1,470. In support of his grant he stated he had a wife and three children and had received no indulgence since his arrival.

If he had been granted land, he had intended to put his father in charge of it while he continued to run the Lamb Inn in Brisbane Street as its owner and licensee. However his land grant application was unsuccessful.

Joseph Bowden's father had arrived at Hobart Town in the brig *Mary Jane* on October 30, 1829, according to the *Colonial Times* of the same date, and he is perhaps the 'Henry Bowden' who applied for a town allotment on September 4, 1830. Joseph and his wife Sophia produced ten children and the fifth was John Gibson Bowden, my grandfather, born on July 28, 1831. I was named after him, and Gibson is my second name.

Although Joseph Bowden seems to have done quite well for himself with property, I can remember Father telling me that his father, John Gibson Bowden, was one of the lads of the village, as it were. He reputedly went through his share of the family fortune quite quickly. At one stage he was racing a coach against another for a bet when his coach capsized and he broke his leg.

Breaking a leg in those days wasn't much fun and the repair job was poor. He was an invalid from then on and I think things went from bad to worse with his financial situation and his health. Earning a living while incapacitated must have been a struggle. There wouldn't have been much in the way of benevolent pensions. He eventually died in 1874 at the age of forty-three. My father, Frank Prosser Bowden, was only thirteen and immediately had to get a job. So the Old Man had a fairly tough and deprived start in life.

My mother, Grace Hill, was a direct descendant of Edward Garth, a convict who came to Australia with the First Fleet on the convict transport *Scarborough*, in January 1788. Of course, being of convict stock has only recently been fashionable and there was some concern in the family—not from me I must say—when my sister Dorothy received confirmation from the Archives Section of the State Library of Tasmania that old Edward Garth had been indicted in England for feloniously stealing on October 29, 1784, two live cows, value £17, the property of Thomas Rhodes the younger, and was found guilty and sentenced to death. On February 23, 1785 his sentence was commuted to transportation to Africa for seven years.

Well, Edward Garth scored Australia instead of Africa and, like many of the felons bound for Botany Bay, saw some hope of a fresh start in a new country once he had done his time. Only a few weeks after the First Fleet arrived in Sydney, Garth volunteered to join Lieutenant Philip Gidley King's party of fifteen to be the first settlers on Norfolk Island—that tiny spot on the map of the South Pacific that Captain Cook had described as a 'paradise'.

The convicts who went to Norfolk Island were chosen mainly for their trades. Edward was described as a sawyer. A young alleged prostitute, who had been transported for stealing 'nine guineas and one half-guinea', named Susannah Gough (or Goff), was also on the HMS *Supply* when it sailed from Port Jackson bound for Norfolk Island on February 15, 1788.

They had all volunteered to go and King assured them that 'if there should arise an affection between any two of them they might marry, the Surgeon performing the ceremony, and when a clergyman should visit the Island he would solemnise it'. The party was made up of eight free men, nine male and six female convicts.

Edward Garth and the young Susannah Gough paired off, and almost immediately began to produce the first of their six children, but things did not start well for Edward. It is recorded that he stole three quarts of wheat in 1789—which was only the second year of settlement—so it was probably seed grain and a very serious offence for which the poor fellow was sentenced to 100 lashes. However, by 1791 he had settled *Grenville Vale* on Norfolk Island.

When Lieutenant King returned to Norfolk in 1792 he made land grants to some of his earliest convicts whose sentences had expired but who were still working for the Government. Edward was given twelve acres of land and later he managed to purchase a further sixty acres from R Styles, a Marine who had left the island. By July 1796 he was the overseer of sawyers, and his family was victualled from the Government Stores. The *Sydney Gazette* of March 11, 1804, reported that in January of that year one John Morris had attempted to murder Edward Garth, then acting gaoler, so he must have had an occasional government job. When the first Norfolk Island settlement was abandoned in 1806, those who had land there were given the opportunity to get a similar amount of land on the Australian mainland. I think Edward, having liked island life, heard about Tasmania and asked for his grant to be there. He arrived in Tasmania on *The Porpoise* on January 27, 1808.

The 1819 register of landholders in the Shire of Buckingham reveals Edward in possession of two substantial grants of land—eighty and sixty acres—and a further seventy acres by purchase. He was growing wheat, barley, potatoes and vegetables and ran seventy head of cattle and 2000 sheep. By then his household consisted of himself, Susannah, three children and a servant, no less.

Amy Rowntree's book *Early Settlement of Sandy Bay* contains many references to the Garth family (Garth Avenue is apparently named after them) and, indeed, old Edward Garth died at his Sandy Bay farm on December 18,1820. I saw a map of his Sandy Bay holding only recently. It takes in the valley where, quite by coincidence, I bought a block of land. My three sisters also owned a block of land and a house just above where Garth Avenue runs off Maning Avenue, also on Edward Garth's old estate. When they died, my second son Nicholas bought the property and now lives there with his wife Fran and their four children. And, in recent years, my youngest daughter Lisa and her husband David Roberts have acquired part of the land on my block further down the valley. It is a curious coincidence.

How Edward Garth, the poor old bugger, or even his sons, managed to farm it I'll never know—it has black heavy clay soil which was hard enough to cultivate into a modest vegetable garden. Edward and Susannah Garth had seven children and the clan proliferated. My connection comes through his eldest son, James, who married Mary Bellett—the daughter of Jacob Bellett who had also come out on the First Fleet and was also an original Norfolk Island settler with Lieutenant King on the *Supply*. They had fourteen kids and one of the sons, another James, married his first cousin, Susannah Garth, on January 5, 1842. Their second daughter (also Susannah) married Walter Thomas Hill on July 3, 1872. Their daughter (my mother), Grace Elizabeth Hill, was born on May 4, 1873, and my grandfather was drowned as I mentioned earlier when the ferry *Excelsior* capsized in the D'Entrecasteaux Channel on January 31, 1875. He was only twenty-seven years old.

Susannah married again, to James Laffer (probably Le Fevre).

So that is our First Fleet connection, through my mother Grace Hill—who was an extremely beautiful woman—back through the Garths to penal servitude on Norfolk Island.

My father's first job was at Walch & Son, the stationers which was then on the corner of Liverpool and Elizabeth streets in Hobart. He had to make spills. You rolled paper into cylinders about six inches long which could be held in the fire and lit. They were used to transfer a flame to gas jets or lamps around the house. Walch's used to sell them. Then he got a job as a messenger boy delivering telegrams and joined the permanent staff as a telegraph boy. The Old Man firmly believed that anyone could make good as long as they got a start somewhere. I think you got a better go with a better start, but he didn't get much of one and he did all right, finishing up as the Manager for Telephones and Telegraphs in Hobart.

He told us later that telegraph boys used to walk around Hobart delivering telegrams unless the distance was over a certain limit, and then they were allowed to take a cab. They didn't use bicycles and I suppose that gave the Old Man his love of walking. The two-horse cabs were lined up on a rank in Elizabeth Street alongside Franklin Square, diagonally opposite the Post Office.

The Old Man told me that the honourable thing was to take the leading cab—the first cab off the rank—but he got on particularly well with one cabbie. He would come out of the Post Office with his telegram and, if Alfie wasn't in the front rank, the Old Man would give him some sort of sign. This bloke would look at his watch to give the impression to the other cabbies that he had an appointment, and would drive to a pre-arranged spot nearby and pick the Old Man up to deliver the telegram.

Eventually the Old Man became a telegraphist, and that is how he met Mother—at a distance. Grace's mother was the Postmistress at Cygnet, south of Hobart. As she grew up, Grace picked up the Morse Code and used to help her mother by taking down telegrams and sending the answers back. They literally struck up an acquaintance over the Morse key and it gave them an advantage in later life. When they wanted to say something at the table that they didn't want the family to know about, they used Morse Code to each other, rapping a knife or fork on the table—much to our chagrin.

In those days you could go through from messenger boy to manager, and that is what Father did. He had a great capacity for getting on with people and he was a highly competent fellow. When he became Manager for Telephones and Telegraphs he had quite a large office on the Elizabeth Street side of the Post Office and this second storey office became a part of our lives. It had two windows which looked right down on Elizabeth Street and since this was a great era for processions, particularly during World War One, we would go down to Father's office and look out at the marches, troops and bands playing.

Along one wall was a set of keys which used to be telegraphing all the time so the Old Man would keep up with what was going on. There were machines with big wheels around which paper tapes were wound so that the dots and dashes could be recorded.

The Old Man always took his lunch to the office and when my sister Nora worked at the legal firm of Dobson Mitchell and Allport, she used to go down and have lunch with him. Philip and I used to walk down Macquarie Street from Hutchins School to join them. At 1 pm he would spread out the daily newspaper which he read while he ate. He never had sandwiches. He liked cold toast. At about 1.30 when he finished his lunch we would go for a walk. We'd usually go down to Hobart wharves and look at the many ships that used to be in—some of them sailing ships in those days—and stroll around discussing the scene there until the Post Office clock struck a quarter-to-two when we would head back to school and the Old Man to his office.

In March 1912 the *Fram* arrived in Hobart with Amundsen's expedition on board. Amundsen had just beaten Scott to the South Pole. He had used dogs, while Scott had largely pinned his hopes on primitive petrol-engined tractors and ponies. The *Fram* was a wonderful old wooden ship which had been specially built by the Norwegian explorer Nansen to resist ice pressures when he tried to drift her across the North Pole from 1893 to 1896 and Amundsen had chartered her for his South Polar expedition.

Anyway, when Amundsen came to Hobart on March 7, 1912 there was no way of knowing whether he had reached the South

The Fram *at anchor in the Derwent Estuary following Amundsen's triumphal return from the South Pole*

Pole ahead of Scott until he told somebody. He expressed a wish that someone very senior from the Post Office should organise a telegram to send to the King of Norway. I remember the Old Man saying later that Amundsen was not a communicative fellow at all, and it was a very stiff and formal meeting. He handed over the telegram, which was sent through the proper channels, but for some days Father was the only person in Australia to know that they had reached the South Pole ahead of Scott. He never made much of that.

There was another first. The chief electrical engineer at the Post Office was a man named Hallam. He was a nice man, but he used to worry me a bit as a kid by asking me testing questions about what I'd learned at school. As he was a communications engineer, he was interested in making a radio which was both a sending and receiving set. They had big spark coils in those days, most complicated things. Hallam wanted to experiment to see if he could transmit and receive a message back from a ship which was sailing down the east coast of Tasmania.

Father was then the head telegraphist and Hallam got him to transmit the Morse Coded message. They set up their equipment near Sandy Bay on the slopes of Mount Nelson and actually managed to transmit to and receive from the ship. It was a great triumph. The Old Man said the ship's captain was very pleased about all this, and wanted to inspect Hallam's equipment. Hallam was a bit nervous because he had bits of wire twisted around and it was a pretty rough sort of an outfit. Then the skipper invited them on board to see the ship's radio gear, and Hallam was most reassured because it made his equipment look better than theirs. That was how the Old Man became involved in the first ship to shore radio message in Tasmania.

Because of the Old Man's position at the Post Office we had the only telephone in the street and the calls were free. It made us a bit of a community centre because whenever anything went wrong, or if a doctor was wanted, people would come up and ask to use the phone, or ask us to phone for them. Our number had only three figures—457. It was installed on the wall in our hall and you didn't have to wind a handle. You picked up the receiver and the exchange answered.

I have a vivid memory of the outbreak of World War One when our next door neighbour, Mr Hurle (his youngest son Alan became the Hobart Town Clerk later on), came in and asked Father if he could stay by the phone on the night in question to 'get some information about what was happening'. There was a German ship in Hobart called the *Oberhausen*—an evil German ship—and she had loaded a big cargo of timber supplied by the firm of Crisp and Gunn (where Mr Hurle worked). As the news was getting around that war was about to be declared, people suddenly became aware that the *Oberhausen* had slipped her cable, cast off, and was heading off to freedom and to take our beautiful timber back to the German nation to further the war effort.

How far the *Oberhausen* thought she was going to get I'll never know, but the Navy despatched a party with a bloke called Russell Young in charge. The Navy did not have much of a presence in Hobart and I think they used the pilot launch of the day. Young was a lawyer in the town and a part-time naval officer. He had a pointed beard and was a rather flamboyant fellow. As I understand it, they went out on the pilot launch and caught up with the *Oberhausen*, climbed the Jacobs ladder—unopposed apparently—and went to the bridge where Young pointed a gun at the captain and said something like: 'I arrest this ship in the name of the King'.

The ship's captain accepted the inevitable and while the *Oberhausen* slowly made her way back up the Derwent again to port—and internment for the captain and crew—Russell Young and his party, with the captain and his senior officers, settled down in the captain's cabin to enjoy his hospitality. They virtually had to be carried off the ship! They were as full as the family po when they got back to the wharves. I can clearly remember Mr Hurle turning away from our phone on the wall, saying excitedly, 'They've got her. They've got her!'

When World War One ended, Hobart geared up to celebrate the signing of the Armistice. Father was involved in those arrangements as the news of the signing was to be telegraphed through. It was worked out that when the news came through officially, the Post Office would ring the man who let off the One O'Clock Gun on the Hobart Domain and he would fire a special shot to signal the end of the war. The ritual of the One O'Clock Gun was linked with a time checking arrangement for mariners to adjust their chronometers. There was a flagpole down on the wharf with a big black ball inside a basket. At the moment the gun went off, the ball would drop. It had to be visual because the sound of the gun could vary depending on the distance the sound travelled. Anyway, it was to be a special shot from the One O'Clock Gun that would signal that the Armistice had been signed.

The whole family went to town that night. Mother came, although she wasn't well, and we all congregated in the Old Man's second floor office, overlooking the celebrations in Elizabeth Street and all around. I had a bugle I remember, and was blowing it around the place.

During the war, all important news was posted in big letters on boards outside the offices of *The Mercury* newspaper, which was next door to the Post Office, in Macquarie Street. About nine that night, *The Mercury* put up a notice saying it had been *unofficially* stated that the Armistice had been signed. The crowd all went mad, including me, blowing bugles and dancing around, yelling and making all kinds of joyful noises. The sound of all this revelry reached the man on the gun at the Domain, and he said, 'What's all that about?'

Someone said, 'The Armistice has been signed'. He said, 'That's good enough for me', and fired the gun!

Father was the man who was to receive the official message that the Armistice had been signed. We went up to his office saying, 'Whacko, the Armistice has been signed . . . Eric's coming home' . . . and so on. But I had never seen the Old Man looking so worried. He said, 'The Armistice has *not* been signed. We're still waiting for the news to come through.'

The crowd boozed on and celebrated until after midnight, and finally everybody went home. About 2 am, with the Old Man still manning his office, the news came through that the Armistice had been signed and it was all official. By that time there was no one left in the streets to celebrate.

Chapter Seven

THE HEADMASTER'S VICE

Father had a theory that no one should start school before the age of seven. How mother put up with us until then I don't know. He wasn't a snob, but he didn't favour State education.

There was a small private school called Miss Aton's Tabernacle School in North Hobart and, in our turn, we all went there. It was called a Tabernacle but it wasn't a Jewish Tabernacle as far as I know. I didn't ever see the inside of a kindergarten.

I hated Miss Aton's Tabernacle School and I only went there for a short while. My eldest sister Dot had all her education there, and it seemed to be good for her. Marge and Nora left eventually and went to the Hobart Ladies College near Trinity Church also in North Hobart—where Aunt Annie told them how to deal with snobs like the Brownell girls. They went there with reasonable success until they were old enough to go to business college.

When the Tabernacle School closed in the middle of the school year, Philip and I had nowhere to go, and since the Old Man wanted us to start at the Hutchins School the following year, he hired a governess to bridge the gap. She was rather nice and did her best with the unsatisfactory business of teaching us in a small house while my sister Dottie chucked her weight around in the background doing the housework. I got kept in once at playtime—no doubt for something I thoroughly deserved—and Dottie's voice could be heard in the background saying 'reeediculous nonsense'. The governess was giving me a lecture with one ear on the kitchen,

The Hutchins School, Macquarie Street, Hobart

and I've no doubt the other ear on her job. Anyway she let me out with five minutes to spare and honour was saved all round.

At the end of the Christmas holidays the day came when Philip and I started at Hutchins. I was about eight, so it was probably 1914 or 1915. Father must have enrolled us some days earlier and it was arranged that we were to walk to school and walk home. I now walk with a sort of rolling gait, because I had to keep step with Philip. He was three and a bit years older than I was, and I *had* to keep step with him! It never occurred to me to revolt over this. The route was explored but on that first morning my eldest brother Eric took us in the sidecar of his Matchless motor bike and dropped us off at the front door of Hutchins School in Macquarie Street.

I was put in a class called the Third Form under a Miss McAlister, who was a kindly person and a good teacher. I know I did well in scripture for which, one term, I got 100 per cent! Philip started two forms ahead in 4B. Our walk home from school was extremely hazardous because we had to walk past two Catholic

Miss G M Elliott and the Hutchins Junior School of 1919

schools, St Mary's for girls, and St Virgil's for boys. We were the little Hutchins Protestant boys. The girls particularly used to give us bloody hell, and after running the gauntlet of the schools we had the lads of the village to contend with. They used to give us bloody hell too, jeering and mucking about.

Philip always had rather an aura of dignity about him but he reinforced this with a little black water pistol which—if things got too bad—he would fill with dirty gutter water. Then he would squirt his tormentors in the face and they would retire in confusion, cursing because of that water pistol. The walk home was not pleasant and there was yet another school, Trinity Hill School, where it started all over again. I had a full-sized kids' fight once going past Trinity Hill School. We had to go through all this every day walking home from Hutchins to North Hobart.

There was no school uniform then and we wore a kind of suit, a pair of short trousers, coat, collar and tie, socks up to the knees held up with elastic garters and boots. There came a time when we wore stiff collars that you studded on to your shirt and that were worn outside the lapels of your coat. They were not very comfortable. As Philip grew out of his suits they just about fitted me, so I spent most of my growing life in his discards. This didn't worry me particularly.

I was at Hutchins School during World War One, and the standard of teaching—with a few exceptions—was not high. The school was divided into two sections, you went to what was known as 5B stage, then you went up into Christs College to do your Junior Public Exam. At that stage you came under a master called Bob Bullow who was probably of German extraction and who was a bloody good master, there was no doubt about that. He was tough, but he had the sort of toughness that people loved, and he was a much loved man. He never physically manhandled boys or caned them, but he used to roar at them and really pushed people through their exams. He was a most conscientious teacher and there was great emotion in the school on the day he left. My brother Philip really blossomed under Bob Bullow. He worked like a son of a bitch, and achieved five credits and four passes in his Junior Public out of nine subjects.

At this time I was in the hands of a silly old bugger called Isherwood. He had me for maths and arithmetic. He was a sarcastic old twit and I did not do well under him. This had unfortunate consequences for me, for the year I was to move up into Christs College to the great Bob Bullow—where you really worked and learned something—Bullow left the school, and they moved Isherwood up with me.

There were, however, some other tremendously good masters. There was a man called Dorsch who had not had his intestines blown out in Flanders for the simple reason he had a withered arm—although he was a handsome and physically splendid fellow in other ways. He probably had paralysis in his right arm as a youth. Despite this he used to row in the masters' crew and he was a very fine bloke. I blossomed under him as a teacher. I think he liked me a bit—I don't know why, I was a silly little bugger in many ways. He understood me and he really made my subjects live. Unfortunately he left, probably at the stage when the army was taking men with any sorts of arms.

Another good teacher was known as Captain Dundas, late of the

Inniskillin Dragoons or whatever. He was a very large florid man, and I now realise George—as we used to call him—was probably an alcoholic. But, oh God, we loved him. He taught us French and made our lessons fairly live. He used to spice his tuition by telling us a highly amusing little anecdote of some sort. And we used to scream with laughter, of course. He would get terribly agitated and say: 'Shut up! Shut up you little bastards, shut up, shut up!' The headmaster's study was very near our classroom.

On one occasion George was doing something on the blackboard, writing out a fairly complicated example of grammar, when a boy in the front row called Ian Miller called out, 'Sir, sir, you're wrong!' Old George put his chalk down, turned around and advanced, putting his florid face within an inch of the by now trembling Ian Miller and clapped his massive hands together with Ian's face in between. In a voice barely under control he growled, 'Don't you *ever* tell me I'm wrong,' and then he went back to his blackboard. Whether he made the correction or not I don't know, but Ian was upset, of course, and as the class dispersed I noticed old George went and had a long talk to him. I've no doubt his conscience troubled him because he was being very nice to the boy. I guess as much as a schoolmaster could, he was apologising.

Usually when a master was sacked from the school there'd be a vacancy on the stage at assembly time and a replacement would arrive the next day or so. In George's case I fear the liquor got too much. The headmaster actually said, 'I have a very sad announcement to make this morning. Owing to circumstances beyond his control, Captain Dundas has had to resign from the school. We know how sad you will be that he has gone, and wish him luck.' We were sad, too.

The headmaster was a man called Lindon, a classical scholar from England, who is remembered for describing Tasmanians and Hutchins boys as 'grubby little colonials'. He had a white walrus moustache and used to call you 'a beastly dog' and similar endearments. He was just a figure in the distance to me. He used to beat people pretty heavily on the back with a cane. One of his prime targets was a friend of mine, Mac Urquhart, who was belted by him a lot and who said being caned on the back was a pretty terrible thing. It was a heavy cane, too.

The Vice-Master was Mr S C Smith—he pronounced it

I'm the twelve-year-old directly to the right of the top of the shield in what we called Room One at Hutchins.

Smythe—and if ever a man's position was appropriately named it was Smith's. He was an awful man, an ex-naval paymaster. I have no doubt he had been cashiered! He was a tall, immaculately dressed fellow with a long pointed beard and a waxed moustache. The Hutchins School Magazine of June 1914 described him as having 'an excellent reputation as a disciplinarian'. This was something of an understatement. He had an absolute love of caning people. He used to hit them on the hands, so I think it was just straight sadism—but he did get an odd expression on his face while he was doing it. I remember noting this as a kid. He held the cane in a particular way between his thumb and forefinger—there was a touch of delicacy about it. He was a connoisseur of caning, and that cane used to swish right throughout the school.

I was pretty lucky, I only got it once. I was scared stiff. Some boys got it a great deal. One boy called Cummins I knew couldn't be in Smith's sight without getting a caning. Smith used to come into our classroom, where our form master Mr Palmer, a nice young man, was teaching us. I was about ten years old by this stage. Smith would come in with his cane under his arm and look all around before walking up to our form master to say:

'Mr Palmer, is there anybody in your class you feel should be caned?' or, 'Do you think caning would do somebody any good?'

Mr Palmer would say, 'No thank you Mr Smith, we're all right thank you'.

He'd just stand there silently in front of the class looking round. And finally he would say, 'Ah Lucock, I think it's time you were given a little urging along to work'.

He'd haul this kid out and give him six, or something horrible like that. Then he'd continue on with four or five other boys. Some wept bitterly, others kept quiet. Then, leaving this train of misery behind him, he'd walk out. It's unthinkable, quite unthinkable, now I look back on it. But you never went to your Daddy in those days and said, 'There's this man who canes people and he's going to cane me, too'.

He did cane me too, the old bugger. He couldn't get me on my behaviour patterns so he set a test in French. I thought I had done very well, but he had obviously made up his mind to cane me, so he told me I'd failed. That was the penalty for failing. I still get angry when I think about Vice-Master Smith.

In the end he caned himself out of house and home and they reduced him to an ordinary master and removed his caning authority. When I moved up into the next class I got him as a form master. He nearly died of frustration not being able to cane, but we were too scared of him to make the most of the situation. He lost control one day, though, and laid into a bloke called Reynolds with his bare fists. I can hear the thumps now as he punched him, I suppose, six or eight times in the body. It must have been very painful for the kid. It broke him up completely.

At one stage, when he was still Vice-Master of Hutchins, I went through a very unhappy period. To be fair, Smith was not my teacher, but I wasn't coping with school work and it was all getting a bit difficult. I suppose having Smith in the background didn't help much either. I did what kids often do in those circumstances, I became too ill to go to school. The family were all very tolerant—they didn't know there was nothing the matter with me. Our family doctor, Dr Hodgkinson—a rosy-cheeked man with a black moustache—came to see me, diagnosed 'indigestion' and put me on a balanced diet of toast and tea. But after some two weeks of this, Dr Hodgkinson said diplomatically that there wasn't much 'supporting evidence' for my illness and the Old Man said I had to go back to school.

I wept and said I was too ill to go to school, but he said I must. I got dressed and left *Hazeldene* but I didn't go to school, I went down to his office at the Post Office and knocked at the door. He said, 'What's the matter son?'

I said, 'I'm ill'. He said, 'I don't think you are, but we'd better go up to the school together'.

He phoned for an appointment and we walked up Macquarie Street together to Hutchins School. We were greeted by the impressively good looking Mr Smith who, in the presence of a parent, was articulate and seemingly full of sympathy. But, in fact, the Old Man sorted it out with him. He had the impression that the class was a bit ahead of me and I dropped back into the class behind, which was a good move, and life came back together again. It was beautiful. I could do the work.

My father had only been gone half an hour, however, when Smith came into my new class and delivered a lecture about me! I was too dumb to appreciate what he was doing. Fortunately, I didn't cotton on until later. He spoke about miserable little twerps who had to be coaxed to work and whose parents had to come to the school. I thought this was a general philosophy on life he was giving to the class. I didn't realise he was talking about me, so his time was wasted. Of course while he was with the Old Man he was saying things to me like, 'Wonderful, wonderful, I like your keenness. Do you want to start now? Splendid, good boy. That's what I want to hear'.

I don't know what happened to Smith in the end. I hope he fell into water somewhere not hot enough to kill him, just to burn him. However, on the whole I think Hutchins was pretty good. It must have been, because Philip found his way through to go to Cambridge University and become a distinguished research physicist. He was taught at Hutchins by the legendary science teacher 'Pooley' Erwin, who did his teaching by setting huge quantities of homework and giving enormous detentions if you didn't finish it all. It's a very simple and easy way of teaching. I didn't find him an attractive man. He was called Pooley because he was an Irishman and called a pulley a 'pooley'. I was pretty scared of him and his lousy detentions. But he seems to have become a

At the Hutchins Sports Ground, 1917

great symbol of the school. They have named a science wing after him, the Erwin Wing.

A school contemporary recently reminded me of an occasion when his behaviour wasn't so great. Some boys were making chlorine gas and they used too many Bunsen burners getting the chemical reaction going and blew the front out of the sealed fume cupboard in the lab. The first man out the door, pushing the pupils aside, was the now venerated science master Pooley Erwin.

Although the Hutchins School did try in its way to explain things to the boys, sex was still a bit of a mystery. There was a terrible man named Bligh who used to come to the school and tell us all sorts of insinuating things about sex that we didn't know anything about. He opened new horizons for us one way or another, I suppose.

On one notable occasion Bligh came to address the whole school. It was a big deal. The headmaster spoke first and then Bligh took the rostrum. I was about fourteen at the time, and I remember Bligh started off with the birds and bees and happiness and that

The Hutchins gymnasium doubled as an Assembly Hall.

kind of thing, and when he was about to move on to more specific talk about reproduction he said, 'Would all boys under the age of ten leave the hall'.

All the under tens trooped out reluctantly, and then it was the turn of the eleven-year-olds, and then the twelves. By the time Bligh got to the thirteen- and fourteen-year-olds it was strong stuff—masturbation, how not to go blind, 'Have a cold shower instead and think of your mother', and so on.

Now, as each age group was sent out they simply clustered around the gymnasium door—and no one thought to prevent this—calling out to the older boys as they came out: 'What did he tell you? What did he say?' Finally only the big strong sixth formers were left and I don't know much detail of what they got because by that time I was milling around the door with my peers waiting for the next bulletin.

As the sixth formers came out with all the dignity of their seniority, they were asked what had been said. One senior, Tommy Lyons, leaned over my shoulder and said to the boy who had enquired about the latest revelations, in a marvellous bit of simplification and masterly condensation now I come to think of it:

'He told us not to fuck tarts!'

Looking back, though, I believe Hutchins School was good in many ways. I met lots of good blokes there and whatever went wrong with my education was probably not the school's fault. It wasn't all Smiths and Isherwoods, and I look back on most of it with great pleasure. I doubt if the Old Man got his money's worth, but I don't know if he could have done better anywhere else.

The reality was that I left Hutchins only semi-educated at the age of fifteen. It was the understood thing that you had to pass the Junior Public Exam. Then you did the Senior Public for qualifications to go to university. I thought I had done pretty well, really, in the Junior Public, because I passed in Physics, Chemistry, Algebra, Geometry and English. I failed in French, and unfortunately failed in Arithmetic, which was a compulsory subject. It was mainly about compound interest, and I still can't do compound interest. So, when the names were put up outside *The Mercury* newspaper as they were in those days, I had failed. There was no way of knowing how well you had done, in general terms; you either passed or failed.

The Old Man had left school himself at the age of twelve to look after his stepmother and he seemed to think that people would just get on in life, somehow, after leaving school. So it was resolved from the moment I failed the Junior Public that I would leave school. It never occurred to anybody that there would be any difficulty about getting a job.

I do regret not being able to go back and do that exam again, because a lot of my friends went on to technical college, where you could do engineering or electricity and get a diploma. There were three things, a Trade Certificate, a Diploma, and the ultimate was a Degree. I'm sure I was diploma material, but I just went home to *Hazeldene* and dug the garden for a while until my eldest brother Eric—who had a diploma and worked as an engineer in the Post Office—said there was a job available as a Junior Motor Mechanic in Training Temporary in a place they called the Line Yard, and that if I applied I'd probably get it.

Chapter Eight

POSTMAN'S KNOCK

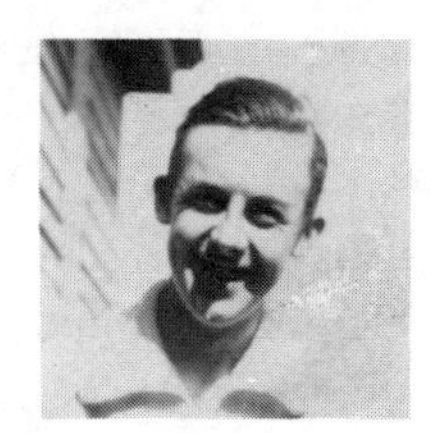

My first job at the Post Office Line Yard was repairing the messengers' pushbikes. I knew bugger all about pushbikes, but I did my best. I don't think that really mattered because the job was temporary, and after a few weeks I was back digging the garden at *Hazeldene*.

Then the big moment came. I'm not sure how it happened, it may have been through some of the Old Man's Masonic connections, but I was apprenticed to a firm called M R Shoobridge and Co, oxy-welders and automotive electrical engineers, on September 15, 1922—ten days after I turned sixteen. My job was on the oxy-welding side and I still have the papers of my indentures, apprenticing me to be instructed in the trade of an oxy acetylene welder and automotive electrical engineer, and to 'truly and faithfully . . . serve the Employer as his Apprentice as aforesaid and shall diligently attend to the business and at all times willingly obey the lawful commands of the Employer . . .'

Father's philosophy was that you got some sort of a job and things would work out all right in the long run. Which they did, I suppose, but it was a bloody awful way to start. My first 'lawful command' was to clean up the yard which was full of old iron castings and rusty buckets and God knows what. Then I was instructed in the art of stoking the acetylene generator, which was used to create acetylene for the welding process. In those days you could only buy oxygen in gas bottles. You had to make your own acetylene in a generator by stuffing carbide into a chute; water dripped on it to create gas. One of my jobs was to clean out the chute that still had the raw carbide in it. Half of the carbide would not be spent and could be used again. The apprentice had to pull out the good carbide from the old fluffy stuff. Well, no one thought of rubber gloves and this used literally to take the skin off the end of my fingers.

This was always considered funny—you know, 'Ha ha, look at his fingers'. I was barely sixteen at this stage and there was no way I would have thought of complaining about it. To add to the joke and to give my fingers a chance to heal, they would tell me to get a cold chisel and chip the slag from old castings. You can imagine a kid with a bloody big hammer and a cold chisel—within a few moments you had no skin on any knuckles.

There weren't many industrial safety rules in those days. I remember one day I was working in the electrical workshop when a muffled but powerful explosion came from the welding shop. The next thing I knew, they were supporting the chief welder, Harry Ikin, through to the garage to take him to the Hobart General Hospital. It shook me, rather, because his right hand was only half a hand and it looked awful. Believe it or not, he'd been welding a petrol tank and thought he had taken sufficient precautions by washing it out with water. Of course what happened was that as soon as the metal got hot, the petrol trapped in the crevices vapourised. He recovered and continued his welding career, with half a hand.

One of my other jobs was working the bellows of the forge. They were about two metres long, great leather bellows with a big handle you pulled up and down to activate the forge and heat the castings. I spent hours and hours pulling those bloody bellows. I don't know why they didn't have an electric motor or a fan, other shops did even in those days.

I had about two years of this, until I had a stroke of luck—lucky for me, not so lucky for a fellow apprentice named Silas. The automotive electrical side of the business was run by a man called Eric Sly. He was a magneto specialist and also a very good fitter and turner. Silas was his apprentice and Silas was hooked on girls. He brought to fruition the things I used to think that one day I might be able to do.

Silas would come to work each day and tell us all about his knee-tremblers against the fence when he took a girl home, and even more lurid details of what happened behind closed doors. He used to fill me with great wonderment and envy. But Silas picked up a dose: he got the clap. Unlike today, it wasn't a matter of discreetly going down to the hospital and getting treatment. Silas had to give himself injections at work and Eric Sly—who was something of a puritan—didn't like Silas getting the clap at all. God forgive him, it was quite wrong, but to my great good fortune, he asked Mr Shoobridge who ran the place if he could swap apprentices. This was agreed to and Jack Bowden went over to the auto-electrical side, while poor old Silas chipped castings and pulled the raw carbide out of the oxy-acetylene generators with his bare hands.

Silas's dose changed my life really. I actually started to learn something. Sly taught me how to operate a lathe, wind armatures and rewind magneto armatures. One of the most regular jobs was to remagnetise the electrical systems of T Model Fords.

The T Model Fords had a beautifully designed ignition and lighting system which worked off the engine flywheel. It had magnets which spun around past a row of coils, inducing current in these coils which fed the ignition and also the lights. Of course, the headlights burned beautifully while you were motoring along, but as soon as you slowed down, the lights slowed with you. As you stopped they would go completely out. After some time, the magnets on the flywheel used to weaken.

Pulling the flywheel off and remagnetising the magnets was a very time consuming and therefore expensive procedure. But Eric Sly evolved a very shrewd method for reconstituting the charge in the magnets without having to dismantle the engine at all. The trick was to use a prismatic compass which you put on the casting of the engine where the electrical terminal came out carrying the current. Then the engine was slowly turned over until the compass pointed due north. This showed that all the magnets were lined up with the coils. All you had to do then was get a 12-volt battery and pass current through the coils. There would be a *pnnnst-thump* sound, and all the magnets would be remagnetised. This used to make an enormous difference to the old engines of these T Model Fords. They would start easily and the lights would be bright—it was just marvellous.

The trouble for us was that people used to like to stay and watch their cars being worked on in those days. We had to go through a certain subterfuge to be able to charge people ten shillings for a procedure that took three minutes because of Eric Sly's ingenuity. We used to get around this by taking people out to look at the view, or by saying, 'Look we can't do it for an hour or so', and so on. Eric's nickname was appropriately enough 'Shrewdy' Sly. He owned a narrow-gutted black speedboat called *The Snake* in which he used to take his family, and sometimes me, on weekend outings on the Derwent estuary.

Through an act of complete stupidity, I nearly brought my apprenticeship and probably my career to a sticky end. A man brought in a little sports Overlander motor car. I've never seen one before or since, and I don't want to. But it was just a little, low open car with a windscreen and no hood. It looked to me the sort of motor car that anybody could drive.

During one lunch hour when nobody was about, I had a fit of madness and decided to take it out for a drive. Incidentally, I had no licence; in fact, I had never driven a car on a road. My only experience was manoeuvring cars around the garage itself. Anyway, I got in and pressed the foot starter button and she started. I put her into first gear and headed out the gate, turned right and took off up Murray Street, going through my gears quite successfully, still thinking, 'This is fine. Anybody can do this.' With my hair streaming in the wind, I drove up Murray Street, came to Warwick Street and turned left, and that goes up quite a hill—a long, fortunately straight, hill. It turns into a road at the top, at right angles. Of course, the traffic in those days, praise God, was not what it is now, even in Hobart. I got to the top of the hill still in top gear, because I was a bit dubious about changing gears, swung around in a glorious U turn and headed off down this rather steep hill.

She gathered speed until I was going a bit too fast, I thought, so I put my foot on the brake. Well, there were no brakes at all! How the owner managed it I don't know. On I went down the hill, my hair really streaming in the wind now, and I could do nothing but just hang on to the wheel, pray, and go straight ahead. Warwick Street goes down this steep hill and levels out at the bottom, at the same time crossing Harrington Street—a fairly busy road—at right angles, and Murray Street a short distance further on. I got across Harrington Street safely and, Lord believe it or not, across Murray. By that time the road was taking a slight lift up towards Elizabeth Street which is *the* busy road of Hobart. But, fortunately, before we got there we lost way. I'd found the handbrake by that time and had pulled it on, so I sat beside the road and breathed heavily for a while.

Then I put it into low gear, turned around and drove back quietly, fortunately it was level all the way back to M R Shoobridge and Co. I turned left in the gate, parked the car exactly where it had been on the garage floor and got out a very subdued and humble young man. Nobody ever remarked on it, nobody saw it, and I got away with it. The Lord indeed was kind to me—if being kind to me meant keeping that awful job at M R Shoobridge and Co.

Apart from pranks like trying to drive someone else's car, I was an innocent in those days about many aspects of the wider world, despite Silas's lurid descriptions of his love life. I did not kiss a girl until I was about sixteen, well after I had left school.

After the camps on Mount Stuart ended about 1921 the Old Man used to take a house at Lindisfarne, on the eastern shore of the River Derwent, for the summer holidays. It was a great success and other families we knew also took cottages. There would be parties at the various houses in the evenings. Mothers had young daughters who were anxious to meet nice young men and we used to play Postman's Knock—I forget the details of the game now, but at some point you went outside into the darkness and kissed a girl. I can still feel that lovely young softness, the body of a young girl. It was the first time I had ever experienced it. It was beautiful. You kissed, and then you went back inside again. It was no more than that but, oh God, we were all fired up with it.

My friend Jack Kalbfell, who lived near us at *Hazeldene*, was staying with us at the time. He was about my age. My sister Nora was also invited to some of these parties and she enjoyed herself. Nora was a very normal girl. She went out and was kissed by someone, I'm sure. They were innocent days. But, unfortunately, Nora went home and told my eldest sister Dotty about the

The Old Man in later life. Not even the party hat robs him of his dignified air.

Summer holidays at Lindisfarne, 1925. From left, Nora, Archie Newell, Claire Hibberd, Bea Elliston, and I can't place the young man on the right.

Postman's Knock parties, and my other sister Marjorie. Well! The bloody heavens fell. You've never heard anything like the fuss that went on. Anyone would think we were all shagging out in the middle of the Common. Dot and Marge said it had to stop, I was not to go and this barmaid behaviour had to stop. It was all very strong stuff. I can laugh about it now, but it was very tense and very terrible, particularly as I made up my mind I would still go. And, indeed, I went.

I would get home from work and Dotty would be waiting. 'You're not going tonight, you are to invite them all around here.' It was just awful. She even wrote to my brother Philip in England as well as tackling the Old Man about it. He was sitting out on the edge of the jetty fishing, and she went down and belted his ear for about

In those days we could leave the city simply by crossing the Derwent River to Lindisfarne and relax in our holiday house as though we were at the seaside.

two hours about how I was being led astray. Anyway, it made no difference, I still went. Nothing stopped this dreadful carnal behaviour! It never developed into anything, but after Postman's Knock we used to go for walks in the moonlight, our arms around the lovely little bodies of these young girls. Nothing more than that, but it gives me great pleasure to remember it.

Of course, it all petered out in the end but, oh, the rows were horrible, they really were. Dotty must have written an impassioned letter to Phil in England because he wrote to me and said, 'I believe you have been behaving in a terrible way, what's going on?' This from Philip—of all people—who, I have no doubt, was having a high old time with the young women around Cambridge.

My sisters were very good to me but their efforts to stop the normal fraternising between young boys and girls was quite misguided. No other families were doing it and the young people were going quite happily to these parties. Their families were quite benign about it but, oh dear, not mine. However, on reflection—and I have only thought about this recently—I do think that Dot's treatment of me did not help my self confidence as a young boy, even through into adolescence. With eight members of the Bowden family, and all the visitors we seemed to have, there were always too many people around the *Hazeldene* table, and I was always asked to sit in the child's high chair. This went on until I was seven and eight! Jesus Christ! I suppose I should have rebelled more, but I didn't.

Dot had a great capacity and reputation for telling funny stories but as the young lad of the family I was basically the butt of most of her funny stories. They were told to adoring audiences and visitors having dinner and I was usually present. I can remember sitting there and pretending to laugh, then going outside afterwards and cursing and swearing. Only to myself, of course. I don't think Dottie ever knew the torment she was causing me. There was a lot of it.

She never did it with my elder brother Philip: he was more awesome. I was the clown in her eyes and I think I played up to it a bit by being a bit of a bloody clown. One of the stories she told again and again was about getting ready to go to Lindisfarne for our family summer holiday. Dottie had to pack up and organise the food and all the things we took—including the family cow, now I come to think of it. It was a sensible way to have plenty of fresh milk. But on this particular pack-up day I was sent to get a thing called an O'Cedar mop, a mop which fitted into a round tin which contained O'Cedar oil to clean and polish the floor. It had a device which squeezed the mop as you took it out.

I went off by tram to get this bloody O'Cedar mop from wherever it had been lent, or sent for repair. I must have been daydreaming, because I got off carrying only the handle of the cursed O'Cedar mop, leaving the round tin, with the actual mop in it, on the tram. I arrived home, and I thought people were most unreasonable about this. Dottie cursed and swore—she didn't hit me with the mop handle although she had cause to. But this became the start of a series of stories told over and over about the day of packing up, and my contribution was to be seen walking up Jordan Hill Road, with 'a fairy wand' in my hand waving it airily above my head—which was the mop handle. I think I was about fourteen at the time, and it would not have been all that long after mother died.

I now realise that Dottie had a lot on her plate for a young woman, having been handed the responsibility of taking over a family of seven—which she did uncomplainingly and managed very well. However, one of the results—unintended I am sure—of this kind of mockery was that I had a low self-esteem. I think I was a reasonably nice sort of a kid, but even the teachers at school used to treat me with a slight element of ridicule. It was not until I was about twenty, and actually left home and went to work in Launceston in northern Tasmania, that I gained a fair measure of self-confidence.

I have not mentioned medical matters at all, but when I was about eighteen and during the period after leaving school with the forbidden pleasures of Postman's Knock, I developed appendicitis.

Surgery of any kind was a serious matter in those days, before antibiotics and what is known now about the nature of infection. One day while I was at work—during my apprenticeship as an auto electrician—I had a terrible stomach ache. I had eaten some tough steak at a hotel the night before and I thought it might be related to that. But the pain became so agonising that I went down to the Royal Hobart Hospital.

Now, the RHH was in a great deal of chaos at the time, concerning a particular Dr Ratten who had become the chief surgeon there. He was a very adventurous and brilliant surgeon but there was a certain jealousy among the ranks of the medical profession in Hobart and they queried his credentials. The Government supported Ratten—they even amended the existing Medical Act in the House of Assembly so he could continue to practise at the Royal Hobart Hospital as chief surgeon and superintendent—so all the doctors walked out. Effectively it was a doctors' strike at the Royal. This was wicked, but it's true. That left only three doctors at the Royal, Ratten, 'Stymie' Gaha and a certain Dr Allport who seemed very old to me—he had a walrus moustache. This was the situation I faced with my pain in the gut. After I had been at the hospital for what seemed a long while, I said, 'Can't I see someone, I'm in agony'.

Finally I was shown in to Dr Allport. I was in my working clothes, a pretty raggedy looking youth with my dirty blue shirt. He said, 'Where's the pain?' I lifted up my shirt and pointed to the centre of my stomach. He pressed around and said, 'Oh, you'd better go and get into bed, you know, if it's as bad as that'.

I said, 'Can't I go home and get my things?' and he said, 'I suppose so', so I went home and got my suitcase and pyjamas, came back on the tram to the hospital—still in screaming agony, walked into a ward and got into bed. The ward was a long high-ceilinged room with about twenty beds in it. There was a sort of cabinet beside each bed and after I got into bed a nurse came around and asked me what was the matter. I said, 'I've got a pain, oooo, an awful pain'. She said a doctor would come and see me soon.

About 9 o'clock that night, who should come around but Dr Ratten himself with Stymie Gaha. He said, 'What's wrong with you son?' I said again, 'I've got this terrible pain . . . it's terrible'. He poked my stomach here and there with one finger and said, 'Does it hurt there?' I said, 'Yes it hurts a bit'. 'Oh, you'll be right till the morning', he said, and they all went off.

Well, that night I can remember going into sweats and nightmares, and in the morning I clung on to the nurse and said, 'Look I'm going to be operated on today—can I go in first?' She said I could, but about 7.30 am the pain stopped. Bliss. I felt like going home, but I didn't, I thought I'd better have this thing done. Of course, what had probably happened was that my infected appendix had finally ruptured but I was out of pain, anyway. I was taken to the theatre and remember a gauze mask being put over my face while they poured chloroform on it.

I was very ill indeed after that and I can remember awful nightmares. I didn't know where I was for about three days. One morning Ratten and Gaha came around and Ratten said to Gaha, 'There you are, I told you he'd be all right'. There was apparently some debate about whether they should have put a drain in me or not. Ratten had resisted it and he proved to be right, God bless him.

One night when I was in severe pain, a nurse I knew, Vera Bryant (she was engaged to my brother Eric at one stage), came in and gave me a glass of red medicine. I remember drinking it and sinking into a glorious feeling of peace. It was probably an opiate-based concoction of some sort. I only mention it because you didn't get much by the way of medicine or nursing care. The nurses were obviously under pressure because of the doctors' strike, but discipline was very strict anyway.

There was an old bloke in the bed next to me who was very sick, indeed he died. I don't know what was wrong with him, but he was in the process of dying and calling out for help. There was no button to press or anything—just a small hand-bell, but God help anybody who rang it. I remember we all got our piss bottles and belted our cabinets. The whole ward kicked up a hell of a row. Finally an irate sister came in—the poor woman doubtlessly was completely overworked—and said, 'What is the meaning of this!' We said, 'That's the meaning of this', pointing to the old dying man. 'He wants something.' They got busy, put up some screens and did something with the poor old boy, but he died not long afterwards.

Anyway, I got better and went home. My sister Marjorie was also operated on by Dr Ratten. She had a very bad hip which could have been congenital or caused by polio or rheumatic fever when she was a baby. It was also said she was dropped down the steps by her nurse on the ferry *Kangaroo*, but I think it was probably polio. She walked with great difficulty and it was a most unfortunate handicap for a young girl. I don't think it gave her any pain but she did walk with a bad limp. After taking a business college course, she joined the Electrolytic Zinc Company as a typist at Risdon, joined the company's health fund and found that she could have an operation at the Royal Hobart Hospital at the expense of the Company.

She went to see Dr Ratten. You name it, he did it. There was no specialisation in those days. He might do an appendix one day and a hip the next. In those days goitre operations were very common and many women in Hobart carried a slight red mark across their throats where Dr Ratten had taken their goitre out. He asked Marge to wait for a while because there was a new instrument he had read about in a medical journal, and he wanted to get it and learn how to use it. He did various tests on her and checked her for TB and so on. Eventually he did operate and it was a disaster. I don't know how long she went through the agonies of it, but it seemed to go on for years. You can imagine what a hip operation was like in those days. Metal pins were put in and God knows what else. She was very ill and suffered for ages. Eventually she had less

The Old Man with his first grandchild, Eric's daughter Peggy. From left, Eric, Phil, Father, Peggy and me

mobility and certainly more pain than before. It was a great disappointment, although no one ever said so.

Ratten was a brave and brilliant surgeon. He no doubt had his failures, but he saved a lot of lives. Poor Marge's operation was unfortunately one of his failures. We'd always hoped that she'd walk better than before it was done. But she never really regained what agility she'd had—which wasn't much—after the operation. Marge was particularly nice to me and I remember her with great affection. She and my sister Nora both started out in life with physical handicaps. Nora, poor girl, was born with very distinct casts in both eyes. Through her childhood she wore the large unattractive glasses of the day, and much of that time was spent with a patch over one eye. It was done to make you use one eye all the time. None of this helped her confidence, of course, but she had a most delightful nature and all she wanted in life was to be nice to people and, in return, for them to be nice to her. She, too, qualified as a shorthand typist and when she worked with the legal firm Dobson, Mitchell and Allport she arranged to have an operation to correct the casts in her eyes. Not Dr Ratten this time, but one Dr J Bruce Hamilton who was the eye man in Hobart in those days. He was a large rather pompous man who bullied not only his patients but anyone else he could see. I always felt he assiduously cultivated the reputation of being 'a great man'. He certainly acted as though he was one. Certainly Nora was swayed by his reputation and went to him for her operation.

She put up with a great deal of the particular bullying that Hamilton seemed to rejoice in dishing out to people and was pretty miserable for some time, and the whole thing did little to help her confidence and self-esteem.

As it happened, I experienced the J Bruce Hamilton treatment myself much later when I was on leave in Tasmania from my unit in Queensland during World War Two, and collected a thing called a virus keratosis in my right eye, which is a very painful condition. I had to report sick and was introduced into the presence of Major Hamilton. Without saying a word, he sat me down and examined my eye for a long period—still saying absolutely nothing. Then he strode to a telephone and I heard him say, 'Is that the Repatriation Hospital? I want a private ward for Major Bowden. Major Bowden has a *very* bad eye.'

He continued the 'I am a great man' technique all the time he was dressing it, clicking his teeth and implying that blindness in that eye was just around the corner. To put it in simple army language, I had the shits—possibly I was going blind in one eye. I spent a couple of anxious days in hospital, where Hamilton had issued instructions that my eye was not to be touched by *anybody*. At the end of the second day he came along and I was in some trepidation as he removed the dressing and looked into my eye through an instrument, as he intoned dramatically, 'Miraculous!' Another cornerstone to his greatness had been erected. However, unlike my poor sisters, that particular medical treatment was successful. And, of course, Dr Ratten undoubtedly saved my life those years before when he operated on my ruptured appendix.

Chapter Nine

ELECTRICAL ADVENTURES

By the fourth year of my apprenticeship, my boss Eric Sly was offered a job by the firm of Medhursts in Hobart to start an auto-electrical department, and I went with him. Medhursts were in Collins Street, not far from the back of Hutchins School.

There was a growing need for auto-electrical work and Medhursts decided to add an auto-electrical workshop to their business in Launceston, in the north of Tasmania. This was about 1927 and I was selected to run it. In fact, I wasn't all that keen to leave Hobart. I had a girlfriend by then and a lot of friends, so when the day came to leave for Launceston I stayed as long as possible, which meant leaving on the 'Midnight Horror', the goods train which left Hobart at 9 pm and got to Launceston at 6 the next morning.

The second last carriage behind the freight trucks was a second-class compartment with hard horsehair seats and if you were foolish enough to buy a ticket you could travel there. So they blew the whistle at 9 on a Sunday night, for me to start work in Launceston at 8 the next morning! It was an awful journey. The train dropped off and picked up trucks all the way to Launceston. I climbed out, with my eyes full of coal dust and grit and feeling absolutely ghastly and took a horse cab from the station to the boarding house I'd booked into for a quick wash and a shave before reporting to Mr Harry Medhurst at Medhurst and Sons, Brisbane Street, Launceston.

Now the family had been dining out on my new appointment: 'John's been made manager of the workshop in Launceston and he's only in the fourth year of his apprenticeship, so how about that!' I was full of pride and my own importance but I had a slight let-down coming to me because Harry Medhurst wasn't a very nice little man. I said, 'Here I am, Mr Medhurst, where's my workshop?'

There was a small lane beside the shop and he said, 'Come up to the top of the lane with me and you'll see'. So we walked up and there was a small double storey, four-roomed cottage there. The two downstairs rooms were kept as a storeroom for the shop with all the wire, screws and things that house wiremen used. The top storey was also two rooms, all solid brick.

Harry Medhurst said to me, 'There's a sledge hammer. What you have to do is knock that wall out to make those two top rooms into one, and there's your workshop'. This was literally the case. So I spent the first week belting into the partition wall. It never occurred to me to say that I wasn't going to do it, and I was going home—this was what I had to do. After I'd knocked the wall down and carted all the bricks away I built some work benches and made up some electrical testing equipment. It wasn't possible to buy test equipment in those days, but somehow I made it. I'm pretty sure I was the first auto electrician to appear in northern Tasmania. The work had been done by motor mechanics before in their own way—people were pretty ingenious and coped as best they could.

While I was building test benches, growlers to test armatures and all that sort of thing, work started to come in. Now, I didn't know very much. I was in the fourth year of an apprenticeship and we really hadn't been taught a great deal. I had never before seen a lot of the equipment that came in for me to repair. Launceston had different motor cars from Hobart. Curious, but true. The Rover agency was in the hands of a bloke named Hollis, and every second car up there was a Rover 9 which I'd never seen in Hobart. They had Lucas equipment and it was fairly complicated. The electrics were also troublesome and frail. Another popular car up there was an Ansaldo, which I hadn't seen in Hobart either. It was an Italian car and had involved electrical equipment, continental stuff.

I used to spend a lot of time finding out how the equipment worked, rather than what was wrong with it. Also, they were the days when customers felt that when they brought a car in, there was none of that business of 'leave it there and come back tonight and it'll be ready'. They felt they had a godalmighty right to stay and look over your shoulder and see what you were doing. I suppose it was fair enough, in a way, if they were paying for it. But they objected to paying for it! They paid you practically nothing for the work you did. You'd work on a job all morning—five shillings an hour was supposed to be the going rate—and if you worked for two hours and said, 'That'll be ten shillings', the heavens fell. Anyway, I learned a tremendous amount during this time.

I think I made the first test bench that had a variable speed drive on it. I built it out of two big cone pulleys. You slid a belt up and down the cone and that slowed it down or speeded it up depending on how far you pushed the belt along. Before that, the only way to see if a repaired generator worked was to put it back on the car. With my beautiful new machine we could test it on the bench. That particular arrangement worked well for a long time and I was very proud of it.

Some of the jobs that came my way were quite curious, and I don't suppose they would ever be likely to come again to someone in my position. Medhursts were the main electrical firm in the town and consequently, if anything went wrong electrically in Launceston, you rang up Medhursts. All the other staff there were wiremen—men who wired houses. I have no doubt that there were many skilled electrical engineering people around Launceston running power stations and so on, but there weren't really any electrical mechanics.

There was a firm in town called D & W Murray, and their building had a lift in it—it was one of the taller buildings in the town. When their lift went wrong they rang Medhursts and, of course, the finger pointed at me. Would I go and fix their lift? I rather enjoyed these offbeat jobs and said I would, while I wondered to myself how the hell a lift worked. I arrived at D & W Murray with my tool bag with pliers and screwdrivers and whatnot. Sure enough, the lift wouldn't go.

First of all I climbed up miles and miles of bloody stairs and then up a ladder into the loft above the lift. There was a room just stacked full of machinery with huge cables, drums, electric motors and circuit breakers on the wall, a maze of equipment none of which I knew the faintest thing about. I said to myself, 'First principles, Bowden—simple things first'. So I went down and talked to the lift driver. He was a rather pompous, beaky little man—although I shouldn't be too critical because it is a job that is unlikely to attract the great brains of the town. He had a handle that he pushed one way to go up, and the other way to go down. So I asked him if he would get into the lift and demonstrate the fault.

He said, 'I'm not getting in there, she's out of order. If you want to do that, do it your bloody self'. So I got in and pulled the little lever and she took off up at a fair speed. I thought maybe there was nothing wrong after all. But just as the lift got near the top it suddenly stopped and descended at a rapidly accelerating rate. Just as I was about to crap myself, she stopped and went up again. This went on for some time. In the end I did find a thing called an emergency switch in the lift and threw it. The lift stopped between two bloody floors, of course, and the little beaky lift driver had to go where there was a handle and winch me up level with a floor so I could get out.

Again I went back to first principles and realised it couldn't be all that equipment up at the top because the lift was working right enough. It had to be a problem of control. Then I remembered there was a big cable that went from the lift control in a big loop up from the machinery loft to underneath the lift. I thought there was probably something wrong with this cable. So I asked the beaky little man if he had smelt any burning in the lift. 'Yes, I did as a matter of fact', he said. 'Right', I said, 'I reckon it's the cable, but I'll have to go back to work and get some more equipment'.

I went back to get a thing called a megger. My plan was to scientifically disconnect all the wires from the control box and with a megger you put a connection on two wires. You could then turn a little handle which generated a high voltage without much current in it and which registered on a meter if there was any leak between the cables. That was the proper and only way to carry this thing out. But by the time I had walked back to Medhursts to get the megger, the beaky bugger who knew every bloody thing had grabbed hold of the cable—bearing in mind that I had asked him if he had smelt burning—and had pulled it past his beaky bloody nose. It was fair enough, I suppose. Finally he came to the faulty part, and said, 'Here it is, I don't know why we worried you, I've found it. Here's the trouble!'

Sure enough, if you smelt it, you could detect burned rubber inside the cable. All my beautiful testing and diagnosis was cast aside by this beaky little bugger. Anyway, modern day regulations would never permit the repair of such a cable, it would have to be replaced and passed by some higher authority or other. But I laboriously stripped it down and re-insulated all the wires. It was quite a big job, actually, and when I bound it all up again, the lift worked. I never did get the whole story, but I think the beaky bugger recommended to D & W Murray that they didn't pay the bill because he found the fault, not me!

One day Harry Medhurst called me into his office and told me that things were bad—it was depression time of course—and that the Government had put on an iniquitous thing called a two-and-a-half per cent sales tax which was going to ruin the country, that things were crook, and we were all going to have to take a cut in salary. My salary, which was five pounds ten shillings a week, was to be reduced to three pounds ten. I thought this was terrible. I was broke to the wide bloody world anyway, because for one reason or another I was still sending a whole pound a week to Hobart to keep *Hazeldene* going. It wasn't really necessary. but I did it, and it was considered the thing. Anyway, I was broke. I had no clothes and I owed a few bob here and there and so on, so I thought I'd have to do something about it.

Incidentally, the depression did not seem to hit Tasmania as hard as it hit big cities like Melbourne or Sydney. An army friend of mine, Dick Durance, told me once that his mother had some valuable books in their Melbourne house. They would be hungry for a long while, and then his mother would put on a slap-up meal. He would notice that one, maybe two or three of these books had disappeared from the bookshelf because she was flogging them to buy food. In those days we didn't seem to bust as hard in Tasmania—we didn't boom as hard either. We seemed to keep more on a level plane.

But I had to do something about my own impossible financial

situation, and I decided to start out in business on my own. I knew this mean little man Harry Medhurst, God rest his soul, would not give me my holidays if he knew I planned to leave. So I asked him if I could have my holidays and be paid before I went. He said, 'Oh yes, all right', a bit grudgingly. So I collected my pay—which was a whole ten pounds—and then gave notice. And I have never heard such a performance in my life.

'My God, you put it over me about your holidays. You wouldn't have got that money if I had known you were going to leave.' I said, 'But it was due'. 'It makes no difference, you wouldn't have got it. But in any case you're ruined—we will break you within three months, I'll promise you that!'

This is indicative of how employees could be treated in those days, and although I tried to be brave externally, I thought it was absolutely terrible that this big firm would be working against me and that I would probably go broke. However, the die was cast.

I had sounded out a bloke called Mick Robson, who owned Robson's Garage in Charles Street, Launceston. It had half a top storey just over the garage which was used for junk and storage. The floor was so rotten you couldn't walk on it in places, but one section had been repaired and Nick Robson said he'd rent it to me for a pound a week. He was a nice man, and he said he'd give me any electrical work that came through his garage.

I had to get busy and make another bloody test bench with the pulleys I was so proud of before, made out of Huon pine blocks pressed on to shafts and turned down to make two tapered pulleys so I could bench-test generators. I also built a switchboard, a growler and a magnetiser—I must admit I had taken patterns off the ones I'd built at Medhursts. So I fitted myself out as best I could and started off in my own business with great trepidation.

A bloke named Max Lovett said he'd look after the accounts for me, and Maxie ruled me with a rod of iron, God bless him. If I took sixpence out of the petty cash to buy myself a packet of cigarettes—I smoked heavily in those days—he used to get very terse and say, 'You can't do that'. I drew £5 a week from the business as salary.

Getting going was hard work. The first thing I did after building my equipment was to borrow Max's motorbike—a little two-and-a-quarter BSA—and drive from Launceston through to Burnie up the north-west coast with a haversack on my back, calling in at all the garages on the way and introducing myself. I knew many of the garage managers and owners from my days at Medhursts, and I told them what I was doing, asked if they would support me and whether they had any generators to be repaired. Some did, and I slowly filled up my haversack with generators and magnetos. They were heavy on my back, too, and the north-west coast highway was not bitumen in those days but corrugated gravel. I left Burnie to drive to Launceston weighed down with my haversack full of repair work, but feeling very proud of myself. It was a bugger of a drive, through heavy rain. The headlights failed . . . I'll never forget that drive.

Back at my new workbench I repaired the magnetos and generators and got started. At this stage I knew a girl named Peggy Lovett (one of Max's younger sisters) who worked at the Telephone Exchange. There was a direct connection with the switchboards on the exchange in those days, and an operator would answer. Peggy would keep an eye on my line and her voice would usually say 'hello', and we'd sometimes talk a bit. There was a supervisor walking up and down behind the girls waiting for them to do just such a thing when she would pounce. But we used to talk a little, and it was very nice—it happened quite often. I like to think about that. Anyway, it led to one of the marriages of the century.

Of course, times were hard and it was difficult to get money out of people, but when I read about what was happening in other parts of Australia, and there I was drawing £5 a week out of my little business in the depression, I knew I was very lucky. I have often wondered, too, what would have happened had I had a real business sense. Any business which could survive during the depression would have been capable of growth if I had borrowed some money and properly financed it. It could have been worth a mint in later years. On the other hand, it would have altered my whole lifestyle and could have meant that I would not have come back to Hobart to live.

I ran my own little business for almost two years, and one day, much to my intense delight and satisfaction, I scored a nice big job from the Cornwall Coal Mine in the Fingal Valley. A large direct current electric motor arrived in my workshop—how they heard of me I'll never know. I dismantled it with great eagerness. It had a burnt out armature and various other things wrong with it. I

J. G. BOWDEN, Specialist in Magnetos, Dynamos and Automobile Electrical Equipment, 42 Charles Street, Launceston, was born in the year 1906, and was educated at the Hutchins School, Hobart. On completing his education he was apprenticed to the firm of Shoobridge and Co., Hobart, general and electrical engineers. After serving a year with this firm his apprenticeship was transferred to the firm of Medhurst and Son, who at that time were opening an Automobile Electrical Service Station. Mr. Bowden was here engaged in armature winding and general electrical work until the firm decided to open a similar branch in Launceston, of which they requested him to take charge, notwithstanding the fact that his apprenticeship had not yet expired. He served in the managerial capacity for a further four years, when he decided to relinquish his connection with the firm and start in business on his own account. He was fortunate in obtaining ideal premises in Robson's Garage at 42 Charles Street, Launceston, where he is now successfully carrying out this highly specialised work.

This flattering account of my skills in the Cyclopedia of Tasmania, *1931, was written by me!*

rewound it, assembled it, and it was picked up and returned to the company and re-installed in the mine.

A few days later I had a ring from the mine manager, Mr Gard, to say that the motor was running a little fast and he thought it was over-heating a little. The main problem was, because it was running fast, a second pump couldn't keep pace with the water it was pumping from a particular level. Would I come and do something about it? I thought about this, armed myself with some resistance wire, test tools, rev counters and various things and prepared to go down there, but it was difficult leaving a one-man business. I found that the St Marys bus left at 4 pm and returned from St Marys the following morning at 7.30 getting me back to Launceston by 11 am which would mean that I wouldn't have to neglect my business.

It was something of a commentary on the public transport of the time, 1927, that the bus was actually a large sedan car in bad repair—an old Buick. I knew it was in bad repair because I had to drive the bloody thing. It was run by a bloke called Russ Hardwick. I think Russ was one of those poor blokes who came out of World War One white faced and tense but who had to earn a living. A lot of those men went into hire car work—anything rather than go back into an office after what they'd been through. Russ wore a trench coat and a felt hat cocked on the side of his head. These buses—they weren't buses at all and were called service-cars—used to ply between major centres like Launceston and country towns. St Marys was about 150 kilometres to the south-east of Launceston.

I boarded the service-car and, as I'd done some work on his car for him from time to time, I had the privilege of sitting next to Russ. It was a full bus. There were dicky seats in the back with three or four passengers, and I sat in the front seat with one other passenger. It was mid winter and we took off on one of those nights when there is a high glass and a hard frosty night coming up. Well, Russ was as full as a boot when we took off, pretty obviously he'd been drowning his sorrows most of the afternoon. We drove just out of Launceston and then he said, 'Come on, cock, you drive. I want a rest'.

This was fine by me, I liked to drive in those days, so we swapped places. Gawd, she was a rough motor car. The brakes, I remember, were bloody awful as we drove out into that frosty night. Russ had me pull up at a pub somewhere to top himself up while we all sat patiently outside, then he fell heavily asleep on my shoulder while I drove. The other passengers just put up with this. No one made any fuss about me—just a bloody youth—doing the driving.

We got to St Marys about 8 pm and I woke Russ up, handed his car back to him and took my overnight bag and booked into the pub. It was freezing by then, a hard frost. The next thing was to find the mine manager, Mr Gard, so I went to the bar of the pub and asked the barman. 'Oh', he said, 'Bill Gard—you won't get him now, he's always passed out by this time of night. But that's his house over there'.

I hammered on his door, but there wasn't a bloody sound. Then I tried somewhere else and finally was told that if I wanted to get into the mine I'd have to see the man who ran the generating plant because I'd have to have lights. So I went and dug him out, poor bloke. He was in bed but not shickered, unlike every other living soul in the town of St Marys who seemed to be roaring drunk by that time of night. The pub had to be seen to be believed. It was a real mining town. Anyway, this nice old bloke agreed to start up the plant which was run by an old steam engine. He unbanked the fires and got up steam, started up the electric plant and on came the lights. Fortunately for me, he also took me into the mine to show me where the motor was. We didn't have to go down in a cage or anything. The Cornwall Coal Mine went straight into the side of the mountain and you just walked straight into the hill. One thing I noticed was the glorious warmth as soon as we got underground, away from the freezing frosty night outside.

My ideas on what had to be done to the motor worked out, so I made the necessary adjustments and returned to the pub. Next morning Russ Hardwick turned up with his service-car, trench coat and felt hat—sober, happy and well—and took me back to Launceston.

After running my own little business for about two years I decided it was a bit precarious, and when the opportunity came up to go to a firm called H C Thompson & Co as workshop foreman in their automotive electrical section, I took the job. They had the Lucas agency and it looked pretty good although it was a miserable sort of place, really. It was a family business. Old H C Thompson managed it, with his daughter doing the office work. Through that particular job I started to do some work on aero engines.

There were various little air services flying out of Launceston—rather like Russ Hardwick's bus to St Marys. A bloke called

Johnson ran a service to Flinders Island via Cape Barren Island in a De Souta monoplane. It was one of the planes that someone famous flew out from England and is now in a glass case at the Launceston Airport. It was a very interesting little aircraft, and he used to bring in his magnetos to Thompsons for me to overhaul. The plane had two magnetos as a dual ignition system. Each magneto fed a separate row of spark plugs. Shortly after take-off Johnson used to switch from two magnetos to one magneto, and if there was any falter in the engine, he would have to come back and land at Western Junction, as Launceston Airport was called then.

These days there are strict rules and regulations laid down about who can work on the repair of aero engines—particularly on passenger aircraft—but no one ever checked my credentials, and I used to test the magnetos on the primitive test bench I'd designed and built. Thank God no aircraft ever crashed because of work I'd done on its magnetos!

One day Vic Holyman walked into my workshop at Thompsons. He was one of the originals of Holyman Airways and brother of the great Ivan. He'd been a sea captain and he was a colourful character—a somewhat florid, bombastic sort of bloke, but I got on well with him. He would wander in with magnetos under his arm off the DH 86 Holyman planes that used to fly across Bass Strait to Melbourne and back. Like a good businessman he'd always haggle about prices. I'd say, 'It needs a new condenser'. 'Why does it? Can't you fix the old one?' Of course, in the end the safety of his aircraft came first and he'd approve any necessary work. Through Vic I did one job I found particularly interesting.

Holyman's were running De Havilland DH 86s on the run to Melbourne and they were a bugger of a plane. They had a habit of folding their wings and diving into the sea every now and then. Anyway, Vic came in one day and said they were installing a radio on their plane. This was quite a radical development—real radio—so they could communicate with Launceston and Melbourne airports. They were having trouble. I wasn't a radio man, but one of the problems was that their system of charging the batteries wasn't working properly, and that was rather in my line.

They had a T Model Ford generator to charge their radio batteries. It was mounted on the wing and operated by a little propeller built on to it which was designed to spin like a windmill in flight. I found it had been wrongly connected up to the generator and fixed that particular problem. They said they were going up on a test and I must have looked longingly at the plane because Vic asked me if I'd like to go and I said I would very much. He said, 'Good, sign here', and produced a document which said that I accepted all responsibility and had no claim on the airline if anything happened to me as a result of the flight. We took off from Western Junction and had a nice little flight right down to the Tamar River heads and back again. But, although my part of the circuit worked, they still couldn't get any results from the radio.

Shortly after this that very same plane—with Vic Holyman on board—just disappeared over Bass Strait. There were all sorts of theories as to what happened to it. There was no radio so nobody ever knew. It was a terrible thing.

Before it vanished and took old Vic with it, I asked him for a reference. I don't quite know why I did. It's on Holyman Airways paper and it recommends me to any airline who wanted the services of a thoroughly competent electrician. I've never used it, but I've still got it.

Chapter Ten

GETTING A GIRL IN LAUNCESTON

When I transferred from Hobart to Launceston in 1927 to sledge-hammer my way into the workshop I was supposed to manage at Medhursts, I was deeply in love with a girl in Hobart called Beatrice. It was a very powerful love affair but, like most love affairs of that day, it was never consummated, although we were very much in love with each other.

Being transferred to Launceston was just a misery. I used to spend my entire life trying to get back to Hobart to see Bea and to spend time with my family at *Hazeldene*. I'd booked myself into the first of a number of boarding houses in Launceston. This was one in St Johns Street at the end of a row of terraces. When you opened the front door to go in you were confronted by a stairway which went straight up, and halfway up the stairway was a lavatory. It was a modern flushing type, but it had a peculiar smell of its own. That was the first thing you noticed when you went in the front door—its distinctive odour reached out to greet you.

I shared a room with another bloke from Hobart, Irwin Knight, who worked at the Rapson Tyre Company. Our room had green wallpaper with white daisies, two black iron bedsteads, a wardrobe and not much else. We lived there and ate our meals in a small dining room. There were about five other boarders there, all men.

The place was run by two spinster sisters, the Misses Goodall.

One of us christened the place 'The Angels' Rest' which we thought was very funny. The house didn't have a name. Unfortunately we started heading our outgoing letters like that and people started writing back to Mr J Bowden, 'The Angels' Rest', St Johns Street, Launceston. The Misses Goodall got very upset and had words with us about it. Our board was twenty-one shillings a week, and it took a bit of finding out of my £5 a week—less the pound I used to send home to the Old Man at *Hazeldene*.

The boarding house was opposite St Johns Church and there was a tennis court there where Irwin Knight and I used to play. That's how I met Max Lovett who became my accountant when I started my own business. One of the other boarders was an electrician named Wally Fewtrell who was a nice man with a keen sense of humour and a most infectious laugh. We used to do silly things. Wally occasionally went out on a jag and he was one of those outgoing blokes who used to talk about it a lot—that he was going somewhere and was going to come back full.

On this particular night we knew he would come home pretty well shickered, so first of all Irwin and I got all the empty beer bottles out of our wardrobe—and there were plenty—and stood them in rows on the stairway, having made sure the Misses Goodall had gone to bed. We didn't put them on every stair, we'd miss a few steps and then plant some more. Then we took the globe out of the light over the stairway and went to bed.

Well, it started about 1.30 am. Wally came in, happily liquored up, and couldn't find the light, so he felt his way carefully to the stairway and started to climb. He toppled the first row of bottles, and you have never heard such a row in all your life. He had this wonderfully distinctive laugh, and he started to giggle. Then he'd come to a few bottle-free stairs and think he was clear, and then he'd knock over some more. The higher up the stairs they were, the more noise they made. Well, the poor Misses Goodall cowered in their beds with horror and terror at what was going on. We managed to sort it all out with them the next morning, but there was a bit of a stinko about it. I can still hear Wally Fewtrell's amazing laugh and the rattle and crash of the bottles.

As an automotive electrician I used to do a lot of work for Heathorns garage in Launceston, and I got to know one of their mechanics, a nice man called Lin Dickens. He had a motor car, a light Overland tourer, and we used to go on night shooting expeditions. We were bloody awful in those days, we used to shoot any game we saw moving with our spotlight—even kangaroos if they showed up. We did eat what we shot but, looking back on it, it was not very good behaviour. Anyway we used to do it.

One night we were out in the White Hills area near Launceston when out popped a rabbit in our spotlight. Lin had a disconcerting habit of slamming his foot on the brake and at the same time getting his 12 bore up to his shoulder and firing a shot. I was holding the spotlight on the poor bloody rabbit—which on this occasion escaped unscathed—but a horse that was grazing in the paddock threw its head up, as a horse does, and I said, 'My God, you were a bit close to that horse, weren't you?' Lin said, 'Oh no, I wasn't'. So we finished our night's shoot and went home with our ill-gotten gains.

The next day a policeman arrived to see Lin at Heathorns. How they got onto it I don't know, but they did.

'Do you own a light Overland car?' they asked. Lin said he did.

'Were you out at White Hills in it last night?' Lin said he was.

'Did you fire a gun?'

'Why, yes', said Lin. 'I shot a rabbit.'

The policeman said, 'Are you aware that you also shot a man, a woman and a horse?'

Poor Lin nearly fell over backwards. Apparently, there had been a man and a woman disporting themselves happily under the hedge, while the man was holding his horse by the bridle rein at the same time. The horse was their means of transport to their meeting place. I think they were mainly hit by chunks of gravel and dirt thrown up by Lin's shot, while the horse was mainly scared. Fortunately for all concerned, the couple shouldn't have been there. Each belonged to another partner, and therefore neither was particularly anxious to have too much fuss made. The policeman gave Lin a severe talking to, and the matter was dropped.

On another occasion we were again doing some night shooting in the White Hills country and had bagged a rabbit or two. We stopped the Overland on top of a hill—fortunately as it happened—to have a beer. Oh dear, shooting from a car and drinking beer at the same time! I was sitting in the back opening the bottle and pouring glasses for the others, and I'd just poured one for myself when we became aware that another motor car with its lights on was coming up the hill.

Lin, being an acute sort of fellow, sensed trouble and dropped his glass. Without putting the headlights on he let the brakes off, ran the car down the hill, got the engine going with a running start and took off like a bloody madman. All this with the lights off! How he did it I'll never know. To our horror, the other car swung around and took off after us. Well, Lin drove like a demented genius. I was still holding my glass and the bottle of beer in the back seat. Eventually Lin shot down a side lane and swung off the road into some cover and we sat there watching the lights of the pursuing car winding around the hilltops looking for us. We got away, but found out later that the other car had belonged to the poor old landowner who, the previous night, had had some stock shot by somebody playing this dastardly spotlighting game. If we'd been caught that night we'd have been in real trouble.

One of the things that made Launceston life easier to cope with after being transplanted from Hobart was the pleasure of owning a good Alsatian dog. My sister Marge had been given an Alsatian bitch called Sappho. She was rather an excitable dog, but Dot, Marge and Nora smoothed her out a bit and they used to show her. Sappho won prizes, too, and Marge got the show dog complex and decided to breed for a hobby. She sent Sappho—at great expense—over to Melbourne in the *Taroona* to mate with a stud German Shepherd rejoicing in the name of Klaus von Uhlengarten. I helped to put her on the boat in Launceston. All went according to plan, and Marge gave me one of her pups which I called Thor. He was about three months old when I took him to Launceston, about a quarter grown. His ears were just starting to stick up. Thor was a very beautiful animal.

I was boarding at a place called 'The Lounge' in Brisbane street, opposite the Brisbane Hotel, at that stage. Old Maude Cleaver, the landlady, would have had a fit had she known I had a dog sleeping in my room. But even as a three-month-old pup, Thor's behaviour patterns were so good that I managed it. I'd wait till things settled down and Maude was in bed and then I'd go up to my room which meant going up three flights of linoleum-covered stairs. Not a sound did Thor make, but his toenails used to click on the lino. So

My Alsatian, Thor, was a once-in-a-lifetime dog.

I used to pick him up, the way you'd carry a calf, for the last flight of stairs past Maude's door.

One night I must have been a bit shickered—quite likely in those days—and I stumbled on the last flight and hit Thor's head against the stair rail just beside her door. Of course he went *woof* and the bedroom door opened and there was Maude Cleaver in her nightdress with her hair in curlers—the classic picture of a landlady. She wasn't a bad old duck, really, but she said, 'Where are you going with that dog?'

'Miss Cleaver, I'm just popping into my room for a minute before I take him back to his kennel.'

'Don't you take him into your room!'

'Just for a minute.'

Anyhow, I did take him into my room and snuck him out the next morning and arranged a kennel for him.

The situation was such that he had to be with me all the time. It was incredible when I look back on it. But I had no real attachments in Launceston, and not many friends. So I spent hours with this great dog training him and teaching him things. Thor had a great capacity for carrying. He would just take a bag in his mouth and carry it. I got him to the stage where, if you said 'sit', he would sit, and stay until he was told to move. I used to show off a bit of course. He was fully grown by this time and I'd go into a restaurant and he'd come with me—they didn't seem to mind in those days, nor did the people eating there. He would sit patiently beside my seat while I ate and when I was ready to leave I'd say 'sit', quietly, and go and pay my bill. This was showing off, really. After paying, I'd walk out with him sitting there watching me. Thor would continue to sit there with the restaurant people doubtless saying how wonderful it was. When I was well out into the street I whistled him. Well, Thor took off at full speed—he was as big as a calf by this time—and chairs and tables went in all directions! There was a bit of a fuss about that, and I never did it again.

In 1929 I had a yen to do something with the lovely long summer evenings we had in Launceston, and I joined the Tamar Rowing Club. At the time I joined it had the distinction of having the senior eight, which had just won the champion eights of Australia, the Kings Cup, and the senior four which had won the Stewards Cup—the senior rowing race in Australia for four oarsmen.

The club officials started you off in some pair-oared skiffs, you found a partner, and were encouraged to row up and down the Gorge, the lower half of which is near the club. I didn't realise that representatives of the club were observing the people who came down and rowed these boats to spot anyone who might have any possible talent in the game. I had always had plenty of contact with boats as a kid, particularly at one stage when we used to go camping out in Prince of Wales Bay on the Derwent. There was a lovely long dinghy with paddles there for our use and we used to kid ourselves that we could really smack her along. This stood me in good stead on the Gorge, also the fact that I was very keen and used to go down every afternoon.

The day came when they had to decide who was going to be in the maiden eight—the eight for beginners—and I was picked as one of the crew. I was very pleased about that and even more surprised when the man who was to be our coach said to me, 'Jack will you sit there, please, for the time being anyway'. And 'there' was the stroke seat. Well, how about that! It all went very well. We had a good crew and a good coach, we were very keen, and we had a tremendous amount of stamina.

It was interesting because at the start of a season you were smoking—everyone smoked all the time—and living a normal life, and after you learned to row a bit, you would begin with the first row of the season. After 100 yeards you had had it but, surprisingly, it only took about a fortnight to settle in and then you could belt the boat along for long periods of time.

We won our first Maiden Eight race at the Tamar Regatta and I can remember it now. Having won a maiden eight, you could only win another if you happened to be entered for another regatta at the time you won the previous one and we had entered for the Devonport Regatta on the Mersey. We had to load our boats on the train, which was quite a ritual, and settle down as a crew like good boys, not smoking or drinking. We won again (whacko!) and then, of course, we got suitably boozed. That was the end of eight-oared rowing, so we moved on to a maiden four and happily did the same thing there, won a lot of races and developed a pretty good reputation. Finally we won a Junior Senior Four race—that's the class under the senior class.

They were successful and happy times, and there was good

camaraderie with the blokes concerned. It was a lovely feeling to go down after work, get a boat out and train, rowing down the river with the coxwain, and rowing back again while the coach told you what was wrong and what was right. We came under a coach called Percy Weetman who had read widely and studied rowing—he was an old oarsman who introduced us to a new theory about 'the short rig'. Normally the rigger sticks out a certain distance from the side of the boat, and common practice was to row very long, reaching forward and pulling right back. The new theory was that by shortening the riggers you shortened the movement in the boat and therefore achieved the same long movement of the paddle in the water, which seemed to be good sense. But it involved a new approach. We had to learn not to reach right out as we'd been taught, and we had to get a certain swing into it that one got used to. We won with that rig very well.

One night in particular sticks in my memory: it was when the Henley on Tamar was coming up about the middle of the season. The practice developed of sending all the crews down the river for a handicapped race home. The good crews, like our beautiful champion eight, would go right down almost to the Grammar School on the Tamar, and the senior four would go just a bit further up. We'd have our place and the maiden eight and fours would be closer to home. At a certain agreed time we would all take off—we were too far apart for anyone to fire a gun—trying to get home first. It was a wonderful experience. You rowed along and thought nothing would ever catch you then around a bend in the river behind you would come the great senior eight with its big square-shouldered men and their beautiful rhythmic swing. They'd just creep up on you. It was a tremendous scene, a lovely calm evening, the thunk of the oars against the outriggers, everyone rowing their hearts out with the coxwains all barking and urging their crews on to even more strenuous efforts. I used to look forward to those nights.

I made some very good friends through rowing. My future brother-in-law Max Lovett rowed with us. Poor chap, he used to suffer from eczema and just before one important race, the Junior Senior Fours for the Henley on Tamar, he had a bad attack which made it quite impossible for him to sit in a boat. Naturally there was a certain amount of dismay, but there was a man in the senior eight called Bob Bain who had never won a senior four, so the night before the race the club organisers said, 'Your race is half-way through the afternoon, and the senior eight race is last. I would suggest we put Bob in your crew as your number 2 man. He'll be fit enough to row in the eights afterwards.' Bob was a very good oarsman, he was about the right weight, and he fitted in very well to our rowing style. But it had one funny side to it.

On Tamar regatta days, the great Jack Artis, who was the coach of the senior eights, would get a dinghy and anchor himself about half-way down the rowing course where he could see all the crews coming down. The half-way point is, in my opinion, where you win or lose the race. But on this occasion all old Jack could think of was his precious Bob Bain tiring himself in our Junior Senior Four race. We started, and it was a pretty close race and hard going, and we were getting to the half-way mark where I always used to call for a sprint and try and get a bit of nose in front. If you did that, you could generally hold it and then bust yourself at the finish to keep it. At the half-way mark I called for a sprint, during which all you can see is death and blackness, while you are really working hard. Through the mists of pain I could hear this voice of bloody old Jack Artis with a megaphone saying, 'Take it easy Bob. Just take it easy, son. You're doing all right. Don't forget you've got the Senior Eight race to come!' I'm glad to say that Bob, being the man he was, didn't take any notice and we won the race. I suppose I should have complained to the committee, but Bob Bain did win his Senior Eight that day, so no harm was done to either crew.

It was a great thrill to compete in Hobart. When you won a race there, they gave you a great long pure silk program, with fringes on the end, that rolled up into a scroll with the names of the crew on it. At one Hobart Regatta, we were rowing a Maiden Junior Four and we were in front. Our coach, Eddie Jack, was standing on the Cattle Jetties just near the finish. Now, when you are leading in the last stages of a race, all you want to hear is the gun signalling the finish, so you can stop and say, 'Hip Hip Hooray—three cheers for the losers'. On this particular occasion we got to that stage, and we heard the bloody gun. So we stopped, and I started to say, 'Three cheers for the losers', when I became aware there was a certain commotion on shore. The silly bastards had fired a gun for the yachts to get ready or something, just as we were about fifty yards from the line. Anyway, we picked her up, which was pretty amazing as we were only a junior crew, and we still managed to win the race. Eddie had a metal megaphone in his hand to 'hoy' us along with at the finish. When it was all over, he realised he had something in his hands, and looked down to see a piece of tangled, twisted tin. The trauma of watching his crew stop and then start again was almost too much for him and certainly too much for the megaphone.

One evening in Launceston we were preparing our boat to row in a distant regatta, and were faced with the problem of getting it across the Tamar River to the North Esk Club before loading it on the train. Because we had to carry bags of straw across the river, to cushion the boat on the racks on the train, there wasn't room for all the crew. The stroke and bow man used to paddle her across the Tamar. But you needed someone to steer it and we didn't have a coxswain. There happened to be a young lad of about ten years old, all dressed up in his school suit and cap, standing on the skidway watching what was going on, and we said, 'Would you like a ride across the river son?' He said, 'Oh, yes!'

I said, 'Can you steer a boat?'

'Oh yes!'

So he got into the coxswain's seat, took hold of the rudder lines and off we went. It was a lovely summer's night, with everything calm and beautiful. As we were entering the North Esk river to unload our boat at the North Esk Club, the *Rowitta*, the one and only river steamer, came up the Tamar at fairly high speed but took no notice of us. With only two oarsmen to hold the boat up, we had no hope and she swamped us!

We collected the boy, rescued his cap as it floated away, grabbed the straw bags and other gear, and swam and struggled our way to the rowing club skidway. This little bloke climbed out of the water in his sodden school suit like a drowned rat and all we could say was, 'Thank you son'. We didn't have any money, we didn't have anything with us! I hope he regarded it as an adventure.

In Launceston in those days, screen advertising—called 'Add-a-Talks'—had just started in the cinema. A fairly typical one was a breakfast scene of a man and his wife, where the man threw his table napkin down, kicked his chair over and walked out the door in a great rage. The voice imposed on this thing said, 'There's something wrong here—he's leaving her, no doubt. She did not get

To my utter astonishment, I was selected as stroke for the Tamar Rowing Club's Maiden Eight.

her meat from Beerman's Butchery!' and that expression, 'There's something wrong here—he's leaving her, no doubt', became a catch-phrase around the rowing club. About that time our very fine champion eight was to compete in the Hobart Regatta and was considered to have their race in the bag. There were, however, a couple of amateur comedians in the crew, and one was a bloke called Merv Ford. The race started, and this great Tamar crew were not doing so well, dropping back in the early stages. At a critical point, a high pitched silly voice was heard to say, 'There's something wrong here—they're leaving us no doubt'. The crew collapsed with laughter, dropped back one length in fifty yards, and never recovered.

They were very good days, and I think they had a great deal to do with the singular good fortune I have now in being pretty fit. You can kill yourself rowing, of course, if you don't train properly, but if you are in good shape with no particular faults with your heart or anything, it can only do you good.

My emotional life was in some turmoil in 1929 because I was deeply in love with Beatrice in Hobart and all I wanted to do—apart from some of the activities just mentioned—was get down there to see her. My sister Dorothy used to arrange an Easter camp at different places and in 1929 we were all to go to Orford on the east coast. We rented a house and shared it with friends. I was particularly looking forward to this because I knew Bea would be there. I spent some of my limited money on clothes to make myself look more desirable and went down to Orford. I thought Bea's manner seemed a little strange, but the reason was not revealed until we went on a walk to Shelley Beach on Good Friday. Sitting on a grassy bank there she told me that it was all over between us, and that she was going to marry a bloke named Irwin Knight, the man with whom I was sharing a room in my Launceston boarding house! There was no turning back, they had a marriage date planned, and so on.

It was one of those things that happen to a bloke once or twice in a lifetime and I went back to Launceston in a very miserable frame of mind. I know it was 1929 because the disastrous Launceston floods were on when I went back, all communications were down and you couldn't ring anyone. I thought I was very badly hit. I was reading *The Forsyte Saga* at the time, oddly enough, about Fleur and her problems, and it seemed to fit in very well. I used to read the bloody thing and smoke Country Life cigarettes through most of the night. And, of course, I was sharing a room with the man who was going to marry Bea. We were quite good friends and we remained so, too.

When I first arrived in Launceston and was moping about like a lost soul, wanting to be in Hobart, a young married man called Alf Gifford—he was something of a pragmatist was Alfie—said to me, 'You ought to get yourself a girl in Launceston'. This was before the bust up with Bea, and I thought that was an awful thing to say. But as time went on I did get myself a girl in Launceston, and life changed dramatically.

Irwin Knight and I continued to be quite friendly and we used to play tennis opposite our boarding house. Max Lovett belonged to the same tennis club and he had a sister called Eileen whom everyone called Mary. When Maxie and I became friendly, he asked me home to tea one night. I was delighted and went up to the

Lovett house in Bain Terrace, Trevallyn, looking out over the Tamar River and the port of Launceston. I met Mother Lovett, who was in her prime, and we ate a meal with sweetcorn out of the garden, French beans and a roast joint. One of Mary's younger sisters was called Peggy. She was a pretty, petite girl, with hazel rather wide-apart eyes, short, dark curly hair and she had almost a schoolgirlish look about her. I remember she didn't take the slightest notice of me. I used to talk to Mary quite a lot, and tell her about Bea in Hobart and so on.

A bloke called Stuart Maslin was courting Mary so our relationship didn't really develop into anything, although we remained good friends—and have all our lives.

Peg and I used to exchange a few words when she was the telephone operator who answered my calls but then an odd thing happened which brought us into contact with each other. Peggy had beautiful teeth and she went to a dentist called Jones to have some minor matter attended to. Jones was a relative of the family and, incidentally, was killed later when Holyman's DH 86 aircraft disappeared over Bass Strait. He opened her mouth and put gags in it and, without any consultation or obvious reason, removed her three front teeth. She tried to stop him, but he pressed on, saying, 'Be quiet girl. I know what's best for you'. He pulled her teeth out, chipped her gums with a bloody chisel, packed it all up with some curious muck and sent her home.

Now, at this stage Peg was going out with the son of a well known Launceston family, reputedly members of the Launceston establishment—Christ knows why, they were as dull as ditchwater. I suppose I'm speaking about my rival of the day, although there was really no rivalry and Peggy wasn't the least bit interested in me. But I think he was considering other interests and the teeth business somehow just turned the scale. So when I arrived at the Lovetts one night I found Peggy with no front teeth, very tearful, and clearly upset because she'd been dumped much in the same way I'd been.

Peggy, teeth or no teeth, seemed all right to me, so we talked, and talked and talked, and formed a very strong friendship. She had a plate made not long after this lunatic dentist had extracted her perfectly sound front teeth, and for me Launceston became a different place, and life started to get very good indeed. The brutal

Bea Elliston is second from left at the back of this holiday group.

pragmatism of my old pal Alfie Gifford was just right. 'Get yourself a girl in Launceston.' And what a girl I got!

We started seeing a lot of each other, playing tennis and going on picnics together. Our love-making was very ardent, refreshing and pleasant, but Queen Victoria reigned supreme. No penetration—no, no, no! No viewing of each other's bodies either, oddly enough. But it was very pleasant indeed and our life together was very good.

When Peggy and I first became friendly I had no transport and lived at a boarding house right out at the far end of Newstead, about six kilometres from Trevallyn and the Lovett house. The innocence of young people in those days meant that the big entertainment was going to a dance or the pictures on Saturday night. I had this enormous problem. The last tram from Trevallyn left town at 11 pm for the terminus which was about a kilometre from where Peggy lived. The driver was so anxious to get back to town that he barely gave you time to get off before he clanged his bell and took off on the final return trip. You either pushed your girl off the tram and said, 'Walk home on your own', which was out of the question in manners and desirability, or you escorted her to the front gate. After some brief but very passionate moments at the gate, I then had to turn around and walk six kilometres at least from the far end of Trevallyn to the distant end of Newstead. I seemed to do this night after night. At least I had my Alsatian, Thor, to keep me company, padding along and carrying whatever I had to carry.

I went to a man called Karl Mantach, who ran a motor bike repair shop, and put what I suppose ought to have been a fairly impossible proposition to him. I was already repairing magnetos for him and I said, 'Could I have a second hand motor bike, something for about thirty pounds. I can't give you any money but I'll go on repairing magnetos until the thirty pounds is paid back'. Quite readily he said, 'Yes that's all right. There's one over there'. It was a little two-and-a-quarter BSA.

This made an enormous difference to life. Although it was only a single seater without a pillion, by careful manoeuvring I could sit forward on the petrol tank and drive it while Peggy sat on the saddle. We used to go to all sorts of places like this, including out to Relbia, north of Launceston, to play bridge with some friends called the Gardners.

Even before I had my own motorbike I had taken part in an event called a Twelve Hour Rally, in about 1930. A bloke named Neil Frith had a very fine big twin-cylinder BSA and side-car, and he belonged to a local motorcycle club. He asked me if I'd go in this trial as his navigator. I was delighted and got busy and mounted a big spotlight on the front of the side-car so I could swivel it around for extra guidance for the road ahead. I had to have an extra battery which I planned to have between my knees in the side-car—a full sized heavy car battery.

We were to start at midnight and then run out through Cressy, I think, around a pre-determined course and finish at midday. Well, we filled in time having a drink or two, which was probably the cause of our later trouble. People weren't so conscious of alcohol and safety in those days. An amazing number of people turned up for the start and formed a double line for almost half a kilometre it seemed. The bikes were flagged off one after the other, and we had quite a hairy start because Neil must have wanted to make his big bike look good so he opened her up and we kind of swayed from side to side as people hurriedly jumped out of the way. Anyway, we didn't hit anybody, thank Christ.

The first leg was from Launceston to the town of Perth, and we came on to the main road at right angles—a T junction. I say this because we were doing about 100 kilometres per hour as we roared down towards it, and I said to myself, 'Neil hasn't seen it'. I opened my mouth to yell but it was too late, we were there! Neil tried to turn left down the main road, which caused the side-car to begin to rise in the air over the bike. Fortunately for me, he did the right thing and swung violently to the right which reversed the procedure and the bike went up over the side-car. My shoulder hit the road, extracting me rather neatly from the side-car. There was a pause, I stood up rather dazed and found I could walk and that all my limbs seemed to work. The bike, oddly enough, had bounced a few times and landed the right way up. By a fluke, it had even propped itself up on its stand. But lying beside it was the rather large figure of Neil, apparently out cold, with not a sound coming from him. It frightened me a bit and I did exactly what the first-aid people say you should never do: I grabbed him and shook him. But he sat up and said, 'What, what . . .', and started to feel himself all over. He seemed to be all right too.

Then we had a look at the bike. Well, my beautiful spotlight I'd so carefully mounted was off and some yards down the road. The battery, which had been between my knees, was thrown out and had busted itself somewhere. Fortunately, the acid hadn't got onto us or the bike. After a short conference, we pushed the bike off its stand, started the engine and off we went again—admittedly a little more carefully this time.

We finished this bloody Twelve Hour Trial, driving through the night and having breakfast in a sleazy little pub somewhere with a

The up-and-coming businessman needed a studio portrait.

number of very strange people, and got back to Launceston. We'd had to pass through check points from time to time, and had to wait at some of them for a clearance. After we finished we rushed to see how we'd done, and the officials said, 'Oh you're not in it, you were disqualified!'

Apparently, at the first check point I'd noticed one of our tyres was a bit low, so I got out to pump it up. Another competitor—either a nice bloke or a bastard, I'm not sure which—said, 'Why not use my pump, it's a better one'. I said, 'Oh, right-oh, thanks', and put a couple of pumps of air in with it, then handed it back. And on that we were disqualified for receiving outside assistance. But nobody told us , they just let us finish. I still feel angry about it!

Eventually I bought myself quite a good second hand BSA from a firm in Launceston called Sim Kings who used to buy up wrecked motorcycles and recondition them. She had a sloping cylinder and a thing called a high-kick piston and was quite a hot bike. Max Lovett, Peggy's brother, bought one at the same time, but it was a standard machine without a high-kick piston. Another friend, Philip Waterworth, bought himself an Ariel and we used to have spirited arguments over whose machine was the best.

The three of us planned a Christmas holiday tour almost round Tasmania, from Launceston to Queenstown on the west coast, back across to Hobart, up the east coast and across to Launceston via what was called the Lake Leake road. In those days, there was no road connecting the Great Lake area with the west coast highway, and you had to navigate over some high and rough mountain country called the Missing Link. A nice bloke called Fred Smithies (known locally as 'The Crag Conqueror' because of his mountaineering and rock climbing exploits) had done this trip over the Missing Link in an A Model Ford, and he gave us a run-down on how to find our way along an old stock route.

We actually set off on Christmas morning, with tents strapped on the back of our bikes, packs on our backs, billies jangling, knee britches and puttees, leather helmets, goggles and big fine fur gloves. The first part was a fairly easy run up the Western Tiers on to the Great Lake plateau. The road continued on past the Great Lake before it suddenly stopped dead, and we dropped off the end of it—to our horror, up to our axles in mud. We knew we were pioneering so we had a cup tea and said, 'OK, here we go'. Our plan was to make our way through the Missing Link and then, when we picked up the west coast road somewhere near Bronte, to have our ceremonial Christmas dinner. Mother Lovett had prepared us a Christmas pudding, turkey with all the trimmings, and we had a bottle of port. We'd imagined enjoying all this in delightful bushland warm sunshine.

The reality was somewhat different. In the first place we made a serious navigational mistake. There was a mountain near the Great Lake called Murderers Hill, and we should have gone around the lake side of it. We buggered it up, went towards the mountain, turned right too soon and got into some very tough country indeed. It also started to snow! We were literally lost in a snowstorm on Christmas afternoon.

We were in marshy, tussock country, weaving our way along—*pon pon pon pon*—in low gear, and then every few minutes the bikes would straddle a tussock, the sump would sit on it and the back wheel would spin. So with pack on back, you'd get off and heave the bike, laden with all the other camping gear, over the tussock and on for another few yards to do it all again. My bike had a high compression and tended to stall, so I'd have to jump on the kick starter to get her going again as well. We kept on like this for some time, hopelessly lost in poor visibility through freezing snow and drizzle, and began to get a bit alarmed. We'd gone too far to turn back so just pushed on hoping it would improve. But it just got worse.

The tussocks ceased as we ran out on to an area aptly called Skittleball Plains. But they were replaced by large rocks, through which we had to thump our prized motorbikes, which was rather a nightmare. Finally we came to a bit of a track and followed it to a road which fortunately led down hill, so we lost altitude and left the cold and the snow behind us. We camped as it was getting dark, lit a fire, drank the port and demolished the turkey and plum pudding . . . and things started to look up. The next morning we found the west coast highway and had a good run to Queenstown.

We'd booked ourselves a trip from Strahan up the Gordon River by steamer so we left our bikes in Queenstown to have some minor work done on them and took a steam train over the ABT cog railway from Queenstown. The train used to take copper concentrate from the Mount Lyell mine over incredibly steep grades to Macquarie Harbour.

After staying overnight at a pub in Strahan, we boarded the SS *Kathleen*, a little steamboat which took off at 8 am for a run across Macquarie Harbour and up the Gordon River and back. The run would take twelve hours providing enough steam was kept in her boilers to keep her moving at six miles per hour, but she'd run out of steam every now and then and they'd have to stir the furnaces up. First class tourist stuff! Apparently there had been some complaints about the quality of food served and we were the first trip after the new catering regime established itself. My God, you've never seen such beautiful food, and we were the right ages and shapes to do it justice. The same river trip, which shows the superb reflections of the surrounding hills on the black, glass-like surface of the Gordon, now takes about two hours in fast hydrofoil catamarans.

We motorcycled to Hobart without any incidents worth noting, but on the run down to the east coast, I observed some very peculiar behaviour from my companions. We rode in single file, with about 100 metres between us. As I came round the top of one hill, I saw Philip Waterworth, who was in the lead, suddenly brake to a skidding stop, let his bike fall on the ground, and start tearing his clothes off! I looked at this with some amazement but, within seconds, Max Lovett, who was riding next, went through the same procedure.

I thought, 'My God, my friends have gone mad', but scarcely had the thought registered when I was doing it, too. We'd run into a swarm of bees! It was warm, and we had open necked shirts on but, amazingly, nobody was stung. I don't know why. Then it was up the east coast through Swansea, and over the rough old Lake Leake road, home to Launceston.

Eventually I fitted a second hand side-car on the high-kick piston BSA, and it could carry not only Peg and me, but Thor as well. Thor used to have to ride in the sidecar while Peg sat in the pillion seat. People used to hurl insults at me as we drove along the road but it was transport and freedom, and very important in our lives.

The group of friends I had in Launceston during 1929 and 1930 was always looking for interesting areas to camp or walk in. Peg's uncle, Norman Hawkins, was the schoolmaster of the one-teacher school on Cape Barren Island, off the north east coast of Tasmania, between Flinders Island and the Tasmanian mainland, so four of us got together and worked out a camping trip. We found that a trading boat left Launceston, steamed down the forty miles of the lovely Tamar River, out through the heads into Bass Strait, and across to Cape Barren Island. To make this expedition more of an adventure we decided to fly back in Johnno Johnson's little De Souta and, as usual, Thor came with us.

Our week's camping trip was a great success and we walked

around the island, did some fishing in Norman Hawkins' little motor boat, and had a few drinks in the evening while we argued and put the world to rights. And when the appointed time came, we struck our tents, packed up our gear, and went to the paddock on Cape Barren Island that served as the landing ground. The little De Souta appeared out of the sky on time, and taxied towards us. To our surprise the pilot wasn't Johnno Johnson but a friend of his, Eric Stewart. Eric was an ex-World War One pilot who, I expect, had flown Sopwith Pups or something similar over the trenches in France not so many years before. He used to do some relief flying for Johnno, but he was obviously surprised by the great pile of gear we had. The first thing he said to us was, 'Is all this to come?'

'Oh yes', we said in all innocence as we began loading it on board.

'Well, I suppose she'll take off', said Eric. Those were his exact words!

Because of the direction of the wind, we had to take off towards a row of quite tall trees. The four of us, Phil and David Waterworth, Bill Evans and me—with Thor sitting on the floor of the plane between my legs—crowded into the cabin and off we went, well, off along the grass anyway. It became very obvious to all of us that the line of trees was looming up and we didn't seem to be airborne. I suppose it was an old pilot's dodge, but at the very last second Eric Stewart literally wrenched the little plane into the air, and we *just* cleared those trees. It certainly seemed pretty dicey to us, but Norman Hawkins told us later that the spectators stood rooted to the ground in horror and almost threw themselves sideways on the ground with relief when we made it.

From then on it was a pleasant flight over the blue waters of Bass Strait. Thor started to fidget. He was a very well behaved dog normally, and I cuffed him on his great head and told him to sit still. But he had what I can only describe as a pained expression on his face and a sudden throught occurred to me: I put my hand down on the metal floor and found it very hot indeed; the De Souta's exhaust system passed directly underneath. I managed to find some packing to put under Thor to insulate him.

We'd hoped for an adventurous holiday, but on looking back at that take-off, it might well have been our last.

This was superior transport—although Peg had to forsake the side-car for the pillion when we travelled with Thor!

Peg and I thought we'd probably be engaged for about three years while we saved up some money for a deposit on a house. But after more than a year of the engagement routine—walking Peggy to the gate and both getting in a mood where we should have been leaping into bed together but having to walk six kilometres home alone instead—we got sick of it and decided it was time to get married.

Chapter Eleven

HONEYMOON WITH THE PICTURE SHOW MAN

We were married at St Oswald's Church in Trevallyn, Launceston, on April 14, 1934 by the Venerable Archdeacon Atkinson. The only people at the wedding were our immediate families and mine all came up from Hobart for the occasion. I found a letter recently that the Old Man had written to me about this time and wondered why I had kept it. It was just a nice note asking me to book him accommodation in Launceston for the wedding, and added, 'By the way, the twenty is OK. Let me know when you would like it'. Which reminded me that I'd borrowed twenty quid from him towards the cost of getting married. I suppose I paid it back. I think I probably did.

The wedding breakfast was at Mother Lovett's house on Trevallyn. It was afternoon tea, actually, and I said I would supply the wine. I had discovered a very fine wine that was revolutionary—only men of great taste and discernment would have discovered it—called sauterne! I bought six bottles, which was quite an outlay in those days, and that was offered to people after the cups of tea, the sandwiches and cakes. The only guests outside immediate family were my best man Brian Richard, Philip Waterworth, and another friend, Bill Evans.

Ernie Lena, who ran a hire car service in Launceston in those days, had been hired to drive us down into town to board the service-car for Deloraine, where we planned to spend the first night of our married life. He insisted on wearing full regalia of white coat

Peg and her bridesmaid Sheila Crick on our wedding day

and cap and dressed his car with white ribbons along the front. It was a clear, cold, frosty evening and we drove on the bus to Deloraine where we'd booked in at a guest house on the banks of the Meander River. There was no champagne glamour about it. We were ushered in to a gloomy, very cold dining room for a meal—and we were soon in bed, of course. We were just in seventh heaven, and absolutely thrilled with ourselves and everything around us. As well we might have been.

However, not to mince words, I was flat broke. I'd had to borrow from the Old Man to get married, and there was no way Peg and I could have gone away on even a short honeymoon. The question of our honeymoon was overcome in an odd way. We didn't think it in any way extraordinary at the time, but other people thought it was odd. A nice bloke called George Record was Secretary of the Agricultural Bureau in those days, and one of his jobs was to travel around Tasmania showing instructional films to farmers, but some areas had no hydro-electricity and George had to find some means of generating enough power to run his projector.

I devised and did the electrical work on a scheme where you dropped a back wheel of the car on a set of rollers which were linked to a pulley, in turn linked to a generator which generated the necessary power to run George's motion picture outfit. George came in to have a trial run. He set his cinematograph up and indeed it all worked, but he said to me, 'Look, it is all very well, but I'm scared of all this. If I paid your wages for a week, and if your company agreed to give you leave, would you come with me on my lecture tour and run it for me?'

I said that all sounded very attractive and pleasant, but I was getting married. 'You're leaving on the Monday, and I'm getting married on the Saturday.' George's face fell, and he left. But an hour later he came back. Looking at his feet—not at me—he said, 'I suppose you wouldn't come on your honeymoon with me in my car?' George had an A Model Ford, not a motorbike and side-car. 'I'll stay at different hotels', he said and then outlined all the different places he planned to visit.

I thought this sounded sensible, so I saw Peg that night and talked it over and she liked the idea too—and that's why we spent the first night of our married life at Deloraine. George Record had arranged to pick us up on the Monday morning from our guest house on the first leg of our honeymoon/picture show holiday. It was a most successful honeymoon in every way. Old George was a nice fellow and we took it in turns to drive, and acted the fool as people did in those days. We drove to Ouse and on to Hobart, Bruny Island and up the east coast to Pyengana. The generating arrangement broke down at Pyengana but I managed to fix it and then we went back to Launceston.

My motorbike, side-car and Alsatian dog were my sole assets, apart from about £30 capital, but I managed to finance a nice little house at 42 David Street, Launceston. In those days lending institutions were having trouble with people who had taken on War Service Homes and defaulted on payments. A bloke called Pop Cooper had one that he couldn't go on with. I enquired about it, although the house wasn't in the best of repair, and it was agreed that I could buy the house for £900. My obligations were to find £20 deposit, and be responsible for paying £4 a month. The War Service Homes Division said they would put it in full repair, which was done.

When Peg and I came back from our honeymoon with George Record in his A Model Ford, the renovations on the house hadn't been completed, so we had to find somewhere to live for a week. I went to the Cornwall Hotel in Launceston, because I knew a bloke who boarded there quite cheaply, asked what double accommodation there was on a weekly basis, and was told £3/10/-. Peg and I talked it over and thought we could just about manage that. We were there for a week but when the time came to pay I found to my bloody horror that it wasn't £3/10/- double accommodation, it was £3/10/- *each*! That was a very serious financial blow. I remember saying to Peg, 'Well, I thought we were going to have a hot water service, but we're not going to have one now'. We had a week in the Cornwall instead.

We did get a hot water service eventually, and friends came on working bees to get the garden in order, and we moved in to our first house.

Peg used to take part in amateur theatricals with the Douglas Caddy Players in Launceston at that time and I helped with the lighting and electrical side of things. Every now and then they'd give me a small walk-on part to keep me interested and possibly to guard against my persuading Peggy not to go on with it. However, it was during one of these brief stage appearances that I perpetrated one of the greatest Spoonerisms of all time in front of a packed house.

I had a small part in which I did a scene with a big business tycoon in a play called *It Pays To Advertise*. One of my three lines was to say to this big shot, 'I'm afraid I'm not quite so far sighted as you are, sir'. It was the last night, and I'd been imbibing a little behind the scenes. I came on in very good form for my last appearance but when I came to this brilliant line, what I actually said was, 'I'm afraid I'm not site so quai farted as you are, sir'. That didn't seem quite right, so I had about three goes: 'Not quite so sai farted . . .' and so on. After my third attempt the entire audience stood up and cheered, and the producer called out from the wings, 'For God's sake, stop him somebody!' and I was led off. I wasn't offered any more parts after that.

When we moved to Hobart not long afterwards we joined the Repertory Society and Peggy used to get some good parts. I became interested in stage lighting, long before the Hobart Repertory Society had its own theatre. They used to hire the Town Hall or other halls to stage plays. I knew damn all about stage lighting, but I made up an auxiliary lighting switchboard which I used to lug around. If we played at the Town Hall, I'd just plug it in to one of their power points and operate from that, turning on the footlights and the overheads.

At one time there was a play-writing competition, where people not only wrote one-act plays, but produced them. Someone had the brilliant idea of doing a play on Noah and the Ark. The script began in bright daylight and, as the play went on, the lights got dimmer and dimmer because the storm was coming—the great deluge—and the finish was in absolute pitch black darkness.

This wasn't easy to arrange without any proper equipment, so I experimented with a glass jar containing a solution of salt and water and put an electrode—a flat copper plate—in the bottom. The second electrode was in the form of a long copper stick with a rubber handle so I wouldn't get a shock. When the metal rod was pushed down through the salt solution to touch the bottom plate, the lights shone brightly. As I lifted the rod a little bit, creating a gap bridged by the salt solution, it created a resistance and the lights dimmed a little. As I lifted the rod further up the jar, the lights dimmed more and more, until I lifted it right out for complete darkness.

I did a trial and it seemed to work just fine. I'm not claiming this was an original idea, it had been done before, but only for instant dimming. Although the idea worked, I hadn't tried it over the whole length of the play which was half an hour. The play began and I had my lighting cue to begin dimming. I lifted the rod a little bit and the lights went down as planned. But as this went on for some time, the solution started to heat up like a hot water jug with an element, and it started to boil. I can see it now . . . *glug glug glug* and it would spit boiling water onto my hand. I'd get an electric shock and jump, causing the electrode to go the bottom and the lights would come on again. Then I'd dim them a bit more, and there'd be more boiling and spitting and jumping and the lights would suddenly go on and off. I was in a hell of a bloody mess. Anyway in the end I pulled the rod right out and switched off, and the play finished in darkness. It must have been a bloody awful play.

I didn't know what was going to happen. I thought the producer might come and slit my throat. As it happened I didn't have to worry because the critic who was judging the play said he was particularly impressed with this play about Noah and the Ark with the darkness coming on, 'particularly the imaginative effects of the lightning flashes that took place'.

When the Repertory Society bought the Playhouse in Bathurst Street—it had been an old church, I think—I was honorary electrician, and a bloke named Dennis Ashton and I designed a switchboard and made all the floodlights and spotlights out of tin buckets with a hole cut in the bottom and a billy screwed on to that, with big globes in them. We had them on stands and in big clusters overhead. They worked there for years.

Peg and I hadn't been married more than about six weeks, when a nice man called Briggs who worked at the Launceston Post Office came to the house at about eleven at night. I think we were in bed as all young married couples should be. His message was simply

A jolly picnic at Low Head. Peg is in the middle of the front row.

that my father was very ill and my eldest brother Eric had passed a message on that we should go to Hobart as quickly as possible. (Eric was now married to an English girl, Ida Hankey, whom he'd met during the war. She came out to Tasmania and they were married when I was about twelve.)

Peg and I got up next morning with a strange feeling of unreality. We left quick messages with her family and my boss at the garage, and set off about 9 o'clock, hammering off down the main Launceston to Hobart road which was unsealed in those days. I drove the motorbike all goggled and gloved and Peg sat in the side-car. The next development was a rear tyre puncture. Mending back wheel punctures on motorbikes in those days was a bugger of a job. You had to take the back wheel off—and that included sprockets, chain and brake connections. I decided I'd pump her up and see what happened: the tyre held pressure so we drove on. After about ten miles I looked down, and it was almost flat again. So, I stopped and pumped. Having started doing this, I had to keep on because by then it was getting late in the afternoon. Eventually the tyre would only stay up for a mile.

I suppose I was a bloody idiot. I should have mended it properly in the first place, but I didn't. There was a certain touch of the frantic about it because we didn't know if the Old Man was still alive. I remember we struggled up Jordan Hill Road towards *Hazeldene* just as the tyre went completely flat. Fortunately the Old Man had by no means died. He was conscious and a bit puzzled why I was there. He said he had a bad attack of flu but in fact it was pneumonia.

The Old Man was particularly fond of Peg and we were able to spend quite a lot of time with him. He had become ill in his office and had taken the West Hobart tram as far as he could then walked home the rest of the way—not a very good thing to do if you have pneumonia. Fortunately for him—in my opinion—penicillin and antibiotics were not available in those days and the next day he went into a kind of a delirium, then a coma and died. We were all with him and he died during the day. He was seventy-three. I often think that if you could get pneumonia now and be left alone, it would be a marvellous way to go. I suppose the Old Man felt ill for about twenty-four hours, became unconscious and that was it.

For the last few years of his life the Old Man had been friendly with a woman called Myra Gillon. They used to go to a musical evening on Sunday nights, and became fond of one another. I didn't know much about this because I was in Launceston, although Dot, Marge and Nora had passed on their misgivings about the relationship. My sisters were not good about that sort of thing as I remember from my own early extremely innocent experiences during the Postman's Knock days at Lindisfarne. They would tell me of the 'terrible state of affairs with Myra Gillon', who was 'casting eyes at the Old Man'. Mind you, Father was everything to them, his life was their life, really. It was understandable they would feel uneasy about this situation altering but I'm sure that never would have happened.

Looking back I wasn't much help either, because I was very involved with our family and tended to say things like 'how terrible' instead of 'how good'. I tended to go along with my sisters' opinions, and it never occurred to me that in some things they could be wrong. Anyway, on the second day of the Old Man's illness, when he was slightly delirious, a friend of the family, Bishop Blackwood, came up with a travelling Holy Communion outfit, including a chalice and bottle of holy liquor, wanting to give the Old Man his last Communion. I said 'fine' because I knew that sort of thing meant a great deal to him. Marge got upset and said no, 'because it will make Father realise he is dying'. We had a bit of a contretemps about this and I'm glad to say the old Bish went in with his load of nonsense and the Old Man did have his Communion. I don't think he knew anything about it, but Marge thought it would have been terrible if he had regained consciousness to have seen the Bishop standing over him—a very proper supposition!

Later in the day Myra Gillon appeared. *Hazeldene* had a white gate and steps down to a short path, and then more steps up to the verandah and the front door. There was a white, wooden-slatted garden seat on the verandah just outside the door. Myra knocked at the door—I think my eldest sister Dot opened it—and she asked to see Father.

Dot said, 'He wouldn't know you, he wouldn't recognise you, and if he did it would make him realise he was dying, otherwise you wouldn't be here'. Absolute bloody nonsense, of course. I remember observing this and being uneasy, but I didn't do anything to stop it. This poor woman just sat on the seat outside the door and quietly wept. Dot stood at the front door like the Rock of Gibraltar and, finally, did go and put her arm around her and said 'never mind' or something. And that was the last I ever saw of her. It was not good really, our treatment of Myra Gillon, but people's attitudes to death seemed different in those days.

So Father died. If I had remembered my mother's funeral as something of a to-do, it was a mere pipe-opener for the Old Man's. Of course, a lot of years had gone by. The Old Man was a prominent churchman, a choirmaster, lay reader and so on. He was the Grand Master of all the Grand Panjandrums of his Masonic Lodge, or whatever they called themselves. He was an extremely popular Mason and the masonry craft is built on ceremonial procedures. Horse-drawn cab after cab was drawn up, we all went to a packed out Holy Trinity Church for the memorial ceremony, and a huge procession set out for the Cornelian Bay cemetery. All the cab drivers wore top hats and had black bows on their whips, and the horses had black trappings.

I was a very sad young man, because we all loved the Old Man.

The newlyweds on a weekend outing at Hagley, near Launceston

Then there was another ceremony at the grave, and everyone seemed to be there—the Bishop, the military commandant, Governor's representative, and the Masonic boys, out in force. I can remember feeling at the time (brilliant man as I was at the age of twenty-seven) that this seemed tremendous, but what did it all mean? When it was all over, it wouldn't affect reality. The next day when the horses were back in the stable, and the Bishop was getting on with something else, we would still have the grief.

That feeling has grown on me as time has gone on: that if you so desire, you can ask your family just quietly to put the notice in the paper that you're dead, and indicate that the funeral has already taken place. Then people can do what they like. I like the idea of a wake—people can have a drink and there is a feeling of relief, and a fresh start.

But Father's funeral was enormous, and after it was over my eldest brother Eric and his wife, Ida, Peg and I and my three sisters all went back to *Hazeldene* (my middle brother Philip was, of course, at Cambridge University in England) and there were distressing scenes the next morning. My three sisters came from their various bedrooms and just wept and said, 'What is going to become of us?' I think it was about 7.30 on a wet morning and a bad time for everyone. They sobbed out their grief and anxieties, life had come to an end, they could never stay at *Hazeldene*, and so on. Eventually they pulled themselves together and their behaviour was impeccable from then on.

The Old Man had left a will but he didn't have any money—how he got what he had I don't know. He owned *Hazeldene* and the acre paddock but there was a problem about the property. He'd left it to the family to be sold and the money divided evenly, but he obviously had his three unmarried daughters on his mind because the will stated the house was not to be sold until the three girls agreed. There were other complications, too, but eventually Eric, Phil and I signed away any interest we had in the estate so it could be sold, and the money was used to buy land and build the girls another, smaller, more suitable house at 27 Maning Avenue, Sandy Bay, Hobart.

Later I was able to raise a small mortgage on that house to buy a block of land further up the hill in the same street at Number 37, where I still live. My second son, Nicholas, bought Number 27 after my sisters died, and my daughter, Lisa, and her husband built their house virtually at the bottom of my garden. The family was back on the old Garth estate.

Father's death fundamentally altered the plans Peg and I had in Launceston. We both decided we wanted to move to Hobart. I was offered a job with the firm of Heathorn & Co, and had the awkward job of disposing of my house in Launceston. I suppose if I had managed to keep that house, just let it to someone and got enough rent to pay the instalments, it would have made a nice little nest egg. But we didn't think that way in those days and it seemed an enormous financial risk. Eventually we found someone to take it over, with the War Service Homes people's permission. Curiously enough, the bloke's name was also Bowden!

Chapter Twelve

RUNNYMEDE

Before I managed to buy a block of land and build a house in Hobart, Peg and I rented a little cottage in the grounds of the *Runnymede* Estate in New Town which is now run by the National Trust. We paid eighteen shillings a week for a little three-roomed cottage in the grounds. It was arranged by Peg's Aunt Mildred Lovett, who was a Hobart artist and knew the rather formidable Misses Bailey who lived in the *Runnymede* stately home.

Mildred told them that she knew a young couple who lived in Launceston and were coming to Hobart and that the cottage would be an ideal place for them to live—but some alterations would have to be made. 'You can't expect a young girl to cope with things as they are', she said. So the Misses Bailey put a new sink in the kitchen and installed a gas hot water service. The little cottage had a cobblestone back yard which you walked across to get to the dunny—at least it had been converted to a flush toilet. There was one bedroom with two tiny living rooms all in line with a verandah at the back. The rooms opened out in the front to a little round garden, with a small patch of lawn and a walnut tree in the centre. It was just a pocket-handkerchief lawn, really, and even that must have been beyond me, because Miss Bailey asked to see me one day and said she was very concerned that the garden was not being maintained as it should be and the lawn cut. I mention this because anything to do with keeping a garden in order was quite beyond me in those days; the important thing to do on Sunday morning was to go and play tennis. A Colonel Elliott had an asphalt court attached to his house nearby, and he had a Sunday morning tennis club. A friend of mine, Neville Richard, and I used to arrive an hour before the others came for a singles match. Neville used to beat me *every* time. Now and then I thought I had him by the short hairs, but I never beat him over the years and years we played. You'd think the bugger might have relented once or twice and sort of pretended I'd won a match. But he never did. It was big time stuff—men's tennis only. After our game the Colonel's older contemporaries would come, we'd play doubles, have a cup of tea and go home to the midday roast.

I had my motorbike to get to my new job with H C Heathorn & Co, but it was also possible to get a monthly ticket on the railways—a penny each way. A nice little steam train used to circle the Domain, along the shore line of the Derwent River past Government House, and on to the New Town railway station. I just had enough time at noon to hop on the train, be met by my young wife who prepared a very nice lunch and sometimes some fringe benefits that could be quickly had on a nice sunny day and board the train to get back to work.

My first son Tim was conceived in that house although I'm not sure if it was at lunch time. The *Runnymede* period was a very happy time for us both. By then I had developed what became a life-long habit of whistling or humming while I was working or concentrating on something. My work mates at H C Heathorn once good humouredly clubbed together and bought a pack of cigarettes which they put on my work bench, saying I could have it if I didn't sing or whistle for half an hour. I lost it before the first ten minutes elapsed.

It was a great relief to be finally married. We had had a long courtship and a pleasant one, but there was no what you might call real sex, although we enjoyed a lot of ardent love-making as I've described. So we were very happy in our little cottage at *Runnymede* once we learned a bit about it. We got along very well from the point of view of the bedroom, as we got along well on most things, really. We had a great feeling for each other. There wasn't much literature about in those days even for married couples to find out about aspects of love-making that they couldn't work out for themselves but we read as widely as we could. A friend of mine lent us a book written by a Dutch fellow. I forget his name and the title. We called it the book by 'the dirty Dutchman'. It was the first thing we ever read that talked explicitly about sexual acts and orgasms and so forth. Our respective mothers would have fainted at people talking about such things, but it wasn't pornography, it was well written and a serious work. Unfortunately there were no illustrations, but we read it with great interest and, in fact, there were occasions when we put down the book during Chapter 4 and tried something out. But I suppose that's not unheard of, anyway.

We considered Aldous Huxley a great find. Both Peg and I read *Point Counterpoint* and the articulation of free thinking made a big impression. It was everything, it was life, it was a new discovery. In my enthusiasm and bloody stupidity I passed it on to Peg's Aunt Mildred Lovett, but although Mildred was a talented artist and sculptor and a woman of considerable sophistication, sex was something I don't think she allowed for in her life. The first chapter of *Point Counterpoint*, as I recall it, has a fairly detailed description of heavy sex with a girl called Marjorie Carling, so, of course, when Mildred read it, she thought it was terrible and actually sent for me: 'John, I'm worried, I want to talk to you.'

When we did meet she said, 'Is this the way you are shaping your life?'

'What, Auntie Mill?'

'You know that awful chapter', she said. 'Is that the way you feel about women?' and so on. I thought, 'Oh, dear God, what a fool I am'. Anyway, it was overcome. Aunt Mill's intellectual interests ranged over a wide area and she had drawn nudes with great delicacy and frankness, but she could not cope with Aldous Huxley.

Peg became a superb and imaginative cook as time went on, but in the beginning she only had a limited repertoire. She knew how to cook a roast leg of lamb, which we had for Sunday lunch after my weekly defeat on the tennis court by Neville Richard, and doubles with Colonel Elliott and his friends. This cut of cold lamb used to carry us on through the week. After several weeks of this I asked if we could have a change from roast lamb, and Peg said, 'What a good idea'.

When the butcher drove up the *Runnymede* drive with his horse and cart for the weekly order he came to the door as usual and said, 'What would you like, lady?'

Peg asked a young architect, John Wilson, to draw the cottage at Runnymede as a present for me.

Peg said, 'I won't have lamb this week; I'd like a leg of beef for a change'.

Barely containing himself, the butcher said, 'And how many people are you expecting to dinner, then, Mrs Bowden?'

'Just my husband and myself'.

Well, he started to laugh at the back door while explaining the difference in size between a leg of lamb and a leg of beef and Peg said she could hear this laughter ringing around the district as he clip-clopped away.

But Peg was always an innovative cook, interested in experimenting with new dishes. There would often be something new either for main course or dessert and one day during one of my lunchtime visits home from work she chose a recipe from a work called the *Davis Gelatine Book*. The particular dessert rejoiced in the name of Lemon Snow, the principal ingredients of which seemed to be sugar, Davis Gelatine, lemon essence and cochineal. There was no refrigeration in the house and it was a warm summer's day.

Peggy hopefully put this slopping dish of pink froth out on the porch to set.

When she produced it at lunch time, an uncontrollable urge came over me because it had just the right texture. I remember reaching over to the dish and washing my hands in the mixture—then wringing my dripping hands out the open window! Well, bless her heart, she didn't burst into tears or tip it over me, as she well might, but she did laugh, and it became one of the funny things because she had had a spoonful by then and realised that's about all it was fit for. But it's rare that a young bride would tolerate the fact that her husband washed his hands in the sweet she had prepared.

Deliveries of commodities to the house were rather similar to those during my boyhood at *Hazeldene*. The milkman drove his horse and cart to the door, and slopped the milk from churns with a ladle into your jug. We were fortunate in having a beautiful Chinaman's garden in the land between *Runnymede* and the crematorium. Peggy would go down there with sixpence and come back with a cabbage, a cauliflower, great bunches of carrots and parsnips. The Chinese were kindly fellows and were a bit intrigued about Peg. She used to come down from the big house on the hill and I think they thought she was part of the staff. After a while they couldn't contain themselves any longer and they said, 'You work there?'

Peggy said, 'No, no, no, no', and added very proudly, 'I'm married'. The head gardener looked at her and said, 'How long you been married?'

'A year.'

'How many children you got?'

And Peggy said, 'I haven't got any'.

All the Chinese broke into peals of laughter and said, 'Oh ho, you no married . . . you no married!'

We used to entertain our friends at *Runnymede* quite a lot and went to their houses for dinner. Solo was a very popular card game, we played it more than bridge. Sometimes we men would get together for poker nights. I liked poker but I didn't do much good. I can remember feeling a little self-conscious about some of the housekeeping disappearing down the drain when I got home from a poker night, but we always had reasonable tolerance with each other. One night when we were totting up our slender finances, Peg said to me: 'What happened to that ten shilling note you brought home a fortnight ago and meant to give me with the housekeeping but you didn't?'

And I said, 'Oh goodness'.

She turned to me with an accusing eye and said, 'You frittered it!' Ten bob, for heaven's sake. 'Yes, you frittered it!' There was great reproof in the air. If I'd raped the next door housemaid I couldn't have come in for more scorn and derision than blowing a ten bob note.

I can remember another occasion when my behaviour left something to be desired. Peg was pregnant and I had dressed in my tennis whites—not shorts in those days—and was twiddling my racquet about to piss off for my usual Sunday game of tennis at the Colonel's tennis club when she had the effrontery to say that she was a little disappointed in me.

I stopped in my tracks and said, 'Why?'

'Well, you just don't give a hoot about me', she said. 'Every Sunday you just go away and play tennis and come back expecting to find your lunch ready.' I remember going off to tennis steaming with righteous indignation that anybody could say such a thing to me. God Almighty, how right the girl was, really. Anyway, I think I did modify it a little bit. But we got on very well, really.

We stayed in our little *Runnymede* cottage for about three or four years. The three rooms in it were all strung along in a row and we asked the Misses Bailey if we could have the wall knocked out between the tiny dining room and living room to make it into one. They agreed to this then they put the rent up from eighteen shillings to £1 a week, which was reasonable in the circumstances, I suppose. I undertook to do the painting if they had the building work done. The alteration made it into a really lovely little house. There was only one drawback and that was the nearby rubbish tip in New Town Bay. The fly problem was horrific. Everything had to have fly-wire doors, and the little back verandah that opened onto the cobblestone yard was wired too. On one occasion we went out and forgot to close the fly-wire door, and when we got back the house was just full of flies. Even the flowers in the vases were black masses of sleeping flies—you've never seen anything like it.

Thor in the prime of life with Janne Maslin, Peggy's niece, circa 1936.

In those days they didn't have these pressurised cans that destroy the ozone layer; instead there was a thing with a pump action and a little tank of Mortein or Shelltox, and we went around and pumped insecticide all through the house. Then we had to get to work and sweep and sweep and sweep. We tipped out buckets full of flies. That was an unpleasant aspect of our stay there, but as long as we maintained our discipline with the wire doors we were all right. We couldn't ever sit out in the open because of the flies.

The crematorium at Cornelian Bay was built while we were at *Runnymede* and local residents were not impressed. A Mrs Frank Johnson, who lived in Risdon Road, was particularly upset. 'It's awful', she said. 'You can smell the burning flesh.' Looking back, her objections were very just. She kept up her protests and one winter she was in an upstairs room when she pulled the window up and sniffed. 'My God', she bellowed from the open window, 'you wait till Frank comes home. I can smell the bodies burning.' She turned round to find a clothes horse full of washing airing in front of the fire just bursting into flames!

But the flies and the nearness of the crematorium did not really concern us all that much, and my memories of *Runnymede* and early married life are happy ones, except that our landladies, the Misses Bailey, poisoned two of my dogs, the old buggers. When we arrived from Launceston I had my beautiful big Alsatian dog Thor. Now the Misses Bailey were crazy about cats and there were cats galore around their house and grounds. The big paling fence that enclosed our little cobblestoned back yard where Thor used to live backed on to their place.

Thor got ill, and just got worse and worse. The vet couldn't find out what was wrong with him, and he died. We were heartbroken of course. But after some time I got Peggy a little fox terrier—again called Spike after the dog Lin Chopping had given me as a boy. He was quite an unusual, happy and beautiful little black and white foxie.

One day he was out in his little back yard—the same place where Thor had lived—looking at me through the fly-wire door when he suddenly went into a strychnine fit and just died in my arms. Obviously the Bailey sisters had been throwing strychnine over the bloody fence because Spike had been chasing their cats. He wouldn't have even hurt them. He used to have a lovely time rooting them around, but I think the last thing in the world he wanted was to actually catch one. Strangely enough, it took a long while for the penny to drop. I didn't realise till much later that the Bailey sisters had poisoned two of my dogs.

The old motorbike and side-car I had brought down from Launceston satisfied out transport needs and we used to go camping from time to time. Some weekends I would take Peg to the Great Lake in the mountain plateau in the centre of the island, pitch a tent, and do some trout fishing. Peg wasn't all that wrapped in camping and fishing but she did at least come. She used to sit by the tent, fight the blow flies and march flies and read a book. Once at a place called Dud Bay, I latched on to a six pound rainbow trout. The tent was pitched only about 200 yards away up in the scrubline with an area leading down into the water. While Peg blissfully read her book, I fought this magnificent fish. It leapt into the air and curvetted, while I nursed my bloody old rod with an over-running reel, agonising over losing it. But eventually I sorted it out and landed this trout—feeling somewhat miffed that Peg had been up there reading and not taking in this great triumph. She liked fish once caught, however, and we took it home and baked it and had a very fine dinner party.

Not long after I landed the fish, a southerly change came in. Now, there are southerly changes and southerly changes and this was a ripper. It came in with a sort of roaring sound and with horizontal, heavy, hard, cold bloody rain. I pulled the tent down, stuffed it into the side-car of the motorbike, put Peggy in on top of it with the fish under her feet, and struggled into my motor bike riding gear, a waterproof coat, leggings, complete with leather cap with the fur inside and goggles. I took off for Hobart on the old BSA straight into this screaming southerly with freezing cold rain.

It took about three hours to get home and I was just about unconscious with cold and stiffness. The only movement I made, other than sitting on the saddle, was the twist grip of the throttle, and my right foot for the brake. I hadn't been going long when a particularly savage gust of wind just whipped my goggles off. I didn't even hesitate. I let them go and went on driving against the wind and sheets of horizontal rain—not because I was being stoic, just because I couldn't move. Peg had a weather screen in front of her in the side-car, but she was sitting on a wet tent with a fish under her feet.

Back at *Runnymede* we lit the gas bath heater and had hot baths and tea round the fire and life seemed very good.

By 1936, when Peg was pregnant, it was time to find a place of our own. I bought land and built a house at 37 Maning Avenue, Sandy Bay. It was a few doors up from my sister's house at Number twenty-seven—financed from the sale of *Hazeldene*. I was able to take out a small mortgage of £250 on my sister's house to negotiate a loan from the Agricultural Bank for a total of £1000. Lester McAulay, who sold me the block, owned most of the land on the old Garth estate. He was most apologetic about charging me £250 for the block, and spent the rest of his life giving me more and more land because he always worried about charging me too much. In the end this remarkable and generous man gave me the equivalent of about three acres of land, because he loved the valley and knew that I would not sell the property to make money.

Tim was born on August 2, 1937. I remember going to collect my young wife with baby from the Queen Alexandra Hospital and, as

Camping at Bicheno, on the East Coast. As it happened, Wilf Jowett (centre) married Peg's younger sister, Dot, many years later.

we walked down the steps, the bloody old matron there—she was the equivalent of a Pommy sergeant major—said in a loud voice for the benefit of all the people in the corridors and everywhere:

'You keep away from that girl for the next three months. You leave her alone!'

We went home to the brick bungalow built with the £1000 which was just ready to move into. It has been added to over the years, of course, but at the time of writing, I am still living in it.

Chapter Thirteen

GOING TO WAR

In 1939 they called for volunteers to join the AIF, and if you were accepted you wore an AUSTRALIA on your arm just at the top of the sleeve. This was a great thing to have, because it meant you were a real soldier. People who had been in the Militia—like I had been—wore uniforms, but we didn't have the AUSTRALIA up. The Militia was Australia's second army and could not be sent overseas, but it wasn't as easy to get into the AIF as I thought it would be.

At the time Peg and I and our two-year-old son Tim were living happily in our house and I had a reasonably good job earning £8 a week. I liked repairing magnetos and generators and dealing with people who owned motor cars. There is a certain amount of diagnostic skill with auto-electrical repairs, and I rather enjoyed that. But when trouble brewed in Europe, most of us knew that Australia would be involved in a war.

I talked to my brother Philip, now a Cambridge-based physicist, who had returned to Australia briefly in the summer of 1939 from a lecture tour in America. He had no doubts that I should go and that it was going to be an enormous affair. At this stage the French were still fighting, Paris had not fallen and I had a feeling I was going to trench warfare. I rather had the picture of a weary young lieutenant leading a convoy of vehicles through France, being shelled and taking shelter in duckboard-floored trenches. Phil had no doubt that if I didn't go to the war I'd probably regret it. He was

Number 37 Maning Avenue, Sandy Bay

very pessimistic and said, 'You are probably joining up to go away for at least ten years, and of course you must face the fact that you probably won't come back'.

You don't have to dig very deeply to know that I was very fond of Philip, and I can get quite emotional even talking about him now. He had become a protege of A L McAulay (later Professor of Physics at the University of Tasmania) and in 1927 was accepted as a Research Student at Gonville and Caius College, Cambridge. Before he left Tasmania he had fallen in love with Margot Hutchison and in 1931 she left Hobart for Cambridge and became his wife. He became extremely fond of Cambridge and the life there, and resisted all offers to move. The only time he spent any significant time away from Caius College and the Cavendish laboratories was during the war, when he was seconded to the Council for Scientific and Industrial Research (forerunner of the CSIRO).

I think Peg and I really knew I would go and we talked it all through. We were very much in love, of course, but she supported me completely, although we went through great trauma. It was not easy deciding. While it was all going on we went to parties and

Number one son, Tim, 1938

had people to dinner, talked about the war, boozed on and behaved like Noel Coward would have expected us to behave. Most of our friends were very supportive, but there were some exceptions. One couple took the 'I thought you two were happily married—are you trying escape' line. They also asked us to dinner which Peg and I thought was to be a farewell, wishing-you-good-luck affair. It wasn't. During dinner they advanced the theory that we were being led down the garden path by the nose on behalf of the rich and wealthy in the world, and why not stay home and not be a mug? We quite liked the people concerned but the timing was bad and it was particularly rough on Peg. I must say that the fellow concerned stuck to his guns and had a very good war. He was a professional man and did very nicely thank you, including building a boat and a house or two.

Peg and I never argued about my going away, but there was a great sadness. I won't ever forget that period. There was no sudden dramatic decision, no call to the colours. There was a kind of unspoken inevitability about it. I'd been commissioned late in 1939 and that seemed to be part of a natural progression of going away. A war was on and I was a King's officer. They were forming the 7th Division, and the 6th had already sailed.

My association with the army went back to schooldays. At twelve years of age you joined the Junior Cadets, and marched around the playground and marched and marched and marched. Then at fourteen you achieved the Senior Cadets and marched even more—but at least you had a uniform and not just your ordinary clothes. At sixteen you joined the Militia for two years, and then you joined a specialist corps like the Artillery or the Engineers. So by the age of sixteen boys had six years military training. I rather liked the Militia part, and stayed in. My brother, Eric, who had served in the Royal Australian Flying Corps in World War One, was the Commanding Officer of the 36th Fortress Co Engineers, and naturally I managed to be drafted into that. I was Sapper Bowden and we used to run the searchlights at the Blinking Billy lighthouse on the River Derwent. There were two units: The Fortress Engineers stayed down at sea level at Long Point, Sandy Bay, where the sewer is, and up on Mount Nelson directly behind Long Point was the Garrison Artillery. We used to run the searchlights across the Derwent at night while the Artillery up top went 'click, got you', type of thing.

They used to aim guns at imaginary targets and at boats coming up the estuary to the port of Hobart. We enjoyed that. There were two big generators run by a couple of beautiful big old Gardiner kerosene diesel engines. Their flywheels were about eight feet in diameter, with a big moving belt connecting the top of the flywheel to the direct current generator. To start them you had to get at least twelve men running with the belt until you got to a certain speed, and then the compression lever was pulled over and they went *cloonk*, *cloonk*, *cloonk*. They were fuelled by kerosene which fed into a little cup on the end of the cylinder head. You could actually see the kerosene being sucked in through a jet. They were hot bulb diesels and you had to have the bulb red hot with a blow lamp before you started. This big slow moving engine also sucked in water with the kerosene, to form a steam cushion when the big piston came up to the top of the cylinder. It was beautiful to watch. If you turned the water off, you'd think someone was hitting the bloody cylinder with a sledge hammer, and as you brought the water up again it would go quieter and quieter until she was just turning over like a great big steam engine.

We used to annoy the ocean liners sometimes when they came to Hobart by keeping the searchlights on them for too long: then we'd get reprimanded. There was an annual camp, which was good fun and since our training was at night, in the afternoon we could wander around Sandy Bay beach and ogle the girls. Simple souls we were. By the time I was eighteen I had become a Corporal in the 36th Fortress Co Engineers, and because we were a technical unit, Corporals were permitted to use the Sergeants' Mess. This was significant, in view of one of the most embarrassing experiences of my life. There was a billiard table in the Sergeants' Mess with two very big electric lights over the top. There were no fluorescent tubes in 1924. They had big incandescent globes of around 1000 watts each, with great big china shades directing the light onto the billiard table. One night I noticed that the flex on one of these lights was sparking—arcing a bit, just above the adaptor that held the globe. I knew that if nothing was done, it would flare up and blow the fuses, perhaps even set fire to the flex.

I was the only one to see this, so I took off my big army boots and climbed on to the green baize of the table in my socks. I had a small piece of cardboard which I planned to wedge in between the arcing wires as a temporary repair—it could be fixed properly the next day. I didn't realise that it had been arcing for some time and, as soon as I touched it, the flex snapped and let this 1000 watt globe with its heavy china shade drop with a shattering crash on to the table. While I was gazing in shock at all the broken glass at my feet, I became aware of a whirring noise going on over my head. The china shades were so heavy that they had counter balances, in this case a porcelain bowl filled with lead shot. They were beautiful things. But the whirring noise was this counter-weight running back through the pulley and it, too, came crashing down to explode and shower broken porcelain and lead shot over the rest of the table.

All this happened in a few seconds, of course, and the others in the Mess didn't know why I had climbed up on the table in the first place. It was all rather dramatic. I remember the senior Sergeant saying, 'Well, thank you very much Bowden. That was a

Snapshots of times like these made it harder to contemplate going to war.

very good job!' Miraculously it hadn't damaged the cloth. Why I'll never know.

I can't ever remember not being in the army. I was bitten by the bug and after I transferred to Launceston I joined the artillery and then the Infantry. My aim was to get a Commission and become an officer and eventually I did—in June 1940. It was a bit of a haul, though. I was in Signals as a transport officer and I was recommended for a Commission and got it. No exams in those days; the war was on. It was a question of your CO recommending, and your local Commandant approving. So, in a way, I was committed. If you accepted a Commission during a war, you assumed you would be continuing with military life.

The troops had an easier time moving from the Militia to the AIF. They would be asked what they did for a living and a motor mechanic would go into Ordinance or the Service Corps, a farmhand or forester would go into the Forestry Unit and so on. But the officers had to 'have a guernsey' as we put it. A unit had to have a vacancy for an officer and a CO prepared to accept him. They weren't taking Signals people but, if they were, they would expect a real died-in-the-wool Signals officer with a knowledge of Morse Code and other skills.

I was a transport bloke. I tried for the Service Corps, missed out first time, but in the end was selected for a Victorian company which rejoiced in the name of the First Australian Corps Petrol Park. It was based on the British army establishment and I thought it a silly name. Actually, its job was to transport petrol but why the 'Park' I'll never know. People would say, 'What's your unit?' and I'd say, 'The First Australian Corps Petrol Park', and feel faintly ashamed. I was posted to Puckapunyal army camp in Victoria in June 1940, and Peg and two-year-old Tim came over to Melbourne to stay with Philip and Margot for the first three months. By that time Philip, who was an expert in the friction and lubrication of solids, had been co-opted from Cambridge for war work in Australia. He and Margot made their house available to us and Peg was able to stay in a little cottage at the bottom of their garden.

But Puckapunyal. What a dreadful place it was, just a collection of brown huts with a sprinkling of parade grounds in the middle of nowhere. It was winter time, it was wet, and we were all inexperienced troops. No one knew anything, all they seemed to think necessary was for everyone to get up and be on parade at 6.30 am—this was essential to being a soldier. It was dark, usually raining, and we all had this dreadful 'Pukka throat', a flu of some sort that swept through the camp. The medical people couldn't cope with it and they had a scheme whereby if your temperature was under 103°F you lay in your hut, and if it went over 103 they shovelled someone out of the hospital back into a hut, and gave you a bed. Fortunately, I had a dose of it just before I went to Puckapunyal and it seemed to make me immune and I didn't get it.

Despite all this we still had to parade at 6.30 am and in the dark and rain of the early morning we sounded like a paddock full of flukey sheep. I suggested that they put the reveille forward an hour for a fortnight until things got better but, oh dear no, suggestions like this from young officers were frowned on. Our Unit Medical Officer, Captain Peter Parsons, a very nice bloke, was concerned about hygeine. All the sick men were lying in their huts and coughing into their blankets—the good old grey army blankets—and some laundry seemed essential under the circumstances. So he went to camp headquarters to see the Brigade Major in charge of all camp routine matters and asked what was being done to have all these blankets washed.

The Brigade Major said, 'Good God man, I served throughout World War One and I never saw a single blanket washed or laundered. And, what is more, I am not going to order any blankets to be washed here in Puckapunyal'. And that was the end of the matter.

My CO was a Major, commonly known as Kim, which was short for 'Fuck'im'. I didn't think he was a nice man and I know he wasn't very impressed with me. But, oh God, nobody knew anything. We were all trying to train troops, and I didn't know what to do. No one had ever trained me. I was in B Company, with two other Lieutenants, and a Captain in charge of us. One morning we were detailed to take our platoons up to have their first anti-tetanus injections. I remember it was a dull, nasty day. Puckapunyal always had dull, nasty days. We marched over to a sleazy hut where there was a Medical Officer waiting. My brother Lieutenant was an Englishman—a small man with a moustache and a rather flamboyant personality. He was a very nice chap, actually, I mustn't get him wrong. I used to be embarrassed when we had to 'do things in front of the men'. But not this little Englishman.

The troops approached the hut with some apprehension, and my fellow officer went to the front to set an example. 'Me first, men, watch me go in. There's nothing to it.'

A few minutes later he strode briskly out of the hut saying, 'Nothing to it, men, nothing to worry about'. He took two more paces, his eyes became glazed and he keeled over splat into the mud, completely out cold. He must have had an allergy to the shot. They loaded him into an ambulance and took him away, shot some adrenalin or something into him and got him going again. But you can imagine the effect this had on the troops. They were reluctant to have the injection, anyway, and they started to waver and fall over. People fainted before they had been in. Somehow we got them all through and went on a short march and back again.

My first real duty was to be put in charge of the weekend leave personnel from Corps Petrol Park. This was a big deal, our first weekend leave in Melbourne. We officers who were to be in charge were taken by the Brigade Major down to the Puckapunyal siding where it was all marked out. 'This is where your troops will detruck and enter the train and nobody must move until the order is given' and so on. Then, on the return, the train would stop and no one would leave the train until ordered. 'They will then fall in alongside the carriage and march over to their embussing points', also marked out. It all looked wonderful—as all exercises do without troops. I was full of fire, and mine were going to be the best troops of the day.

To add to this, my CO gave me elaborate orders along the lines that 'the First Australian Corps Petrol Park troops will not be as other troops, they will not just walk down to the train on Sunday night and get on board—you will fall them in a block away and march down to the train at Spencer Street Station'. In my naivety this all sounded pretty good to me. I wasn't wearing a trench coat leading convoys of petrol being shelled in France, but I would be marching in front of real Australian troops through Melbourne to get on the train.

Well, the embussing bit went pretty well. Most things go well with troops if they are going in the direction they want to go—like bloody horses. I do not mean to be superior, but in those days officers were somewhat apart. There was a vague but constant uneasiness that I had to hold my poor miserable bloody little end up in front of the troops. We got on the train and on to Melbourne where I went into Peggy's arms and, oh dear, it was beautiful. We went back to Philip and Margot's house, and Peg and I put the little hut in the garden to good use.

Then came Sunday night and, with it, two things. First, I had had a vaccination two days before and that had really come onto the boil. I don't think sex is good for vaccination because I was a really sick guy. Second, it was raining like buggery when I set off by tram for Spencer Street Railway Station. There I found a bedraggled lot of troops all complaining that they didn't want to go back to camp, they had domestic problems, they wanted extra leave—all of which was a bit hard for a young officer. A year or two later I would have said, 'Look, get stuffed, just fall in will you and get cracking'. But I was listening to blokes saying that there was someone in bed with their wife when they left and they had to go back and do something about it.

I did not lead my troops through the streets of Melbourne, we straggled down in a mob to get on the train. Happily my CO wasn't there. Everybody on the train was pissed to the eyebrows. There was vomit in all the corridors and the noise was unbelievable. Everything was completely out of control. Troops were still coming up to me and saying, 'Look I'm not coming back to camp, I'm going home. You can do what you bloody like.' I should have said, 'Well, piss off, it's your own fault, and you'll be up on a charge before the CO in the morning but that's your own business'. But I tried to reason with them.

I remember one of the soldiery coming up to me in the murky pouring rain and telling me he wasn't coming back to camp that night because, 'Me wife's at a party and there's a bloke trying to interfere with her'.

'You've got to come back to camp, your leave's expired,' I said with all the power and authority of a second lieutenant and holder of the King's Commission.

'I'm not.'

'Yes you are, I'm ordering you to get on that train and go back to camp.'

He said, 'You can get fucked!' And disappeared into the night. Others went and some came. The rain poured down, and this malodorous train was packed with shickered troops.

It all seemed to go on and on, but eventually the train blew its

Lieutenant John Bowden of the quaintly named First Australian Corps Petrol Park

whistle and the engine moved off, but nothing else did. Someone had uncoupled the engine. In the army there is always someone who knows how to do something. If you ever call for a volunteer to organise a ski run, someone will come along and say 'I used to run a ski operation'. There were obviously some railway men on this train who knew how to uncouple carriages. They brought the engine back and hooked it on again, blew the whistle and started off again. This time the engine and first three carriages went, and the rest stayed behind. This went on, I think, for two hours. In the end the whole train got going except the guards van. But finally they got it all away.

Of course, if I'd been one of the boys I'd have been in it up to my testicles, too, but I was the young officer with a court martial looming when the CO heard about all this. But I thought everything was going to be mended at the Puckapunyal railway siding, because my troops were going to fall in and do all the right things.

When we got there I got my blokes together and said, 'You have got to do as you're bloody told. Enough of this nonsense now. Fall in outside the train.' Then we were supposed to march over to embuss. Unfortunately, I was the only officer to do this. The train pulled up, the carriage doors flew open and what seemed like 5000 troops rushed out into the rain and just ran helter-skelter—with good sense, too, when you come to think about it—to any available transport. All the trucks and buses immediately took off for Puckapunyal about twenty miles away, leaving me and my men standing in the pouring pissing rain with nothing. Everything had gone. Incidentally, I was pretty sick as well. While I was wondering what to do, I thought that since we had been told to stand fast, we would stand fast and wait for some transport to return.

The next thing my Captain appeared and said, 'What have you got those men standing in the rain for? You don't keep men standing in the rain, get them marching.' So I led my men up a country lane. I can see it now, wet gum trees, rain pelting down. I had my best Sunday-go-to-meeting uniform on, too. We finally got up to the Hume Highway as the convoy returned to pick us up.

By this time, thank God, the idiot Captain had taken over. I was considered useless by then and he started to turn a convoy on the Hume Highway on a wet Sunday night. Well, he had one truck right across the road and there was someone hurtling from Melbourne to Sydney, or wherever, and there was an awful screech of brakes and a thump as he hit the truck. I don't think anyone was killed. It was sorted out and we got back to camp.

That exercise represented to me the difference between what you think you are going to do when you join an army, and the way it actually works out. There was a bit of a rumpus the next day. The officers were considered responsible for the pulling apart of the train and not properly controlling the men. We were reprimanded, talked to and told to pull our bloody socks up. There was no disciplinary action. There couldn't be, I suppose.

We didn't have any courses for officers in those days. Anyway, at this stage, a Colonel Max Dollery (the creator of the Corps Petrol Park) had an idea which turned out to be good. He designed a unit called the First Australian Mobile School of Mechanisation. It had to have three officers, a Major, Captain and Lieutenant. Its function was to move into active units and train drivers and mechanics. A bloke named John Goggs from South Australia was the Major, one Captain (I'll call him T) was from Sydney and I was the Lieutenant. We had to get busy and put a unit together, happily not at Puckapunyal but in Melbourne.

To equip a unit you had to go to a barracks and see people and get equipment. No one knew quite how to give it to you, no one wanted to give you anything, anyway, and the invariable answer was, 'No, you can't have it'. It was ludicrous when I think what we went through, but eventually we got our unit together with a pretty good bunch of blokes, mainly Warrant Officers as instructors, Sergeant draughtsmen and so on, and an odd lot of vehicles. We were pretty lucky because we also scored a staff car. So, while colonels and such were driving around in utilities, old John Goggs had a staff car because it was considered we should have every form of vehicle in our unit for training purposes.

On the day we got our unit together we set up our headquarters in the Guinea Stand of the Caulfield Racecourse. I used to wake up in the mornings, sleeping in the grandstand looking out, and watch a horse called Ajax—one of the great horses of the day—having his morning exercise.

Finally we got an embarkation order to move overseas and were also ordered to put our trunks—our precious personal officers' trunks—on a ship called the *City of Lille*. This was a worry, as we were to sail on the great liner *Aquitania*. Our trunks had all our important worldly goods, including greatcoats, and a list (probably dating back to World War One) including a valise, spare wrist watch, spare glass for wrist watch and so on. When we heard our trunks were to go on another ship we said, 'Bugger this, we won't do that—we'll never see them again'. But arguments went back and forth and, cowards that we were, we obeyed orders and put our three trunks on the *City of Lille*. We drove sadly back to headquarters to be told that the order had been countermanded and we were to bring our trunks with us to Sydney and the *Aquitania*. We hurtled back to the docks just in time to see the *City of Lille* heading out into Port Phillip Bay! Just another early experience of army organisation.

Eventually we boarded a troop train for Sydney where the four-funneller *Aquitania* was waiting at the Sydney docks. They'd taken this beautiful old ship off the Atlantic run and this was her first trip as a troopship. The *Queen Mary* was also in the harbour, and we learned later that we were to meet the *Mauretania* out at sea, somewhere in the Bight.

This was probably the most exhilarating part of army life. We left Sydney one fine morning—it was supposed to be a secret but every privately owned boat in Sydney Harbour was out—and the *Queen Mary* led the convoy down towards the Heads. There were bands on the forepark playing 'Now Is The Hour', people were cheering and the boats were tooting their sirens as we headed out to sea. Every craft that could float turned out to see us off, from canoes to packed ferry steamers; whistles were blowing and the lads were all cheering. It was a highly emotional scene as we went charging off to fight for our country and do what others had done before us.

Chapter Fourteen

TO THE MIDDLE EAST

October 22, 1940

My dear Peg,

This is our third day at sea, and we have settled down into our routine. The convoy was joined by another big ship yesterday [the *Mauretania*]. We have a cruiser [*Perth*] as an escort. All the orders as to formation came from this little warship and it is amusing to watch her hoist a signal flag, and three hulking liners manoeuvre into a new formation like small yachts.

Last night my CO, Major John Goggs, and I spent a long time on the boat deck. Everything was blacked out, of course, and the other ships looked like great dark shadows with long phosphorescent streaks in their wake. Today there is a good swell running and we are heaving about quite a bit. I spent hours standing up as close to the bow as they will let us, watching her bucking into them. I really think I should have joined the Navy.

Three of us share the same stateroom, on B Deck. This is the posh part of the ship and it really is absolutely luxurious.

We steamed close to Wilson's Promontory and pushed on through the Great Australian Bight. We had beautiful weather but there was an enormous swell rolling in from the Southern Ocean. As we bucketed along during the day, the old *Aquitania* would put her noble nose down and down into the swell, and rise up again. I didn't think such a big ship would do that. The *Queen Mary* was running beside us at one stage and I actually saw her bow go down into a swell and lift and water actually run out her hawse holes. Some of the troops were seasick.

As shipboard life settled down, the bullshit started. I don't mean the training and lifeboat drill which were very necessary, but the formal messes which impressed me at the time. The *Aquitania* was taken off the Atlantic run and sent straight out to do this job of troop carrying to the Middle East or anywhere else. She had a full complement of stewards and her wine cellars and larders were stacked with the luxuries that the cross-Atlantic travellers used to enjoy. Incidentally the lifeboat drill did not instil great feelings of confidence. The lifeboats were wooden and old. They filled them with water each day and they leaked dry in about twenty minutes.

The procedures we followed were based on British army tradition and certain standards of dress were demanded. In peacetime we would have worn dress uniforms. Certain topics of conversation were taboo. You were forbidden, I think, to mention a woman's name. At a given time the mess president would call on the most junior officer present (who by tradition was always the mess vice-president) to pass the port. It went from left to right, of course. The Colonel sat at the head of the table and the port had to go right around without touching the table. After the glasses were filled the president would say, 'Mr Vice'. And the junior officer would call out, 'Gentlemen!' People would stand and say 'The King', to drink the Loyal Toast. All this was a lot of bullshit really, but we thought it was Christmas at the time. And it was in the first class dining room, attended by white-coated stewards.

Being a commissioned officer had great advantages, believe me. But looking back the contrast was too great, and that sort of thing didn't go on for long during the war.

Dear Peg,

An idea has struck me: what about you cutting out the parts of my letters that you would care for others to read, and sending them round to our numerous friends? I would like you to keep these originals as in years to come they might be interesting.

The letters of the men of the unit have to be censored by an officer. It's probably a compliment, as they all give them in to me with the request that I do them personally. [What pomposity!] It is also a bloody nuisance, a hateful job and I feel uncomfortable all the time I am doing it. My brother officer Captain T is a queer mixture. One minute he tries to play the comedian, big pal with the blokes; the next minute he is the big chief disciplinarian—both without much success, I think.

[My attitudes towards T were starting to show. He was a curious mixture, and I let him get well and truly under my skin. And, for the record, he was a prick of the first water.]

The more I have to do with John Goggs the more I like him. Unfortunately at the moment he is allowing things to be run too much by T. Things will settle down well in the end. He is a man of surprising firmness when he likes.

[Later] They have a wet canteen for the troops and there has been an officer on duty to see that they all behave themselves. I had the job the other night. Actually the blokes behaved as one would expect and there was no bother. The arrangements were bad: for each beer drunk, the drinker had to stand in a queue for the best part of half an hour. As it is a blackout all the windows are closed and the atmosphere I leave to your imagination. It was so hot that the sweat was actually running down my legs and my shirt was soaked. The air was so thick that you could barely see across the room for smoke. It was calm, fortunately.

The blighters are not going to let us ashore at the next port. Actually, we can't blame them; there are a lot of men and something is sure to happen to some of them. [The real reason was that the Sixth Division which preceded us—the Seventh—took Perth and Fremantle apart so no more troops were allowed ashore.]

This will be the last letter I will write to you from Australia, for some time anyway, but it won't be long before we get to another port. I've been discussing this convoy with ship's officer, gunners and engineers and they are all unanimous that it is practically impregnable. [Oh yeah?] It is too fast for submarines and the combined armament of the cruiser and the big ships would prove difficult for any raider. [All nonsense, of course, but it was a nice thought and a good idea telling Peg.]

We lived high off the hog as officers and gentlemen on the Aquitania. *I found my new CO, Major John Goggs (left), an agreeable companion.*

We touched briefly at Fremantle and headed up through the Indian Ocean. One day these three great liners formed a line ahead during the day, which was unusual. Then we saw that the cruiser *Canberra* was taking over from the *Perth* as our escort. The *Perth* dressed ship with all the ship's company in white and flags from stem to stern, and steamed straight down past the line of ships while their crew gave three cheers for each troopship as they went past. To see a cruiser at full bore coming down through a trade wind with everything blue and beautiful was very stirring indeed. Poor old *Perth*, she copped it in the end in Sunda Strait on March 1, 1942.

Monday October 28, 1940

This is our second day at sea again and I am sitting up on the boat deck in the glorious sun, getting hotter every hour. Soon it will be too hot; at the moment it's perfect. The sea is deep turquoise blue and there is a gentle breeze. How you would love it all!

We are running an instructional course for one of the units on board. Tomorrow I have to give a lecture to twenty men on the basic principles of the automotive ignition system. I think T is definitely improving and he certainly is a brilliant instructor on Fords.

There was rather an amusing incident while I was canteen officer the other night. One of the military police, a lance corporal, got a little uppish and finished up by tearing his stripe off his arm and hurling it at his sergeant. Unfortunately it was in front of a lot of men and I had to put him under arrest. He was brought up today for trial and reduced to the ranks. I think there must have been a blood feud between them, because every time the sergeant opened his mouth at the trial, the poor bloke got absolutely livid with rage.

October 29, 1940

It has been as hot as hell today and I have seen my first flying fish. The ship seems to scare them and up near the bow they are hopping out of the water continually. They fly very efficiently and the first one I saw looked like a small bird. According to the books I read as a small boy they should be rattling against the rigging and making savoury breakfasts for the captain. They'll have to fly high to land on the deck of this ship.

This is my first taste of the tropics. We wear shorts all day and a light drill uniform for mess at night. The outfit is extremely comfortable. The early mornings and evenings are absolutely perfect. I rise quite early, about six, don a pair of shorts and indulge in violent exercises with the troops. I find it strange to be able to stand practically unclad in the morning breeze and not be cold. I would like to be able to sleep up there, but it is forbidden.

Before we got to Bombay, the troops rebelled over the amount of money they were permitted to take ashore. The idea was, I suppose, to limit their spending power so they wouldn't get shickered, go crazy and belt the place up. Australian troops are not slow to come forward when they think they are getting a raw deal and they demanded to see the OC Ship. The Officer Commanding Ship was Brigadier Jacky Stevens who I thought was a most impressive bloke. The troops assembled in the main stateroom of the *Aquitania* with its great pillars and lofty ceiling. Jacky Stevens said they were getting enough money and that was that. The troops said, 'That's not good enough, we want more. Why should you bastards go ashore with a pocket full of money? We've got the money, it's in our pay books. Why can't we have it?' A compromise was worked out, which probably wouldn't have been the case with the British army but the Australians did have their own way of doing things.

When we got to Bombay, the *Aquitania* anchored out in the harbour and the usual flotilla of bumboats came out to try and sell things to the troops. One particular boat, full of gesticulating and shouting Indians, was piled high with black leather boots. Imagine trying to sell black boots to troops who were all kitted out with brown boots! They threw up lines to the troops crowding the rails and the idea was to send down either money or something to trade. The troops had already been issued with their long woollen underwear for the winter campaign in the Middle East. These seemed rather superfluous in the tropics and were flogged off to the Indians at a great rate while we were in Bombay. But the main sport with the Indian entrepreneurs trying to flog their boat load of black boots was to pull them up on a line and not send anything back in return. You can imagine the caterwauling and indignation of the frustrated traders, and the remarks of the troops can be imagined too. Suddenly this dialogue was cut short, from the Indian side at least, when a huge hatch opened in the side of the ship and what seemed like several tons of potato peelings and other less fragrant kitchen scraps were dumped straight into the boat full of black boots and shouting Indians. It was terrible looking back on it, and I hope it wasn't done on purpose, but it seemed very funny at the time. After a few seconds' silence, a few brown hands could be seen scrabbling through the potato peelings to the surface, to be followed by angry faces screaming impotent abuse at the Australian troops by then almost helpless with mirth. Not good really. We were a superior bloody lot in those days.

I copped the job of Baggage Officer for our unit and in company with other Lieutenants from other groups the task was to make sure that all our gear came off the ship and was put on the wharf in the designated place. It was quite an experience. There was Bombay, gateway to Clive's India, and there was I landed on the wharf in the stinking heat and trying to do my job in some curious sort of way. There was an English officer in charge of the whole operation and he was pretty good at what he was doing. There seemed to me to be an enormous number of Indians doing very little in the way of effective work. Six of them would stand around a box that two could lift easily while they all screamed at one another, presumably arguing about who was to have first lift. Eventually they would all grab a corner and walk off, but the yelling never stopped. I passed some remark in rather a condescending way to the Englishman about the way these very stupid buggers, the Indians, were handling our gear. He was a British India Officer and a member of the Staff Corps as well. He turned on me and said, 'Do you know what you're saying? See that fellow there?' And he pointed to an Indian who had a sort of cloak around his shoulders and was pretending to lift something.

'That cloak around his shoulders is probably the only possession that poor fellow has in the world. And when he finishes from this dock he'll go and find the nearest street and lie down in that street to sleep.'

This rather impressed me because I thought they were 'kicking the niggers' in those days but he certainly resented the colonial's ignorance in these matters. The Baggage Officers were quartered in the Taj Mahal Hotel while everyone else went off to an army camp somewhere. We thought this was going to be wonderful, but didn't realise that we had to pay a certain amount of the bill ourselves from our field allowance.

November 7, 1940

I have not put a word on paper since the night before we arrived in Bombay. Well, this is in all the most amazing place I have seen as yet. We are staying in a sumptuous hotel where a whisky and soda costs about four shillings and a lemon squash three and six. I am drinking iced water which costs nothing.

There are six of us quartered in one large room with an anteroom attached. I have just about the best spot in it, right beside a large window. The best part of the show is our room steward, a native called Filipe, quite a young lad and most attractive. He is the essence of honesty and shrewdness combined. For instance, the other night a few of us wanted to go to the pictures. We said, 'Filipe, pictures. Where and how much?'

He explained the different prices very clearly and we said, 'How do we get there?'

He said, 'If the master likes I will come in taxi and show you'. We were duly grateful and asked how much when we got back. He said, 'I will wait and bring master home. I wait in pictures. It will cost six annas.' (That's about ninepence.)

We took him with us and when we came out he was waiting. There was a terrific rush on taxis, but our Filipe walked up to one that was apparently engaged by a couple of sheikhs and just ordered them out of the way and we got in. All very simple. We take him wherever we go now. Last night he took us to a Hindu temple. It was just as one expects all Hindu temples to be except that it was surrounded by more filth and squalor than I thought possible.

November 10, 1940

I had a very interesting evening last night. The local manager of the Ford Motor Company asked T and me to dinner at his bungalow. A car called for us at 7.30. We sat in the open porch and had whisky. They are obviously pretty well in and have a Gurkha to act as a sort of sentry around the place and oodles of native servants. We dined at 9 pm and for your information had tomato soup, a joint, fruit pie, savouries, coffee and liqueurs. After that they took us to the pictures and, strangely enough, I had to sit through Errol Flynn in *The Sea Hawk*. You may remember that criticism we read in *The New Yorker.* Well, believe me, they treated it too kindly. The pictures here don't start till 10 pm and come out about 12.30.

I took this portrait of Peg to Palestine.

A Canadian bloke in the party was a member of the local yacht club, which is super-pukka and exclusive. He took us there to supper and we had a few drinks and a dance each with the hostess. The 'haw haw' crowd were there and I noticed that they were so busy being pukka that they didn't even seem to enjoy themselves! Our party, being colonials, was not so bloody pukka and we were thoroughly enjoying it. Apparently these people do their sleeping in the day time.

You can imagine how late it was after the pictures at 12.30. They then drove us through the low native quarters. Hell, it gave me the creeps. The prostitutes sit behind iron grilles and you see the natives bargaining with them through the bars. The place is lousy with disease and filth. I was rather glad when we got out of it. You daren't stop your car. Interesting to see, none the less.

I am practically sure to see Allen in the next week or ten days. [Peg and I had worked out code names for the places I might be sent, and Allen was Palestine.] When I last wrote I was a bit off my tucker owing to the heat and what not; now I am eating like a horse and feel absolutely bouncing. I am getting all brown and tropical and can even ask for a cup of tea without milk or sugar in the local lingo. I'm sure a few weeks more would see me kicking the natives out of my way and having tiffin at regular intervals and calling a whisky *chota peg*.

We enjoyed the enormous rooms at the Taj Mahal Hotel and the legions of Indian staff attending our every whim. We were changing ships in Bombay and when the morning came to leave, there was a procession of about twelve people outside my bedroom door waiting for their tips—the laundry wallah, the boot cleaner, the sweeper and so on. I didn't have a cracker! You didn't really need spending money in the army and I didn't have any anyway. Almost all my pay was allocated to my family in Australia. I just had to walk along that line of people looking straight ahead. It was awful and even more so when I found out later that they actually paid the hotel a small sum of money just for the privilege of looking after us and to be able to receive the tips we great white masters would dispense. I often think of that. I just had to walk past the bloody lot—I couldn't do anything else.

From Bombay we embarked on smaller ships for the voyage up the Indian Ocean through the Red Sea to Port Tewfik and Suez. We were marched onto a ship called the *Nevassa*. She had obviously been a troop transport between England and India before the war. As you walked up the gangway there was a big notice at the top which said 'Servants and Governesses Second Class Only'. That annoyed me rather a lot. But she was a nice little ship, beautifully run but in the best Pommy style. That is, the officers had nice cabins, a beautiful dining room and superb food, while the troops had hammocks slung 'tween-decks so close they were almost touching and all the portholes were shut. The foetid atmosphere can be imagined.

The food for the troops was terrible. On one occasion when I was orderly officer I had to go to the cookhouse at six am and breakfast on the food being prepared for the troops to prove it was fit to eat. And by God it was only just fit. They were getting boiled liver and hard-boiled eggs that morning. Imagine how attractive that was in the Red Sea with inadequate refrigeration. Looking back now, over the years, I should have taken a stand on that breakfast and made them improve it. Australian troops will only take so much, though, and eventually they did demand and get better food. Meanwhile the officers were sitting down to four-course meals served on starched linen table cloths, with Stilton cheese and port. It was quite unfair and wrong, and as the war forced realism on the army class structure that kind of pre-war absurdity vanished.

November 16, 1940

We are still moving slowly but surely across a dead calm sea and everything is precisely the same as the morning before. There is a much more friendly atmosphere on this ship than on the *Aquitania*, and I have met some old friends from Puckapunyal. From tomorrow we have to wear our tin hats and carry lifebelts with us at all times. Apparently they raid a bit from now on. I suppose nearly all of us are silly enough to hope that we will see a bit of action soon, a wish that no doubt will alter once we do. We have practice alarms during the day and we all have to proceed below, where we are shut in with the watertight compartments. It all works very smoothly and well. It is fortunate I don't suffer from claustrophobia.

November 19, 1940

Bob [the code name Peg and I had agreed on for the Red Sea] asked me to tell you he is well and not making things too hot. He is a peaceful sort of bloke and our association so far has been pleasant. Last night and today have been pleasantly exciting. We have stood on deck and gazed at enemy territory, waiting for large squadrons of bombers to come and get shot down, and they won't do it. Why, God only knows. You would think they would simply love to have a crack at this lot.

The sunset last night was absolutely superb—great banks of cumulus cloud and the colouring bold and weird, tapering away to delicate shades right down to the horizon. It was nice, too, to see it disappear behind a mountain and not dip into the sea. I thought of you; you would be asleep, well after midnight in the civilised portions of the world. I have made a point of watching the sun disappear every day since we sailed, just quietly by myself. I find it very soothing and there is no need to tell you where my thoughts are.

[Next day] Well, well. Soon after I had finished passing disparaging remarks about the enemy yesterday he had us all scuttling below, in the words of the instructors 'smartly and without confusion'. I couldn't, of course, see anything and we all stood about wondering what happens next. There was a spot of ack-ack fire and a long wait, during which we all said funny things to show how brave we were. Then we got the all clear.

When we got into the Red Sea we were actually looking at a part of Africa which was in Italian hands and I can't understand why we weren't bombed out of existence. We were bombed a bit, but it was of no particular consequence, and the whole enormous convoy of some fifty vessels got to Port Tewfik without losing a ship. One was a French ship, the *President Dumas*, whose commander never seemed to master convoy manoeuvres.

As we steamed through the Indian ocean you would hear a *ding* from the bridge, which was the signal for every ship in the convoy to change course and zigzag as an anti-torpedo tactic. The *President Dumas* was always in some sort of trouble because she had a habit of zagging when she should have zigged. I copped the job of officer of the watch one night, which meant I had to go round with the sentries to various parts of the ship to make sure everything was OK. By this time they had taken all the carpets out of the staterooms and dining rooms and run fire hoses everywhere. As I walked along the deck, I heard the *ding* of the signal to change course. I also became aware that the *President Dumas* next to us either had *not* changed course, or was heading the wrong way, because she was getting closer and closer. The only lights allowed were rudimentary navigation ones and they looked almost on board the *Nevassa*. It was quite hair-raising to have a ship closing on you like that in the dark. They managed to sort it out and the next day the commodore of the fleet signalled by flags that he would like to see the captain of the *President Dumas* on board his ship for a conference when the convoy reached Suez. I have no doubt it was a monumental pull-through.

When we got to Port Tewfik we sat around for a few days and, again, I'll never know why we weren't bombed out of existence. Then we went up the Suez Canal, ship by ship, to Kantara where we disembarked and took a train across the Sinai Desert to Palestine. We arrived there in December 1940. The bloke in charge of the Army Service Corps, Frank Watts, issued an order that we were to go ashore in our dress uniforms with ties and all that crap—I thought that was just bloody nonsense. Then we sat in a train for two days when we could have been in our more relaxed battle dress. I suppose this was a hangover from World War One when officers wore Sam Brownes in the trenches.

When we arrived in Palestine it was cold and raining. We thought we were going to a hot tropical country! The troops who had flogged their winter clothing in Bombay now had to suffer. My fantasy of Flanders, duckboards, and mud was coming closer to reality. Fortunately they work a system where a unit already there is called the foster unit, and they have tents pitched and food in the cookhouse ready when you arrive. The tents were magnificent and were known by the acronym EPIP. Someone once said it stood for European Personnel, Indian Pattern. They were so well lined you could black them out, and keep a light burning even in a blackout, but on this occasion they were full of mud, having been pitched after the rain, and this was a bit of a drawback.

Friday, November 27, 1940

Here I am safe and sound at my destination. We are in Palestine. The censor doesn't mind me telling you that, now we are actually here. We are here after a wearying train journey. We arrived at the ghastly hour of 3 a.m. in pouring rain, were led to the cookhouse and given a large feed of curry and gallons of tea which made us feel fine. We even had beds made up for us in our muddy-floored tents.

A word or two about the camp. [It was near Gaza but I couldn't say so at the time.] It is situated in a fairly pleasant region and is surrounded by orange groves. The weather is starting to break up and the rainy season is just starting. You have no idea how good it is to feel cold again. We wear shorts in the day time and our serge uniforms at night. To be able to snuggle into blankets again is just bliss.

Meanwhile my brother officers and I were terribly worried about our trunks. This may sound trivial to someone like C E W Bean writing a war history, but to a young Lieutenant who had paid £50 for the equipment it contained when he was only issued with £25, it was a matter of great trauma. Particularly as it had gone sailing off on the wrong ship.

There were vehicle parks everywhere, trucks arriving and troops sloshing around in the mud. Both T and Goggs were quite happy because their trunks had arrived—as they thought—and they said, 'We're right, thank you very much'.

I said, 'Where's mine?'

'Oh, yours isn't here, Johnny. Don't worry; it'll turn up sometime.'

I grabbed some nice guy with a ute and he offered to help me find it. We drove around the area which was all a mystery to me, but at the back of one of the vehicle parks there was a utility, and in the back of it were three trunks, mine, bloody T's and, indeed, the one belonging to our leader, Major Goggs. I remembered that they didn't give a stuff about my trunk not being there when they thought they had theirs.

We drove back to camp and I said to them, 'By the way I've just had a look at those two trunks over there, and they aren't yours'. Well, I've never seen two men change quite so quickly! Anyway, I said, 'Calm down, I've got mine, and here are yours, too'. Jesus, it all sounds so trivial with a war on.

Chapter Fifteen

PALESTINE, 1940

Now when I read over the letters I wrote to Peg at that time they reflect a great unease about the value of what I was doing. Certain friends who didn't join up had said to me in Tasmania, 'You are bloody mad, what are you leaving your wife and child for?' And they seemed to be right. Here we were buggering around in this foreign country where I had no idea there would be so much non-effective work. I thought we'd either be fighting someone, or someone would be fighting us. But we just spent months trying to get our unit together and properly trained, and then finding someone to give us a job of work to do. My letters reveal me trying to justify what we were doing, that we were going to be important and necessary, to train people and so on. In the end we did achieve a lot, because none of us knew a great deal in those days. There were few trained drivers and even fewer mechanics. Even though I was frustrated professionally in the early days at Gaza, and desperately resentful of being away from Peg and my baby son Tim, I did enjoy experiencing other cultures in an area of the world I would never have seen had it not been for the war.

November 28, 1940

Yesterday T and I went to Tel Aviv about thirty miles from where we are. At the camp we just gaze on flat country, while at Tel Aviv you only have to cross the road for a swim. T got on the bust as usual—he does it on every available occasion, but takes it for granted that I don't join in now. It took him a while to realise that I could actually want to do anything else.

I got tickets and went to a performance of the Palestine Symphony Orchestra assisted by the Palestine Choir. It was absolutely terrific. Practically every performer was an Austrian Jew and it was the biggest and finest orchestra that I have seen, or am likely to see for some time anyway. These Jews seem to do things properly, but I don't like the blighters. With the exception of a pleasant few I have met, the majority hate the sight of anybody whose nose hasn't a thirty-five degree kink in it, and are most unfriendly towards us in general.

[I am ashamed of these comments now, but it's part of the racist outlook young lieutenants had in those days. I was actually more attracted to the Arabs than the Jews as a race, although I did get to know some immigrant Jews running a kibbutz later on.]

The most attractive people I have seen here are members of a Polish regiment. Their manners make me blush with the realisation of how uncouth we are on the whole. I happened to nod good evening to a table full of Polish captains in a restaurant. They all rose and bowed very solemnly and sat down again.

There are pictures in the camp here, and there is a change of program every night but I have not been yet. It is run by the Jews. I believe the other night the projector broke down and the lads amused themselves by inflating French letters, blowing them up in the air, then heaving clay—pulled off their muddy boots—at them.

December 12, 1940

After getting settled in here the practical joke department of the Army sent us orders to move to another part of the camp, only a short distance from where we are now. Actually we like our new spot in the camp much better than the last. The three of us have a very large tent between us and our batmen have built us wardrobes, shelves and all sorts of fittings, and we have large grass mats on the floor. The mess is a quiet one and I like the chaps in it.

So far the only trip I have had was to Tel Aviv, but I hope to go to Jerusalem in a few days time with John Goggs. What I have seen of the country so far puts me in mind of an age-old vegetable garden: every inch of tillable soil looks as though it has been ploughed and planted for centuries, which indeed it has. I haven't seen a vestige of natural bush anywhere and, save for olive trees, I don't think there is any.

The orange groves are pretty and you can see them everywhere. Speaking generally the Jews and Arabs can fight over the bloody place as hard as they like as far as I am concerned. At the present moment there is peace between them. The Arab has promised to be a good boy as long as there is a war on. The poor blighter hasn't much chance to do anything else with the whole country packed with British troops. I am afraid my sympathies are with him.

We heard a very cheerful news service last night. It seems that we are giving the Italians a pretty fair push back in the desert. It is rather galling to be here, so close, and not have a hand in it.

This morning John Goggs and I went for a walk after breakfast across towards the sea. It was very pleasant. In the fields there were Arabs ploughing with a piece of bent wood towed by a camel, large fat Arabs riding tiny little donkeys and a shepherd minding a small flock of sheep. I expected a dove to appear in a beam of light down onto my head. I felt my chin to see if my beard had suddenly grown long, but it hadn't.

December 15, 1940

After lunch we took the car and drove through a town called El Megdel down to the beach and spent some hours looking over an old Roman town called Ascalon. When I say Roman town, it used to be so once. Now it is only heaps of rubble and fallen marble pillars half buried in the earth. There are also a number of wells, beautifully built in with stone and incredibly deep. It was rather interesting: you looked from the ruins across a belt of fertile ground about a quarter of a mile wide to the blue Mediterranean Sea. One can imagine how it must have looked in the days of the Romans, all set out in gardens. They have dug out quite a number of statues, some of which are still lying about in the sand.

We were accompanied by the RC padre, quite a pleasant young bloke, and by hordes of young Arab lads all taking on the job as guide. You simply can't shake them off. One young devil about ten years old attached himself to me; every few moments he would stroke my arm and say, 'Good

Peggy wrote on the back of this photo: 'I don't always walk along the street grinning like this on my own. I did it "a'purpose" hoping to get a good one to send to you.'

captain, very good captain. [Of course I was a lieutenant.] Baksheesh, baksheesh, yes?'

It is pretty evident that they are used to showing the Australians round because every time another 'guide' tried to take me over, my lad would say, 'Go! Fuck off!', and look at me with pride written all over his face.

We returned to the camp and had a corking hot shower and here I am in my tent clad in a warm dressing gown which, incidentally, still has the left sleeve turned up at the cuff from the last time you wore it. [It stayed like that right through the war too!]

December 16, 1940

I have just read your letter No. 6; it was handed to me when we got back from Tel Aviv. On the way John Goggs and I went off the track a bit to visit Ramleh, a Moslem stronghold. From it you look over the plain of Sharon into the hills of Judea. Here there are some striking relics of the Saracens, the people we used to fight in the Crusades. There is a huge watch tower looking as good as the day it was built close on one thousand years ago and around it are the ruins of quite large buildings. John Goggs was saying that he has never been able to find out much about them and he is a bit of an authority on this part of the world. [I should mention that John Goggs was a member of the Palestine gendarmerie, shortly after World War One.]

We then went to Lydda. This is a very hostile village and you don't go far into it if you have any sense. Here the fight between St George and the dragon is supposed to have taken place and there are many Christian Arabs living in Lydda and a church dedicated to St George. Then to Damascus, one of the oldest cities in history. Perseus slew Andromeda on the beach here. I had a look around but couldn't find any evidence to substantiate the claim. Now the city is a mixture of ancient and modern plus a lot of dirt. Motor car showrooms on one side of the road and Jesus standing on the other.

Tel Aviv is completely Jew. Here we had some beer and lunch and wandered around. I found a little place with some exceedingly nice prints of Gaugin and Van Gogh which I am posting by ordinary mail. The boats on the beach by Van Gogh I think is lovely. Can you have it framed and tell Tim it's his?

December 21, 1940

Today I was lucky enough to get to Haifa with a convoy. We left at 5 am in pitch dark and cold. It was too dark to see anything for the first part of the trip, but as it got lighter things improved. Lots of the country we passed through could have been Tasmanian lake country, alternating with patches as fertile as the Derwent Valley, only instead of hops you have orange groves. These look lovely, the dark green of the trees and the orange of the oranges as well as grapefruit orchards all along the coast.

We saw the *Patria*, the ship that the Jewish refugees sank in the harbour in November 1940. The story is this: they were not allowed to land and the ship was going to take them away to some other place. They conceived the idea of busting the engines, but they rather underestimated the effect of the explosives and instead of just disabling the engines, they blew the side clean out of her. She rolled over and sank in ten minutes and more than two hundred men, women and children were drowned and many more injured. About half of her is still sticking out of the water and most of the victims were caught below. She is a stone's throw from the shore and they were still recovering bodies today, I believe.

We saw some thousand or so Italian prisoners; the poor beggars looked motheaten and all seemed very glad to be out of it. Our lads were doing a great trade buying their badges and buttons as souvenirs. Gazing on the captured does not give me a great deal of enjoyment and I was glad when we moved off to see the town. We only had two-and-a-half hours.

Three of us, the padre and a YMCA bloke, a Methodist parson, hired a taxi and drove up Mt Carmel. I wanted to see the view and the parson wanted to see the Church of St Something or other. Actually both were good. You can see the pipeline and the refineries and the town is at your feet, the harbour, sunken ship and all. Across the bay you can see the town of Acre where Napoleon landed and made a conquest of some sort.

We then went to the church, or rather monastery. The chapel is built over the cave that I think Elijah took refuge in when Jezebel or some such was after his blood. Actually it is rather good, not all tinsel and tawdry as some of the Catholic chapels are. We were shown over by a Carmelite Father who seemed a very nice sort of bloke with a good grip on world affairs. He was Irish, and very pro-British and anti-Jew. Like me, he likes the Arabs and when he was showing us the chapel he said he thought it was probable that Elijah did actually live in that particular cave. The place had been busted up and re-built through the centuries and on the floor are brass plates with the names of English lords who fell in the Crusades.

The Father then suggested we walk further up. There are twelve tablets depicting the story of the Cross which are very ancient and interesting, and anyway the view is good. I warmed to the Carmelite Father. The tablets were interesting in that the silly old Arab had been up there in his last riot and solemnly put the eyes out of every Jew. I noticed with interest that they left Christ severely alone, also any women. They only put one of Pilate's eyes out. He was in his Roman rig-out and they must have been rather doubtful about him.

On the way back to Haifa we were stopped by a smart young thing in a blue uniform and badges of the Palestine police. She asked us for a lift into the city. Thirsty for information, we all fired questions at her—rather rudely I fear, thinking back on it. By piecing her replies together the following story unfolds. She is a Pole. Her bloke was a Jew who fled from Poland before the invasion and came to Palestine. She followed him to find that he had been killed in the riots some weeks before she arrived. She has no word or news of her people since the invasion of Poland, and doesn't know whether they are alive or dead. After a long spin of hunger and difficulty she landed her present job and considers herself fortunate. I don't think any comment is needed. With a solemn handshake all round and a cheerful goodbye, she left us rather shaken.

When we arrived back in Haifa the convoy was loaded and ready for the return and as I am supposed to have a little mechanical knowledge I was asked to go in the rear truck in case there was any trouble. Well, there was. After we had been going some time I saw the vehicle in front of me swerve out to miss a donkey, swerve in again to miss a car, go into a beautiful skid and gracefully take a header over a six foot drop, roll over twice and come to rest facing the opposite direction on its side. We pulled up and made a rush towards it, not quite knowing what sort of mess we were going to find in the cab. To my intense relief the uppermost windows opened and out popped the driver with a greenish-coloured face and one small bruise on his knee. The rest of the convoy sailed on merrily not knowing anything of what had happened. So there I was, and it was getting dark and starting to rain.

I got all business-like and took all particulars, measured skid marks and drew a sketch. The next thing was to get a repair gang out. In places like Australia this isn't very difficult, but here it was a bit of a problem. I

Tim—almost a war-time orphan

had to find a means of ringing the camp, so I left the driver to mind his mess and got my driver to take me down the road. After some time we came to a village full of Arabs who applauded the efforts of an Australian officer who amused them for some time by putting one hand to his ear and talking into the other hand. I gave up disgusted and we went further down the road looking for some British troops. I didn't have a map with me and had no idea where we were as the convoy had returned by a different route.

After a while I came to a railway station and to my delight saw smartly dressed troops all over the place. I went over to an officer and as I couldn't see his rank because he wore a raincoat, to play it safe I heaved him a salute and poured out my troubles. He was all attention and things went well until I asked him to take me to a telephone. He bowed politely and said, 'No English'. He was a bloody Pole. So the antics started all over again. By this time he thought I had earache and wanted something to take for it. I simply got nowhere. Suddenly a thought struck him. He sent an orderly to get some other bloke, and when he came in beamed at me as though to say, 'All is well'. I explained slowly and carefully that there had been an accident and I wanted to telephone. He said, 'Yes, do you want a first or second class carriage?' Anyway, to cut it short I *finally* got to a phone and fixed the whole business up. I felt like carrying it away with me!

December 25, 1940

Christmas Day. I started the day by going for a walk with John Goggs before breakfast. A lovely morning and everything looked fresh and clean. We then both went to church parade and both came away slightly irritated with the nonsense that the padre talked. The lads of our unit arranged a dinner and they did it splendidly. They found a vacant hut in the camp, decorated it out with the usual Christmas streamers and whatnots, and fixed up menus. It was quite a jolly affair and we all got a bit tight. The troops organised the whole thing and reduced all the officers to the ranks and promoted our batmen to generals etc. Each one had to act his part. I was one of the waiters and was fined fifty mils (one shilling) for insolence to my batman who had accepted the exalted rank of a field marshal and looked strangely like one. The alcohol had made him slightly pompous and gave him the necessary vacuous look.

December 26, 1940

Boxing Day. Work as usual. My lecture went quite well the other day. Apart from the fact that the workshop crowd seemed to get a lot from it, it also broke down the suspicion which you invariably find when trying to assist anybody, particularly workshop personnel. Unfortunately T does not assist this situation very much; his main objective is to be impressive and amusing and I blush to say I have seen him score off some rather dull, nervous questioner.

This evening John Goggs and I are going to a Masonic meeting at Tel Aviv which should be interesting.

[I was then at the stage of Master Mason, but I had already begun to move away from Masonry. It may have been this meeting that sowed the seeds that suggested it was time I was out of this sort of thing.]

December 28, 1940

The Masonic meeting in Tel Aviv was rather interesting. We had been invited by a Palestinian Jew, I forget the bloke's name now. By the way the Arab and the Palestinian Jew are friends, they have lived together for centuries; it is the immigrant Jew that the Arab has all the grudges against. We met him in the afternoon and walked around the place together with afternoon tea at a wine shop which was filled with very beautiful Jewesses, usually accompanied by old and revolting-looking men. I had the impression that money counts for more than physical attractiveness here. It was all very Continental with much kissing of hands and shoulder shrugging.

We arrived at the Masonic Temple at 6.30 p.m. and they made us very welcome. The supper which followed I thoroughly enjoyed. Being Boxing Day, it coincided with a big Jewish Festival of the Light, celebrating the day many years BC that the Jews drove the Greeks from Palestine. Their womenfolk were present at the dinner and there was speech making, some of which was translated into English for our benefit. The most imposing figure was an Arab big shot of some kind, one of the most handsome men I have ever seen. His personality was terrific. I found myself listening attentively and imagining that I could understand him. There was music, too, and we heard old Jewish folk songs sung by the people who had sung in Berlin and Austrian opera houses. Most of the songs were in a minor key and most attractive.

They are queer people; what a mixture now I come to think about it. In the room there were Australians, Englishmen, Americans, Frenchmen, Jews, Arabs, all having wassail together. We ate traditional dishes, a flat fish cake with a salad of olives, prunes and some kind of cress, followed by another flat cake as heavy as hell, washed down by the hock of the country. You would have loved it—I mean the evening not the hock. I spent most of the evening picturing your reactions.

January 1, 1941

Four of us last night did some heavy mathematics and worked out that 5 p.m. here would be new year at home. We gathered in the mess, charged our glasses and drank to our wives and families. Tell me what you were doing at that time. I am not going to try and describe my thoughts, you will understand and know what they were. After this the sergeants threw dinner and invited the officers: soup, turkey and plum pudding. We all let ourselves go and there was lots of riotous fun. For some reason I was called on for a song and obliged with great ease and aplomb. I sang Botany Bay. The chorus nearly lifted the roof.

Tomorrow we are on the move. We go to Egypt for a short while to observe a British Army school for a few days, then we come and get to work. My electrical course has been approved and we are starting straight off with it. I will be going like hell for some time. Praise be to heaven. Please don't think we are rushing off to the front line, actually we will be near the Canal. T is as bloody as usual, but he is more than counterbalanced by the decency of John Goggs. When you think of it, it is pretty bloody. Six months ago the show was first formed, and we are now going to start our first useful job. In that six months we have been consistently buggered about as you know. Now we are actually getting down to it. The big shots seem very interested in us, and we are going to be kept very busy.

One of the things that hadn't been thought through with the First Australian Mobile School of Mechanisation was that we were on our own, and we had to find a unit to attach ourselves to, and begin our training role.

Lieutenant Colonel Max Dollery, who had created our experimental unit, was an energetic young staff officer who had won his MC in France in World War One, and had graduated from Duntroon Military College. He'd drawn heavily on those early war experiences. He believed it was better to take training to the troops

I wrote on the back of this snap for Peg: 'Goofy the goop—looking natural and unfazed. The bush in the background is a castor oil tree.'

in the front line rather than bring them out to a base camp. The idea was you moved in with a particular unit and worked with them and trained them in the process. In many ways it had a lot to be said for it, but we weren't in a trench-warfare situation with a clearly defined front line and the idea was not popular with the average commanding officer. Units are rather clannish and tended to think they could train their own people best. We were an odds and sods outfit in some ways, but we battled on and did find units who welcomed us, gave their transport troops to train, and co-operated well. I think we did a pretty useful job, really.

We did get a movement order to accompany the first wave of troops into Greece. Why they wanted to send a mobile school into

Greece I'll never know. But for some incredible reason—thank Christ I can say now—it was buggered up in Signals and we didn't get our orders until five days later. And to demonstrate how great this Greek campaign was, by then Greece had fallen! I can imagine what chance we'd have had getting out. There they were trying to salvage their artillery and infantry and the cutting edge of the army. The priority of a mobile workshops school can be imagined. But at the time we were silly enough to be disappointed that we hadn't gone.

Chapter Sixteen

SCHMIDT DER SPY

January 3, 1941

Since I posted my letter No 12 I have travelled many miles and am at present near the town of Ismailia, and very pleasant it is too. It was the Mobile School's first bit of mobility and everything went well. The crossing of the Suez Canal is done by punt but to our dismay we found a large convoy in front of us and had to wait about three-and-a-half hours. I was rather amused with the remark of our Corporal Peter Milne. We had distributed our personnel in the vehicles to see that our precious gear didn't get damaged on the first run. At the first stop I opened the door of our main van and enquired anxiously, 'Is everything OK?' One thing about our blokes is that they will be comfortable under all conditions. They had fixed up deck chairs on the floor and were lolling in luxury having a pleasant game of cards. Peter Milne said: 'There is one thing, sir, that is rather bad: we forgot to bring any sugar for our grapefruit!'

This Ismailia is the nearest thing to paradise that I have seen. If it were in the middle of a fertile country it would still be good, but to come into it after travelling miles of desert is simply breathtaking. It is situated beside a lake in the Canal. Roughly speaking the lake is a couple of miles square. The beauty of the place is brought about by the sweet water canal system which brings water from the Nile about ninety miles away. The

Captain Bowden conducting an automotive electrical course. We felt we were earning our money at this stage.

town is the headquarters of the big shots of the Canal administration and the gardens and trees are superb. I can't name all the brilliant shrubs and flowers I have seen, but poinsettias seem to be the most prominent. Acres of green lawns and masses of rich colouring and, to cap it up, the native canal barges, the feluccas, are all different colours with high graceful bows, big sails, and great long sixty or seventy foot masts.

We are quartered with the British Army school and it is excellent. This whole business is rather a break, one of the few good ones you get in this life. The idea of sending us was really one of liaison and to let them see the Australian ideas. We are making a bit of a hit and brigadiers and upwards are coming to have a look at our turn-out. It is possible they will start a similar show of their own. I will have to give a lecture tomorrow and we are going to show them some of our films. There is no doubt these Tommies are charming blokes; they have put themselves out in every way to look after us and the conversation in the mess is almost as much an oasis in the desert as Ismailia is. Four of us sat late into the night arguing on more or less abstract ideas—a contrast to the usual arguments in the

Australian mess, which are usually whether Victoria is a better place than New South Wales or some such.

Yesterday afternoon John Goggs, T and I went up to Port Said, some fifty miles or so, to try and get some gear we wanted for our projector. John has a little bellows-type camera and as we were driving along the Canal a few big ships were on their way through. One of them looked so good that we stopped the car, had a look around, and as there was nobody around for miles, John Goggs took some photos. Just as we were approaching Port Said half an hour later, a guard firmly but politely stopped the car and said that the naval authorities had issued instructions that we were to be held for questioning. We were a little staggered and couldn't think why. The photo incident never crossed our minds as we knew nobody but the ship had seen us and she was miles down the Canal, travelling our way.

It transpired that the pilot wirelessed back to Ismailia, they phoned through—and there we were. John Goggs got in touch with the naval people by phone and we were allowed to proceed. He saw them today and surrendered his film and all was OK. They were quite nice about it. When he introduced himself, the naval type turned to the chief of the place and said: 'Here's Schmidt der spy'. We were quite pleased to see the efficiency of the place and, incidentally, the courtesy of it, because John was a long while getting his film and when he finally appeared he smelt very strongly of whisky, but we didn't say a word.

['Schmidt der Spy' was a popular comic strip character of the day—I think in *Smith's Weekly.* He was a heavy jowled fellow with an astonishing similarity to my CO John Goggs.]

We had dinner at the Eastern Exchange Hotel and then came home in the moonlight. It was so good that even T couldn't spoil it, despite the fact that all the way back he told us the famous things he had done. He had driven London tube trains at sixty miles per hour during the big strike, knocked down four men one after the other zung! just like that, and galloped round Kings Cross on a circus horse in tails. John Goggs and I just looked at one another and spurred him on to fresh ones. Lies, all bloody lies. The silly bastard couldn't knock a fly off a jam pot. In our PT business we do a certain amount of wrestling and that sort of nonsense, and even I could do him like a dinner. I also know he can't ride. Goggs is an authority on London tube trains and tells me that they are governed to about 30 m.p.h.

January 6, 1941

Bardia has fallen and the Australians have had a hand in it. I saw some photographs yesterday taken from a looted Italian camera and they were quite interesting—bearded generals at Mass all looking very pious under the hand of the priest and so on. What the hell they are going to do with all these prisoners I don't know. T, of course, says the only thing to do is to machine gun them.

The most intelligent scheme was put up by a young subaltern I know who suggested that they be taken over by a convoy and for the last three days of their trip that their rations be stopped to get them really hungry and angry, allow them one pair of trousers each, land them in Italy and let them be fed and clothed and soothed by their own people.

January 8, 1941

Yesterday John Goggs and I visited Cairo. It's about 100 miles from here. We had to get some equipment that we want. The road follows, as usual, the sweet water canal which gets wider as you go along. We passed King Farouk's summer residence. You can't see the palace but there are acres of garden and parkland. As you go in to Cairo you pass his palace, his real one. What the little blighter must cost the Treasury I don't know. The palace is a huge affair and covers about four blocks of the city. His private bodyguard patrols every few feet of the walls.

Yes, of course we went to the pyramids and the Sphinx. It is well known to be one of the biggest tourist rackets in the world and justifiably so. If you think, as I did, that out in the middle of a desert with the Nile running by you find these incredible remnants and structures, well, wash that idea right out. You drive through the city into the suburbs and at the end of the bitumen road they are on a rise on the outskirts of the town. You push your way through a mob of evil-smelling people who offer you the opportunity to ride the last few hundred yards on a camel and have your photograph taken with the Sphinx in the background.
[Poor bastards; I mean it's their living isn't it! What superior young men some of us Australian subalterns were.]

One guide will pass you over to another who will tell you your fortune; in turn he passes you on to another who sells dirty postcards and so on. By dint of screaming and hitting people with my stick [Oh dear God!] I managed to nail one bloke who commended me on my judgement by saying, 'He can only show you five coffins, I can show you seven coffins'. I told him firmly that I didn't want to see any coffins; I wanted to have a quick look at the Sphinx, go to the big pyramid and then, if time allowed, climb to the top of it, also that it was getting towards dusk and to get going. I might as well have saved my breath; we were led, raging and objecting, into squalid little holes in the ground until we had seen seven coffins, and not until then could I lead him to the pyramid. Here we were passed over to racketeer No 2. He was unavoidable and we fought our way past the dirty postcards into the Cheops, the biggest of the three.

It was rather good. You climb up a very narrow and steep passage until you finally come to two large chambers. I'm not sure what they were as the guide yelled bad English as though he were addressing a multitude in a high wind and I couldn't possibly understand him because of the echoes. Normally it is lit with electric lights but owing to the lack of tourists the guide now carried a candle and a bit of magnesium ribbon to bung off when you came to the high spots of the tour. It was rather eerie plunging along, bent double, despite all their efforts to ruin any atmosphere there is about them. I noticed in the King's Chamber that one wall, twenty feet long by twenty feet high, was one solid piece of granite, cut perfectly square and fitting perfectly with the block next to it. I came to the conclusion that they couldn't possibly have built them, they must have just found them there.

During the earlier part of the day I was looking through the shops for some interesting prints, but couldn't find any. All I could find were coloured photos of the pyramids with a red sky as the sun set behind them. When I came out I found it was too late to climb, so I walked away some distance and was greeted with a view of the pyramids with a red sky and the sunset behind them—its beauty completely spoiled by its horrible likeness to the coloured photos. The run home by moonlight was magnificent.

While I was in Kodaks I met a war correspondent and another chap who was official photographer to the attack on Bardia. He was assisting Frank Hurley. He was very scathing about the Italian infantry but spoke glowingly of the accuracy and skill of the artillery. They mistook his car with its photographic apparatus for some kind of secret weapon, he thinks, because they concentrated on him wherever he went. He said that if the shells had been any good they would have been blown to kingdom come. I think that under the circumstances his high opinion of their fire accuracy might justifiably be a little exaggerated. The stories you hear about large numbers of fully armed officers and men walking about looking for somebody to capture them are quite true. I can't say whether they were being cowardly or just sensible, but I think it's very evident that they had put up a very poor show indeed.

January 9, 1941

We leave for Palestine again on Saturday. Already I am busting to get back because I am sure that there's some mail waiting there for me. We told them not to send it on. I am dying to know how you are getting on back in dear, lovely Hobart. Forgive my adjectives, but my feelings for the place and all that it holds are pretty powerful. When I get back nothing is going to shift me out of it, even if I have to work as a labourer.
[What I said was quite true. I think my entrance back into civilian life was pretty close to that.]

It is good to feel that you and Tim are there. As far as work is concerned, yes, we are doing a bit, although you could be forgiven for not thinking so. I have been attending British lectures here and I like their methods, in spots far ahead of us, and in others well behind. Our equipment has staggered them and we have shown them some of the instructional films we have. They have met with enthusiasm. Already three brigadiers have inspected us and another one is expected today.

January 29, 1941 [Back in Palestine]

John Goggs had to go to Jerusalem and he took me with him. It has been most interesting. The road goes through Ramleh across the plain of Sharon to the Judean Hills. Jerusalem lies at the top of these hills, 2000 odd feet above sea level, and the old city is walled right around. The wall is comparatively modern; it was built by the Saracens in the days of the Crusades and is not, as some people think, the same one that Christ used to walk around. The new city is outside the walls and is quite imposing. I cashed a bank draft in a bank so modern and magnificent that I felt I was in New York.

As we only had one day we had to make up our minds whether to spend a day going around old spots in Jerusalem, or going to the Mount of Olives

Peg and Tim, January 1941

and down to the Jordan valley to the Dead Sea. I voted for the latter and so did John Goggs.

The Dead Sea is the lowest spot on the world's surface, actually 1200 feet below sea level and I think one of the most dreadful and hottest spots on the earth. It is approximately twenty miles from Jerusalem so that in that distance you drop from 2000 feet above sea level to 1200 feet below. It is winter here and from the icy blasts on the Mount of Olives to the muggy heat of the valley takes about three quarters of an hour. I have heard it described as the valley of baked brown plaster of Paris and the description is rather good. I don't know exactly, but I believe the Dead Sea is about seventy miles long and lies on a plain with the Judean hills on one side, and the mountains of Moab on the other. Trickling into it is the thrice holy and equally squalid River Jordan. There is no outlet. The evaporation of the sea keeps it the same level. We stood on the beach and threw sticks in and noticed how high they floated. I decided that I had heard so many stories of the buoyancy of the water I would try it. Our driver, Scott, and I peeled off and went in. It was very queer. You can sit in the water out of your depth and stick your feet and arms out and just float about in the region of your chest. It was quite warm. I got some in my eyes and it was like vitriol.

When we came out we were in a bad way: we had no towels, and as the water dried it left us coated with salt which was most uncomfortable. We were able to wash our faces under a tap in a police post, but felt awful for the rest of the day. It struck me as I was floating about in the brine that I have swum in Tasmania's Great Lake 3000 feet above sea level, and in the Dead Sea 1200 feet below.

We then drove up the valley to Jericho, which is a funny little place irrigated by the Jordan which we crossed by the Allenby Bridge constructed by the Royal Engineers in World War One. We couldn't take the car across as you require passports and there were queer little native police with spiked helmets whose sole occupation, apart from examining passports, seemed to be standing arm in arm with Australian troops being photographed with them. We strolled along the banks, which are just a mass of mud, and I nearly fell in. If being baptised in the Jordan was one of the essentials of becoming a Christian, I can understand the reluctance of the ancient people in entering the faith. It resembles pea soup. I didn't see the spot where Christ was baptised; I am told that the guides' association holds a meeting and fixes a new place each year.

February 21, 1941

Last night the mess invited a number of Polish officers down to dinner and for the evening. I had to miss it unfortunately as I was on duty. In a way it was a blessing in disguise as it would have cost the best part of £1. There were Polish generals, brigadiers and what have you. One of them was an ex-Premier of Poland. When I got back to my tent it was going in full swing. Our chaps would sing 'Roll Out the Barrel' and 'Waltzing Matilda' all in unison and out of tune; then the Poles would sing something and it would sound like a Russian choir—all in full parts from the bass to the male alto. I suppose they are folk songs of some sort, but they sounded damn good. I saw them arrive, and such saluting, bowing and scraping you never did see. But I'm sorry I missed it.

March 2, 1941

We have been on convoy duty to Beersheba, through Gaza and back to camp. I have decided I should at least try and learn a little of the language. For instance, the other day I was standing near an Arab village well off the beaten track when two of the local residents came down and solemnly and courteously shook hands. I offered them cigarettes. They expressed gratitude by touching their foreheads in a very gracious and effective movement. We did a little sign talking, but with very little effect. I would have given anything to have been able to talk to them and get their angle on things.

March 3, 1941

I had a day in Bethlehem. I went into the chapel which is supposed to be built over the stable, saw the spot where Christ was born and where the manger was. Found it a revolting mass of tinsel candles and coloured glass, and glass balls mixed up with priests passing you plates to put money in. It really is frightful.

A few days ago I did manage to get to Jerusalem to do some sight-seeing. The streets are seething with a conglomerate mass of Australians, New Zealand, Polish and British troops in their different uniforms, Greeks, Jews, Arabs, pukka English colonels with wives and daughters, harlots and priests. Goggs and I hired a small boy as guide to take us to the famous Wailing Wall. This is a very queer business. It is a large stone wall, the bottom tier of which is supposed to be the stone from Solomon's temple and is very sacred to the Jews, so sacred that they come in large numbers, place their foreheads against it and wail.

I saw one fat-looking old swine with a bewhiskered face sitting down in some comfort, wailing very effectively, but in a rather pre-occupied manner. I made enquiries from the Tommy police who were there and it appears that this bloke is a professional wailer. If you live in a far country you send him the money and he wails for you. If you send him a little he just sort of grizzles a bit, but for a decent sum he will howl the place down.

I wish I had taken more photographs of Palestine. This is a road tunnel between Beirut and Tripoli, in Syria.

One of the reasons for our trip to Jerusalem was to see the film *The Great Dictator.* There were the usual priceless bits of Charlie Chaplin but the general atmosphere in the audience was a little strained, not unnaturally, as I suppose seventy-five per cent of them were Jews and many of them have had plenty to do with storm troopers. I agree with most of the criticisms I have read about it, that sudden jumps from farce to reality were not good and made most of us feel rather embarrassed. Still, it was good stuff.

A bloke named Ted Holloway and I were in a Jerusalem shop when a padre came in and told us confidentially he was making a purchase that he really couldn't afford, but in doing so was fulfilling an ambition he had for nearly a year. The object he wanted was so beautiful the man didn't want to sell it, but he finally decided to part with it for £3/10/-. We were agog to see what this was.

It is to our everlasting credit that we didn't give way to rude and raucous laughter when it was dug out. It was an ink stand made from some white metal stuff and consisted of Joseph and Mary kneeling one each side of the cradle, with their palms together in the prayerful manner taught to small children. In the cradle was a little baby Christ complete with halo, and on the top of the cradle perched three doves. The whole thing when lifted up and placed down again, played the first three bars of O Come All Ye Faithful—until it ran down. The padre couldn't bear to have it wrapped up and we left him leaning on the counter listening to it with rapture, which made us creep out on tiptoe.

There was an amusing incident a few days ago. Our quartermaster, a staff sergeant, is a very quiet and sensible chap but the owner of the most revolting set of false teeth that you ever did see—the kind where you have an inch and a half of bright red gum with black specks on it before you come to the teeth part. Well he met some old school friends and got a bit tight and came back and got into an argument with our sergeant-major who is a very garrulous bloke. The poor quartermaster couldn't get a word in edgeways, but on the few chances he did get, his teeth took charge, and by the time he had them under control his chance had gone.

Finally he got fed up, and with a gesture, took out both sets, put them on the table and won the argument hands (or teeth) down.

March 5, 1941

This afternoon one Warrant Officer Stooke and I armed ourselves with compasses and maps, climbed into a truck and set out to reconnoitre a cross-country route for an all-day convoy exercise which I have to run. We took the main road to Beersheba for some twenty miles and then turned off to an Arab track and, with the aid of the map, did about a fifty mile circuit using only tracks. It was good fun and we passed through the villages of Al Faluge, Beriare, Beit Hanoon, Sum Sum, Dimra and, of course, Gaza. In fact, we lost ourselves at Al Faluge but sailed merrily in thrusting our way past donkeys, camels and the usual rabble into an absolute maze of mud houses and finally had to stop because the track was too narrow.

As soon as we came to a standstill the complete infant population of the village mobbed the truck, all screaming and yelling. The view from the cab window consisted of bright dark eyes, open mouths and snotty noses to an infinite depth. I wasn't too keen on doing the heavy white master act with a stick in the middle of an Arab village but somehow managed to get them clear enough to be able to back the truck out and we got going, the children dropping off at intervals as we went over bumps or round corners. We got on to the right track a little later and the grass on each side of us was a mass of miniature blue iris and wild anemones. Palestine at the moment is absolutely at its best. I would love you to see the wild flowers. I'm afraid I keep harping on them, but they really are something to remember, every type and kind of rare and lovely flower just grows wild in the fields. I can seldom resist picking them, but they are of little use in this masculine atmosphere.

March 23, 1941

I didn't write yesterday; we were out on a convoy exercise all day and I didn't get back until about 9 pm and went straight to bed. It rained like stinking hell all the time and was so misty that you couldn't see a thing which was a pity as it was interesting country. We came to Rehovath, a pretty little Jewish town, about 6 pm and stopped and gave everybody an hour off. John Goggs and I went to a little cafe and had fried chicken and green peas. It was delightful and we consumed two bottles of wine, one hock and one sauterne. Our views on life altered considerably. We entered cold, wet and rather embittered and came out warm and benign.

You know Peg, I must again utter the platitude that this war is absolute nonsense. In that little cafe were two Arabs who couldn't speak English, two Jews and two Australian officers. Ethnically speaking nobody was supposed to like anybody. But we shared drinks and cigarettes and talked and chatted, chiefly by signs. I had one of the most amusing hours that has come my way in this country. The Jews asked us to meet them there on Tuesday to take us over to the vineyards where they make all the local wines. We are going of course; it so happens that this course will be finished by then.

March 25, 1941

After lunch I am going with a few other chaps to have a look at a Jewish communal settlement which should be interesting. They settle in groups in some spot, build their houses and live as a complete unit. Everything is pooled: for instance, the entire washing for the community is done by one section and the clothes actually belong to nobody, you just grab a garment that fits. They have some form of contract marriage; I think you agree to live together for a minimum of two years. One section looks after the children and they have a scientifically run creche. Everybody works, including the women, on the land or road building or what have you, and you collect your family when you come home at night. I will know more about it tonight. We chose our party carefully; each one of us has decidedly leftish views and we are looking forward to it.

I am going to eat some lunch and then head off for the 'Love Farm' as the troops have dubbed the communal settlements—a name which is characteristically descriptive of the attitude of mind of the ordinary individual to any reform in the mode of living.

March 26, 1941

Well, it was all very interesting. We had some difficulty finding the place and had to enlist the services of an Arab to guide us there. We traversed some five miles of unmade road which was just a quagmire, and we got bogged occasionally. There were four of us in the back of a closed one-ton van and we rattled about and spent our time hitting our heads on the roof or falling full length on the floor in a struggling mass. I had borrowed a cane chair, the very precious property of T. He didn't know I had it. It wouldn't stand the strain and slowly shed its legs and things until finally I used it to pack the back wheel when we once got bogged. It did the job splendidly; in fact, I will recommend that they become standard equipment for this purpose. We then took its photo and I am presenting it to T as proof that it wasn't wasted. He is inclined to take rather a poor view of the whole matter.

We were met by a man called Israel, believe it or not. He is a Canadian Jew and spoke with an attractive soft accent. The first thing that takes the eye is the defence tower. When they started the settlement things were pretty bad. It consisted of a rickety wooden tower some sixty feet high with a bullet-proof top and a searchlight. I noticed some bullet holes in the woodwork. They had built some huts round this, then a concrete fortress, with a stone wall around the lot. Since then they have moved their site to the top of a nearby hill and use the old fortress as a laundry. They have what in Australia would be a very small amount of farm land, but they don't waste much of it.

As we walked up to the new settlement Israel gave us a brief outline of the idea. When you join, everything you possess, including clothes, is put in the common pool. There is definitely no private ownership of anything. The children are looked after in a nursery school and lovely kids they are, too. The parents can see and collect them any time within reason. I noticed that the reaction of the kiddies to their parents was particularly marked: they were terribly thrilled to see them, but worried not a jot when they were returned to the creche. Israel said that they consider the job of feeding and teaching young children is far too important to leave to the haphazard method of allowing it to be done by individual mothers. So they have it done by people who know the job. It seemed sensible to me.

They took us in and gave us tea in the communal dining room. This was a shed, very draughty and rather bleak. They will build a better one when they have some money. We sat down and had coffee, brown bread and cream cheese and a lovely sweet. With the exception of the coffee, everything was grown and made on the farm. As we ate, many of the others came in; they were a curious crowd, but looked interesting. Those that could speak English would come and talk to us. The women were particularly attractive and sensible. One forgot after a while that they were wearing anything from dungaree overalls to attractive jumpers and skirts, depending on what particular job they had been on that day.

I became a little uneasy at that stage. Our friend the Arab guide, who seemed a rather dignified type of bloke, followed us round wherever we went. With my mind running on the bullet holes in the fortress and the searchlights, I thought it just possible that our hosts might not like to have that Arab wandering around. I cornered Israel and shared my concern. He replied that at one stage they were careful not to let the Arabs see anything, but it didn't matter now. I noticed that he extended the same courtesies to our guide as he did to us, there was not a look of resentment anywhere, and yet I am sure that they hated his being there like hell.

After the feed we were invited down to see some of the private living rooms. They are fitted out very simply and are quite attractive. The young marrieds have a room each. What their code of morals is I do not know. One rather amusing thing: Bill Kingdon, one of our party, poked his head around the door of one room and jumped back as though someone had hit him. I was standing close to him and he looked quite startled and shaken. It appears there was a young woman having a shower. He told me afterwards that after some twelve months of celibacy, to be confronted with the completely naked body of a beautiful young woman quite unexpectedly was a bit shattering. I asked him what her reactions were. He said she had soap in her eyes!

Israel asked me to go again and stay for a few days. I have a few days' leave due at the end of the present course and I'm considering it. I think it would be damned interesting.

We had the same trouble getting bogged on the way back, and when we

The spring flowers of Palestine

dropped our Arab guide at his village he refused any payment. He gave us a pressing invitation to eat at his house which we had to refuse.

One of the pluses of army life is that it enables you to develop quite extraordinary friendships. I can imagine the strength of the bonds between men in active fighting units—that aspect makes the RSL understandable. I became friendly with a bloke called Vernon Lawrence, a rather unusual fellow who went by the nickname of 'Lachrymonious' Lawrence. At one stage he was sent to a gas school in Cairo—gas wasn't used in the war, thank Christ, but both sides were fairly well equipped for it. No one really gave a stuff about gas drill. You had respirators which were always at the bottom of your trunk and never used and although there were supposed to be gas warning systems in all the camps, nobody bothered. But when Vern came back from this Pommy-run gas school he was all fired up about it, and he wrote a letter to the colonel in charge of our area reprimanding him for not having any gas precautions! Not a very tactful thing for a captain to do to a colonel and it got the sort of reply you might expect. Vern was undeterred and insisted on giving lectures to all the troops. Some varieties were called lachrymonious gases, hence the nickname.

'Lachrymonious' and I became friendly with Israel and the people in the kibbutz. It was called Kfar Menahem and we used to go there whenever we could. Then the kibbutz was put out of bounds because the Intelligence people had detected certain activities going on there—people trying to find out too much information from Allied soldiers. Vern and I were upset about this because we looked forward to our visits to these pleasant and civilised people and we put up with the new edict for quite a long while. But one night we decided to sneak out and see them. We behaved like a couple of schoolboys, although it could have been more serious. We got a driver and a ute and drove to within about twelve kilometres of this place then walked the rest of the way so we wouldn't be detected. We had to go in through their guards because of the possibility of an Arab attack. Well, we got in and there was great rejoicing. 'John and Vern have come', so orange juice and some kind of alcohol they mixed with it was produced, and we had a ball.

Then a message came through somehow that the Military Police were on their way. 'Quick', they said, 'come this way'. Vern and I were rushed into one of their sleeping huts and up through a trapdoor into the roof where we had to wait. Every now and then someone would sneak down to the hut we were in and say, 'They're still here, but it's good news. They have come to tell us that we are not out of bounds anymore.' But that was of little comfort to Vern and me. Had the bloody provos found us hiding under a hut roof there, it would have been extremely awkward. The provost colonel who had come out to give them the message was treated hospitably, and he enjoyed his orange juice and alcohol while we sat up under the bloody hut roof until about 2 am! At last they drove off and

Lachrymonious Lawrence and I snuck out and began the long walk back to our ute which was fortunately still there. The driver had about given us up.

The kibbutz people were very keen to keep up contact with Australians and wrote to me for many years afterwards. I have a feeling they were keen to perhaps form kibbutzim in Australia, but this was never said.

May, 1941

In Jerusalem I bumped into a young lieutenant who had been to one of our earlier courses. He was on a few days' leave to get the smell of Greece out of his nostrils. [Greece fell at the end of April.] He is very cheerful despite the fact that his worldly possessions consisted of a pair of slacks and a shirt, boots and socks. His praise for the Navy is unstinted, also for our chaps and the New Zealanders. He said we have learned a lot and we agreed we would like to meet the bloke who thought two Divisions would be effective against fifty highly mechanised Divisions, plus air force to burn.

The amount of Fifth Column in Greece was terrific and they were under orders to shoot all shepherds in their vicinity. The arrival of a flock of sheep coincided too often with the arrival of aircraft.

Down on the beach yesterday there were some fellows with a queer little dog of nondescript make. He was marvellous at keeping the pestering Arab hawkers out of the way. When one of the blighters came near with the everlasting, 'Lemonade, very sweet, very clean. Chewing gum, very American, very hygiene', the lads just pointed at him and the dog drove him away. They told me he had been to Greece and Crete with them and they managed to evacuate him by stuffing him inside one of their tunics. They said, 'He's a crack first-line trooper now'. At the first sign of any trouble from the air, one look skywards and he is into the nearest slit trench like a streak. He is a traitor, though. They pinched him from the Arabs, and when they first got him he used to wag his tail at the Arabs and bite all men in uniform on principle. Now he bites the Arabs and is pally with everyone in uniform.

At one stage we moved to Syria, still performing our transport training role, and operated in all sorts of odd areas. We were

FRANÇAIS,

On vous trompe

On vous dit que des formations aériennes allemandes occupent les aérodromes de Syrie.

C'est Faux !

Seuls quelques appareils ont transité par la Syrie pour aller en Irak. Ils font actuellement le trajet en sens inverse.

Dans quelques jours il ne restera plus un seul appareil allemand en Syrie.

On vous dit que des troupes Allemandes sont venues relever les troupes Françaises à la frontière de Palestine.

C'est Faux !

Il n'y a pas un seul soldat allemand de l'armée de terre en Syrie et au Liban.

A la frontière il n'y a que des troupes Françaises décidées à remplir leur mission, c'est à dire à défendre la Syrie et le Liban contre toute agression d'où qu'elle vienne.

Si vous voulez vous battre contre les Allemands, ce n'est ni en Syrie ni au Liban qu'il faut aller, mais en Egypte.

En attaquant les territoires du Levant, vous vous battrez contre des Français pour le plus grand profit de l'étranger.

(translation)

FRENCH PEOPLE

You are being deceived

They tell you that German aerial training uses the Syrian aerodromes,

It is false

Only a few aircraft have passed in transit through Syria on their way to Irak. At present, their course is in the opposite direction.

In a few days there will no longer be a single German plane in Syria.

They tell you that the German Army have come to relieve the French army at the Palestine frontier.

It is false

There is not a single German soldier in Syria or Lebanon. At the frontier there are only French troops determined to fulfil their mission, that is, to defend Syria and Lebanon against any aggression wherever it comes from.

If you want to fight against the Germans it is not necessary to go to either Syria or Lebanon but to Egypt.

In attacking the territory of the Levant, you fight against the French for the greatest advantage of the foreigner.

camped in a deserted monastery up in the hills. Hostilities had ended, I'm glad to say, although at the time we thought it was terrible to have missed the action. We also camped in an olive grove at the notorious Damour which has featured in the news quite a lot recently. The previous occupants had been the Vichy French army who, incidentally, had killed a lot of our blokes, the bastards. After being used to British military standards of hygiene it was a shock to move into the olive grove where they had camped. It was just one mess of poop and muck. Anyway it was all cleaned up and proper latrines and garbage pits dug, and there was a campaign to interview the Vichys and invite or persuade them to join the Free French and stay in the Middle East. Some did, but most of the Vichy got on their boats to steam back to France. I thought that was terrible at the time. I didn't like the Vichys anyway. I still have a pamphlet that was circulated to the Vichy French at that time.

September 3, 1941

We have finished our first course in Syria and we are all packed up ready to move to fresh woods tomorrow. It is a glorious night, a crescent moon, calm and still. Someone unearthed an old portable gramophone and we are sitting round a table by the light of a hurricane lamp, listening to *No No Nannette* records and quite enjoying it. Simple souls aren't we?

Two telegrams came today. I haven't opened them, just snuck a look to make sure everything was all right and shut them up again. I will officially open them on the fifth. [My birthday.] By the way, I was doing some mental calculation today on the subject of a captain's pay. It appears, my darling, that instead of being some twenty-four shillings per week better off, it amounts to thirty shillings per week, so with great delight I will be able to increase your allotment by fifteen shillings a week instead of ten shillings as I originally stated. There is a Gazette due tomorrow, and I have a feeling. [Promotions, demotions and everything came out in the Army Gazette which appeared once a month, I think. 'To be Captain: Lieutenant J.G. Bowden'—whacko!]

Peg used to cut out the personal bits from our letters before passing them on to friends to read. I came across this excerpt recently among some other papers.

[Undated]

Letters are impersonal things. On reading this through, it does not convey the feeling that I have inside me when I am writing to you; just a warm satisfactory feeling that I am talking to the only woman in the world. To say that I love you sounds weak and paltry compared with how I actually do feel. Yet it is the nearest I can get to in words, and I like the sensation of saying it as I write. I love you Peggy darling.

We were at the Syrian coast for a while and often went to Beirut on leave. Australian officers were made honorary members of the Beirut Swimming Club, which was a great privilege, to swim in the beautiful Mediterranean. I forget many of the places we visited now, but I was at Baalbeck at one stage. I visited the old Krak des Chevaliers, a superb Crusader castle stuck on a hill.

The old Roman watering place of Ascalon on the Mediterranean coast made a big impression on me. It had old Roman statues lying, half covered in the sand, and Roman pillars lying on the beach. In later years when I built a weekend cottage on the east coast of Tasmania, I named it *Askelon* (there are different spellings) because I was reminded of the Mediterranean Ascalon. The army map had it as 'Askelon'.

Then Japan came into the war. I can remember one dismal night in December 1941 because we had just heard that the British battleship the *Prince of Wales* had been sunk near Singapore. We were camped at Beitjurja in Palestine and I went to see a bloke called Ted Holloway—he was a good bloke, but a rather gloomy fellow. It was raining like buggery and he was sitting in his tent with a hurricane lamp burning. I was feeling rather low and dropped in for a chat.

'Good day Ted. I'm a bit fed up with life in general, and I could do with a cheer-up talk.'

He said, 'You don't think you're going to see you wife and child any more do you? This is the end of it. We'll never see our families again.'

I've never forgotten the utter desolation of that night, with the rain beating on the tent.

Chapter Seventeen

GOING HOME

If it hadn't been for Prime Minister John Curtin, I don't know where we'd have finished up. But he had his row with Churchill when Singapore fell in February 1942 and pulled the 7th, 6th and 9th Divisions back from the Middle East to defend Australia against the Japanese threat from the north. Anyway, thank Christ I still had my testicles and whatever intelligence I possessed, and these were the things I hoped I'd get back to Peggy with.

While my period in the Middle East had its fair share of frustrations, I shouldn't leave the impression that the First Mobile School of Mechanisation had been in any way ineffective. We did carry out a lot of training. At the time there were no automotive electricians in army workshops and I started a course to train some. I had to fight to get permission to do it, but the course eventually ran very well. It was probably the most satisfactory thing I did while in the Middle East.

Word got around there was a big move on back to Australia. It was known as the 'Step Sister' move and the first to go were the fighting units, infantry and artillery. The odds and sods bits like the schools and training units and some artillery schools were shunted down to a place called Nusarat, further down the coast from Gaza.

At Nusarat we came under the command of one Colonel McDonald, a Staff Corps man, and we thought he was the greatest shit of all time. Of course it is sometimes better to have a difficult character in command at times like that to stir things up a bit. We could have sat there and vegetated. But not under Colonel McDonald who decided he would mould us into a strong fighting force. All the ingredients were there, artillery, infantry, the Army Service Corps—he had the lot. A meeting of all officers was called and he said we would be temporarily divested of all rank and be students in this Bandy Force as it was known. We still had certain privileges like our own mess, but otherwise we were simply units of Bandy Force.

To our great horror we were ordered not to go near our beloved vehicles. Not a wheel would turn without the CO's special permission. We had been used to pissing off into Gaza or Tel Aviv when time was available. No more of that. We were out at 5 am on cold winter mornings doing PT and unarmed combat. We had to go on five-mile runs, and do simulated attacks with live ammunition whizzing around our ears. We became very fit.

McDonald decided he would have a review parade. There weren't many senior people left but he found some high ranking dreary old poop who was still in Palestine and we did have the review. I noticed that the senior officer had brought a nurse with him, and she also observed our display as we marched past the official dais.

Our one big relaxing point was the Gaza Officers Club—our rank was returned to us for that. I remember going there one night and getting so full that I nearly terminated my army career. If it hadn't been for a well developed musical ear, I would have. I had just reached the stage when the smoke-filled room had started to revolve, and I said to myself, 'You're pissed. You'd better get out of here while you can.' This was excellent self-given advice and I attempted to walk briskly—more like a stagger as it turned out—to get my cap and lurch out the bloody door. In the middle of this hazardous procedure I became dimly aware that God Save The King was being played. I dragged my right foot up against my left, put my arms down by my sides, stiffened them, and came to attention. As I precariously swayed backwards and forwards I became conscious of a great mass of colour in front of my eyes. This puzzled me rather, and I peered bleerily, attempting to focus, only to discover the colours belonged to a great mass of ribbons on someone's chest. I raised my head further, and found myself gazing

We didn't care about overcrowding on the Dorset*—we were coming home!*

into the steely blue eyes of the Australian Commander in Chief, General Thomas Blamey!

Well, if a shickered captain had lurched across the room while the National Anthem was being played, Blamey was the sort of man who would have said, 'Who is that?' Which could better be expressed as, 'Who *was* that'. I think the career of temporary Captain Bowden could have easily come to an end that night.

Finally our marching orders came and we entrained at Gaza to cross the Sinai Desert, across the Suez Canal at Kantara, and down to Suez and Port Tewfik. Then we marched into a Pommy staging camp quite some distance out into the desert. There we found rows of tents with the sides rolled up. It was blowing hard, and a great cold mass of gritty sand was blowing straight through about a metre off the ground. We Australians generally made sure that if a unit came in to our area, the tents were secure and the food was all right. We sat down to sandy, gritty, tinned bully beef dumped on to a plate with nothing else and a loaf of white bread on the table. God bless the bloody Poms!

One thing had changed for the better, though, since those palmy days of white table cloths, four course meals, port and Stilton cheese on the *Aquitania* and the *Nevassa*, coming from Australia. By this stage we were a proper army and that nonsense of better food for the officers and worse for the men had disappeared. Even so, the staging camp was so bad that had the troops not been going in the direction they wanted to go, there would have been a revolt. We didn't really know where we were going, it was all very secret. But we had a feeling we were going back to Australia. Then the rumours got around that the biggest convoy ever was about to leave Port Tewfik within a week or so, bound for Australia, and there would be an aircraft carrier, cruisers, hundreds of ships and so on.

While we were waiting we did manage to escape from that awful bloody Pommy-run staging camp and have a few simple meals at the Suez YWCA that had been started for army nurses. But we ran out of money and had to go back to the gritty bully beef in that dreadful camp.

At last, early in March 1942, we marched towards the docks. But there was no big convoy, no aircraft carrier—there didn't seem to be anything. There was, however, a tiny little ship called the *Dorset*. Oh, how we loved the look of her just the same. Apparently they had asked the Captain how many troops he could carry and he said, 'Well I could take about thirty at a pinch', so the Australian military command said, 'Think again mate, because we're going to put a thousand on board,' and that is precisely what happened.

The *Dorset* was a typical little merchant ship with a well-deck forward, and a well-deck aft, and with some ingenuity they built an army cook house in each of these decks. Things were fairly primitive, with latrines built out over the side of the ship so you crapped straight down into the water. God knows what would have happened had we run into really bad weather. Fortunately they loaded a lot of beer on board her, too. The Australian army always seemed to be able to find plenty of beer. They might have been short of ammunition and rifles at times, but never beer. I'm not complaining either, although I did sometimes when I couldn't get urgently needed training equipment.

An extremely fortunate thing happened to me at this stage. While we were in the last dying days of our Palestine period, we were running a school for motor mechanics and I had a visit from an Ordnance officer. Now, traditionally, Ordnance and Army

Service Corps officers love one another like a hole in the head. I don't know why, it's traditional, like the Artillery looks down on the Infantry, and everybody looks down on the ASC, and even the ASC looks down on Ordnance—there's a kind of pecking order.

Anyway, this Ordnance captain came to me one day and told me he'd been ordered to organise a course for mechanics. He had no equipment but hoped I could help him. He seemed a decent bloke, and I rallied around and showed him our set-up and what our instructors were doing. I even loaded him up with some précis of our lectures, and our draughtsmen found some spare diagrams and charts. Then we gave him a beer in the mess, and sent him on his way a very happy man. The point of all this was that when we were rafted out to the *Dorset* and marched up the gangway to be allocated living space, the Ordnance captain I'd helped only a few weeks before was the man dishing out the accommodation. Most were being directed down into the hold, but he said to me, 'Stand over there'. This also included my new CO Major Dick Durance who was also a close friend. So while everyone else filed down into the hold, we stood there on deck and looked out to sea.

They'd built a small wooden shed on the boat deck and crammed twelve bunks in it. My Ordnance friend said, 'Put your gear in there'. Everybody else was down in the hold and Dick Durance, ten other blokes and me—I don't know how they were selected—were in this shed on the deck. So this voyage, which would have been a nightmare, turned into one of those bits of army life that I just like thinking about it. We had nothing much to eat but stew and you had to take your dixie up to the cook house to get it. Again, there was no distinction really between soldiers and officers when it came to the basics of living. And, of course, soldiers going the way they want to go can behave bloody well. They were all seasoned troops, light years removed from the men who had disconnected the carriages from the engine at Spencer Street Railway Station in mid 1940.

The water situation was critical. We had one ordinary army water bottle per man per day for everything. We washed in sea water from hydrants on the deck. Washing in sea water is awful, you always feel sticky. But it wasn't awful because the *Dorset* was a bloody good little ship and we were going home. The Captain's name was Almond—not surprisingly known to the ships company

My sister Dottie wrote on the back of this snap: 'I'm sorry my face is so big and so like me, but it has always been like that. Anyway, it is a good foil to Timothy. Taken at Xmas, at Blackmans Bay. Timothy had just had measles.

as 'Nutty'. Nutty Almond was a Pom, but there are Poms and Poms, and he gave us a good go.

These were precarious times to be at sea and we had to have a complete blackout at night. The twelve of us would cram into our little hut to smoke and talk, and have a beer. We were all smokers in those days. I'm glad I was when I think of the atmosphere in that hut. In order to have the light on, the door had to be closed. If someone wanted to go in or out, the light was switched off while the door was opened and closed. As we got into the Red Sea the atmosphere in that closed up little hut with twelve sweaty blokes smoking and drinking beer can only be imagined.

One night we asked the Chief Officer to come and have a drink with us. He knocked on the door to give the signal to turn the light out. He moved into this sweaty smoke-filled box, and we switched the light on. He said, 'Christ', turned the light off, opened the door, and fled. We never saw him again. I don't blame him.

I did get to know the Chief Engineer. Now the *Dorset*'s crew did not have to put up with our conditions. They were doing their job as merchant seamen and living under great danger all the time. The ship's officers used to ask one Australian army officer to dinner each evening in their mess where they put on their whites and had stewards serve the food. When my turn came someone lent me a pair of clean socks, and another of the hut fraternity wiped the muck off the back of my neck and passed me smart enough to go. I went to the engineers' mess and, oh God, they had beautiful masses of white freshly baked bread on the table. We only had army biscuits. It was just an ordinary meal, but it looked like heaven. I was just starting to get into the fringes of this, when I looked around and everyone had finished. They weren't very hungry as they had similar food every night. I had to gobble up what I could and leave a lot of unfinished food on the plate.

Then the nice Chief Engineer said, 'Would you like a bath?' He took me to his cabin and there was a nice little bathroom with a porcelain bath and fresh hot water. Oh Jesus, I've never forgotten the luxury of that. Sadly the *Dorset* was sunk on the way back from Australia.

Although it was a wonderful feeling to sit on the deck during those soft lovely nights in the Indian Ocean knowing every throb of the engine was taking us closer to Australia, we were one lone little ship in a situation of some danger. I think our course was controlled from London or some other strategic communication centre. Every now and then we would change course suddenly and the bridge ladders and ship rails would start to shake as we crammed on all speed. It was likely a submarine had been reported or a ship sunk. The *Dorset* would receive signals but did not reply. This speeding up and changing course happened quite a lot and we'd know something was on. But we made it home without incident.

Fremantle was our first port of call, on February 5, 1942, and a number of us went to the Adelphi for a light-hearted night of eating real food and boozing. It's difficult to describe the sheer delight of knowing that I was on the same continent as Peggy, my son and family. We got back on the *Dorset* as full as boots with six cooked chooks in a brown paper bag, given to us by a waitress at the Adelphi after we had told her how bad things were on board. Although we had eaten and drunk our fill, we brought those six warm chooks on to the boat deck and ate them.

Peg wrote: 'John, for September 5 [my birthday] love from Tim'.

We had had no mail for three months. The authorities that ruled our destinies in those days had decided that the best way of handling the censorship and security at this time was to cancel all incoming and outgoing mail. As it happened, that was not the great deprivation it might have seemed. Our poor wives didn't know and went on writing, but for two years we had been writing home and although it was easy enough in the beginning with the excitement of new countries and different experiences, as the months went on, it was difficult to enjoy writing. There was some sense of relief in knowing we couldn't write. Peggy, of course, knew nothing about the 'Step Sister' move and was still writing to me in the Middle East. She worked in censorship so she had an idea that something was going on but didn't know what. I can remember sitting in the sun and catching up with three months of family news.

When we got to Adelaide we were allowed to ring our homes and reveal that we were back in Australia. I've never forgotten that. We were given seven days' leave and I will also never forget the feeling of standing on the deck of the little Bass Strait steamer *Nairana* and seeing the shoreline of northern Tasmania heaving up in the February dawn. We meandered up the Tamar River to the Launceston wharf where Peg and my five-year-old son Tim were waiting to meet me.

Chapter Eighteen

MUTINY IN ALICE SPRINGS

Before the *Nairana* pulled into the wharf at Launceston in April 1942, I had been lumbered with the job of being in charge of all the returning troops on the boat. I was standing there with all the paper work, nominal rolls and various travel documents. Then I looked down on the wharf and saw Peggy and my five-year-old son Tim standing there, and I just let it all fall to the deck and ran down the gangway to embrace them for the first time in two-and-a-half years.

We all had seven days' disembarkation leave. When I think of it, what I should have done was to take Peg and Tim away to a seaside hide-away like Coles Bay and just spend that time catching up. But no, the idea with my seven days' leave seemed to be to see as many relatives and friends as possible. There was lots of boozing and catching up, but the seven days were squandered really. The absurdity of what we were doing with that precious time was well illustrated by the visit to Peg's aunt, Jessica Lovett. 'Come on John, you haven't seen Aunty Jessie yet.' So off we went.

Aunty Jessie was a bit of a nut, really. She had a cleanliness fetish. It was always family lore that she actually went around scraping out the dust from cracks in the skirting boards with a hairpin. Certainly the house was always spotless. She was a little bird-like woman with white hair and when we knocked at the door we heard the pitter patter of her feet running down the hall.

Captain Bowden was standing on the porch resplendent in full uniform as the door was flung open. 'John! How wonderful to see you. Wait a minute, you have a spot on you lapel!' She disappeared, pitter patter again down the bloody hall, to reappear with a face-washer from the bathroom and some special soap. She dabbed phut-phut-phut-phut on my chest and inspected the result. 'Ah, that's better.' Then she threw her arms around me to welcome me home! Poor Aunty Jessie. She finally lost her mind and I believe finished up in a nursing home tearing newspapers into little squares. They would have been neat little squares, I've no doubt, and swept up afterwards. But she was a cheerful soul and always very hospitable.

Peg had lived in our house at 37 Maning Avenue with a woman companion for a time, and then rented the house while she lived with friends. She worked in censorship during the war and that meant sitting at a desk and reading other people's letters to wives, to husbands and so on. She told me that she became quite immune to intimate personal details after a while. They had to be on the look out to block any information of possible military value such as the name of a visiting warship coming to Hobart. I don't think there was much, really, that could have done any harm, but it had to be done.

I never asked what she did on other fronts. In fact, we both avoided any other relationships during those years of separation. We did discuss this before I went away. Peg said, 'The important thing about it is that if something does occur in your life caused through absence of man from wife—I don't mind as long as you don't tell me'. Curiously, almost unbelievably I suppose, it never did. Mind you, we were in the Middle East and any misbehaviour there had more than a slight risk attached to it, not only of getting your bloody throat cut but getting the clap, as I remember. What might have happened if we'd been sent to Tahiti or somewhere like that I don't know.

Anyway, after seven all-too-short days of leave, I reverted to being Captain Bowden, second in command of the First Australian Mobile School of Mechanisation, attached to 1 Australian Corps Troops. Unlike our experiences when we arrived in the Middle

On leave, April 1944

East and had to establish ourselves and find a job to do, we were now in demand. By mid-1942 we were sent for by Brigadier 'Tommy' Loutit who was the commander of the Alice Springs area, and responsible for the great lift of supplies and war materials up to a big depot being established in Darwin. (His name was actually Noel Medway Loutit but he was always known as 'Tommy'.) There were a number of transport companies in the Alice with all their attached gear, workshops and so on, and the vehicles were three-ton Ford and Chevrolet trucks. The roads were corrugated and dusty and they were having appalling tyre troubles because nearly all the tyres we had at that stage were designed for desert work in the Middle East and wouldn't do the job.

Before the war Brigadier Loutit was a senior executive with an oil company. He was well equipped for the war job he had and ran the area extremely well. He had the reputation, though, of being a little Napoleon. He sent for us because they had problems with their drivers, mechanics and repairs and he wanted us to help sort it out. This was just the sort thing we liked doing. Dick Durance was in charge of our unit, and off we went to Alice Springs, driving by convoy to Adelaide and up through Port Augusta to a staging camp called Terowie to board the Ghan steam train for the final haul. There was no road to the Alice from the south in those days.

I have vivid memories of Terowie because it was dark, raining and miserable when we arrived. Staging camps are terrible places, no one loves anybody much and we were given the usual diabolical feed of bully beef and sloshed off to our tents. Dick and I had scored a bottle of whisky somehow, and on this pouring wet bloody night we went to bed around 7 pm, put two glasses, a pannikin of water and a bottle of whisky between the two beds and quietly put that bottle away. It was a classic case of how to turn an appalling situation into a pleasant one. You didn't have to worry about camp hygiene because it was raining heavily, so we just stood at the tent door and piddled out into the rain. Lovely.

After four days on the rattling lurching old Ghan train, we approached Alice Springs. One morning we had one of those golden central Australian sunrises and the train was pulled up at a water point siding where bore water was pumped up into one of those square tanks on legs. We were all filthy by this time as there was no way of washing on the train. The pump had been left on, and a big overflow of water was splashing down. I can see it now, in this golden dawn. The whole train load of troops just disembarked and peeled off and went over to this cascading water with their little cakes of soap. It impressed me very much indeed. It made a fine picture, these fit young troops with their brown slim bodies. I even added my miserable body to it, somewhat ashamed of it compared with the others.

To our amazement, when we arrived in the Alice, we were told to proceed to a staging camp as we were to go straight on to Darwin. The army is always full of surprises. We thought we were going to Alice Springs at Brigadier Loutit's request. We had an hour's respite before facing up to the staging camp so Dick Durance said he would pay a courtesy visit on the Brigadier. Dick was always a man for doing the right thing. He presented himself to the Brigadier in a formal way and said, 'We are just passing through the area sir, and I would like to pay our respects.'

The Brig said, 'What's this passing through business?'

Dick explained we had been ordered to proceed to Darwin. Well, bloody hell broke loose. It was just the sort of scene Napoleon loved. He pressed a button and all his G staff and his A staff and his Q staff assembled while he blew the tripe out of them—in front of Dick, unfortunately. Then Loutit said, 'You are staying here Durance, and you will move into Headquarters Camp forthwith'. Which we did, but it concerned us a bit because it was not a good start. We had to work with Loutit's staff and you need a bit of co-operation when you are getting established in an area. However, it settled itself down.

Part of our job was to train automotive electricians for the workshop. It was a course I had started in the Middle East and, fortunately, it had taken on. There was also some driver training. We had a busy time there. The brief included convoy duty up to Larrimah, the staging camp at the end of the Darwin rail. A driver's routine would be: four days' driving to get up there; a day to unload; four days back and one day's rest. They did a day's infantry training because after all there was a war on somewhere around the place, although it didn't seem like it up there, then a day's vehicle maintenance and off again. The convoys drove at twenty miles per hour and it was dead boring on this dreadfully corrugated road with the dust, heat and flies. There was nothing to do at the staging camps, and no wonder the troops got a bit skinned off. From our unit's point of view, though, it was a fairly satisfactory time. We did some useful work, and this was recognised in the area.

On Sunday we had a day's rest, war or no bloody war, and we used to drive out into the bush with our vehicles and have unit picnics. The cookhouse would be raided for chops and so on and we'd go out to Standley Chasm or Emily Gap and grill them. On one notable occasion we were given permission for a day's outing and convoys of troops went out to Standley Chasm. We all drove in through a narrow gap in the rocky hills and everyone settled down kicking footballs, playing games, and eating their grilled chops. There was no boozing, of course, but people were having a lovely time.

A poor miserable looking Lieutenant came up in a ute, talking with each group of troops. He said, 'I regret to say you have to leave the area. Brigadier's orders'. Well, you can imagine! Some of the

Driving an Army DUKW at Trinity Beach, Cairns, Queensland.

blokes were walking away in the bush, on the northern side of the chasm. They all had to be hunted up and chased out and their food packed up and put back in the trucks. Everybody was abusing each other and in a foul temper. Then we took off, back to Alice Springs. And there at the entrance to the chasm area waiting to drive in was Tommy Loutit in his staff car with his companion—I'll call her Flora. She was well known in Alice Springs and a friend of the Brig's, and I think she just said, 'I'd like that place on our own today, Tommy'. And Tommy probably said, 'That's easy. I'm the Brigadier'. So he issued an order that all troops were to get out. They actually stood there as though they were reviewing a parade as these steaming angry troops drove out. It says a great deal for army discipline that nobody called out anything on this occasion, and off we went back to camp.

Alice Springs wasn't a bad area to be in, really. The food was good and there was even a reasonable beer supply for the troops.

They were given a ration in the evening and they had a permanent two-up school in the dry bed of the Todd River. That was supervised to a degree and they used to go there by the bloody hundreds to play two-up. There was even a picture theatre later.

The trouble really was the lack of any home leave. I don't think it was Brigadier Loutit's fault. Headquarters have a tendency to ignore requests which don't suit them and I understand he pointed out fairly clearly that unless they did something about giving the troops some regular leave there would be trouble. He got duck-shoved and duck-shoved and told there were no trains and no replacement drivers and so on. So there was a riot—a full scale riot. The blokes had a case, really, and they weren't being listened to.

It started at about 10 o'clock one night, I can't recall the exact date but it was not long after I arrived in Alice Springs in the winter of 1942. Troops broke into the band room and stole a couple of big drums and a lot of kettle drums. A bit like the French Revolution, they started off boom boom, rattle rattle, rattle. And they marched through all the camps and the blokes just fell in behind. I can remember the uneasy feeling those bloody drums gave me, irrespective of where one's sympathies are now. These were troops and they were rioting and we were the King's officers. There was no way we could be in favour of what they were doing.

They marched through all the transport camps and they must have been a couple of thousand strong I suppose. And they then came marching into Headquarters Camp. I remember I was a bit concerned because I had got myself a brand new radio and they were knocking tents over and kicking possessions about. But for some reason or other they left our tents alone. I can't believe it was deliberate, but they did. Then I joined some fifty officers and gentlemen from Headquarters Camp who linked arms to form a ring around the Brigadier who was standing outside his tent.

The troops didn't offer any violence to us, they just pushed us around a bit and moved on. But then they formed into a big group and demanded that the Brig speak to them. And he did. He got up on something—he wasn't a very big man—so he could be seen above the crowd. It was about 2 am by then and he asked the troops to voice their demands. Then he spoke to them. 'I have been trying to get leave and I will somehow be successful in getting you leave. But first you have to stop this bloody nonsense and go back to your quarters and quieten down and get on with the job.' That was the gist of his message.

Someone shouted out, 'We want leave!'

Loutit repeated that he had not only been trying, but would continue to apply for leave on their behalf. Someone else yelled out, 'Oh don't tell fuckin' lies'.

Brigadier Loutit said, 'I do not tell lies'.

The same voice then said, 'Well, what do you tell your missus about Flora!'

If ever you want to break a riot, humour is the way to do it. I can still hear that laugh that went up from a couple of thousand blokes in the still of the night. Roars of laughter, followed by mutterings of, 'Oh bugger this, let's go back to camp. I'm sick of this,' and it just faded away.

Next day the Brig had to cope with it, and the first thing he did was borrow our big instructional tent—I wasn't very happy about this—and assemble all the transport officers from the transport companies in the area who had not turned out on that night. They had remained in bed or stayed in their camps. I wasn't in the tent, but I could hear his voice and when the Brig was really steamed up he had a tongue, and I know a very unhappy mob of blokes came out of that tent.

Shortly after that a squadron of Spitfires flew low over the camp, very low, and did repeat runs before they pissed off. Also the intelligence people moved into the area and sorted out some ringleaders who were under suspicion of being subversive fellows—it wasn't altogether a simple matter of not having leave—and they were collected and taken away. At the same time, almost within twenty-four hours, leave trains started. Once the leaves were organised life became peaceful again.

Eventually we did move up 'the track' to Darwin towards the end of 1942, and settled in at a training camp called Winnellie. We carried on with the same kind of mechanic and driver training which I hope did some good. We worked hard enough at it, God knows. We had a little bit of attention from the Japanese air force there but it was all pretty pathetic really.

Living in Darwin under service conditions was not pleasant. Dick Durance and I lived in a little tin hut on the outskirts of the camp, rather than under the auspices of the camp commander, one

Our big instructional tent at Alice Springs—in which Brigadier Loutit tore strips off the officers who had not been on hand during the riot.

Major McLeod, with whom we did not have much in common. There was no refrigeration and we had to suffer such horrors of war as warm beer, if there was any. The sandflies and mosquitoes had to be experienced to be believed. It was not pleasant living, but the work went on, noble men that we were.

My CO Dick Durance hated flying. He was always sick and was therefore less than delighted when an urgent order came to 'report forthwith' to the Director of Supply and Transport in Melbourne. Captain Bowden was to take over command of the workshop wing. We got busy and sorted things out, went to Movements and arranged for Dick to fly down on what was known as the 'cabbage plane', a DC3 which flew fresh vegetables up from the south. Well I've no doubt they were fresh when they left Adelaide, but . . .

We gave Dick a great party on warm beer to send him off. He was to leave at the uncivilised hour of 2 am so we drove down to the airport at Katherine in our staff car, with a completely full Dick Durance in the back. And there the cabbage plane waited. It was well named: God, it just stank of stale cabbages. I remember ushering Dick's large inebriated figure into this vile plane. While they shut the door, we drove away. Dick reckoned that was the worst journey in the world. He spewed his way to Adelaide, got himself cleaned up and moved on to Melbourne. 'Here I am sir', he said proudly as he burst through the door of the Brigadier's office.

The Brigadier looked up with obvious surprise and said: 'Hello Durance, what are you doing here?' Dick produced the signal from his pocket that had started him on his travels.

'Oh God,' said the Brigadier, 'that was fourteen days ago—it's all over now. Didn't they send you a cancelling order?'

'No sir, they didn't.'

'Oh well, you're here now, I expect they'll find you a job.' Which they did, and I've no doubt Dick did very well. I think he was given command of a transport company.

Mention of the cabbage plane reminds me of the doleful food situation in Darwin. A university professor, Stanton Hicks, became interested in the troops' diet up there and did a great deal of very good work. Some of the troops in the Darwin area were showing signs of a lack of vitamins, due to the absence of fresh fruit and vegetables. So Stanton Hicks got busy and with considerable care organised a convoy of fresh vegetables to be shipped to the area. There was to be a special convoy from Adelaide to the railhead at Terowie and then a high priority train would shift it to Alice Springs. A special convoy would be waiting, road speed limits waived and night driving allowed so the vegetables would come through to Darwin in the quickest possible time. This all went according to plan, and the vegetables did arrive in very good order.

But one vital thing had been overlooked. The quartermasters of these particular units took their duties extremely seriously and had an inbuilt problem of never being able to pass anything out of their stores straight away. Each had, in his own store, a list of what they called fresh vegetables, which were some pretty mouldy potatoes and pumpkins that had seen better days, and a few shrivelled carrots. But they were still 'fresh vegetables' to them. Therefore, they couldn't issue the new lot, of course until these were all used up! So in most cases this beautiful fresh produce was put on one side and when it got rotten enough and the old stocks had gone, it was dished out. I got the story from a bloke called Morris Wilson who was running a catering course in the same area I worked in. It was a sad tale. But they did eventually improve things.

One day we had a signal that General Lavarack and General Stevens would be pleased to inspect our area. A time was given and we all got busy and swept out the corners and stirred things up a bit as one should do when a couple of generals are planning to visit. I thought I had my show in pretty good shape and I posted my Orderly Room Corporal, one Snowy Walton, to give me warning when the staff car pulled up and two generals stepped out. Snowy was a nice lad, rather like an Australian Cockney: he always had a cigarette hanging out of the side of his mouth. Well, Snowy had in his mind the red tabs and flashes of colour, bands and trumpets and things. He didn't know these blokes would arrive in normal tropical dress with turned-down slouch hats and rather grubby open-neck shirts.

I had the pleasure of looking up from my table in the Orderly Room, past Corporal Walton who was puffing away on a cigarette, to see through the doorway two generals who were standing outside waiting to be asked to come in. I can remember getting up and treading heavily on Snowy's foot and saying the equivalent of piss off. Fortunately they were good blokes, these two generals, and I think they were sick of doing whatever they normally did, and wanted a change of scene. I found them helpful and interested in what was going on.

My friend Morris Wilson, the catering instructor, had similar problems when they arrived to see his side of the business. Morrie was a pretty alert, ingenious sort of cove and he had designed some field ovens himself which were made of mud and odd things you found lying around camps like 44 gallon drums. He built three or four experimental models on the basis that wherever you were and you had a battalion to cook for, you could always find some way of doing it. All very commendable.

When the two generals arrived on their inspection tour they asked Morrie what these things were. Morrie explained his theories and the generals became very interested indeed. Could they see one? They all stood around while Morrie whipped off the lid to show the oven's interior. What he did not know was that the troops who had cleaned up the camp specially for the generals' arrival had dumped all the rubbish, bottles and gunk in Morrie's prized experimental oven. Anyway after his embarrassment had died down he thought he did notice a twinkle of amusement in both generals' eyes.

Eventually the glorious day dawned, in late November 1942,

when Temporary Captain Bowden, now in charge of the unit following Dick Durance's exit on the cabbage plane, was ordered to move south for re-organisation and refit. The wet season had started, the sandflies were getting worse and we were all developing great yearnings for our wives and children and the things that go with civilian life. It was about a year since I had had my glorious seven days' leave. So we got ready to load our vehicles on the train where they stood all day at Winnellie while the Commonwealth Construction Corps loaded some old tractors and things on board that had to be taken south for overhaul. I can still remember the feeling the night the old train blew its whistle and we set off on the journey south, sleeping in our vehicles.

We fared better than those who stayed behind. A Japanese reconnaissance plane had flown over and spotted our trucks and the old tractors waiting at the railhead and decided this was a great troop movement of considerable importance. That night, after our train pulled out and we were heading down the line singing glorious songs about seeing our wives and families again, the buggers came over and belted the daylights out of the camp we'd just left. They low-level strafed it, bombed it and only one bright happening took place. Oddly enough, no one was hurt—except the camp commander Major McLeod. He apparently leaped into a slit trench as the first wave of Japanese planes came over, closely followed by his adjutant who unfortunately stepped on his face.

I don't know why it gave us so much satisfaction, but we hadn't got on all that well with Major McLeod and we thought it rather ironic.

Chapter Nineteen

WAITING FOR HOLDENS

By 1943 the war had a different feel about it. We were winning it and troops were training to launch further offensives against the Japanese in New Guinea and the Pacific. I remember hearing news of the Battle of the Coral Sea in 1942, and as the reports filtered through we heard of more Japanese ships being sunk and thousands of the enemy drowned which we thought was magnificent news in those days.

After returning from Darwin we went back to our base in Geelong—Land Headquarters Army Service Corps School—with an Irish adjutant and more bludgers and skulduggery to the square inch than you could find anywhere. To our considerable delight we found that our mobile workshop unit was posted to Queensland early in 1943, where we were to teach the handling and maintenance of army DUKWs, a most ingenious and well known amphibious vehicle. The acronym stood for date of manufacture (D), utility (U), front-wheel drive (K), with winch (W).

Not long after the news came through of our move to Queensland, an old bloke called Jim Winfield came to see me. God knows how old Jim was, he was much too elderly to be in the army, really, but he was one of the more pleasant people at the Geelong Headquarters School. He had a job as a kind of batman and looked

Major Bowden about to leave the army in the back of a truck

after about a dozen officers, making their beds, doing the washing and cleaning their quarters. I used to talk to Jim a bit, and was interested to find he was a former Tasmanian axeman.

'Major Bowden, you are moving out, going up to Queensland?'

I said, 'That's right Jim.'

'Would you take me with yer? I know I'm old, but I'm in good shape. I can do all kinds of jobs.' He went on. 'In this place I make beds, I do washin', I iron. In fact, the only difference between me and a bloody old woman is that nobody roots me at night!'

I thought that was a touchingly eloquent plea and after talking it over further with him I decided to do what I could. The doctor looked him over and then I started a little bit of a campaign to get old Jim into our unit. Oh God, it was the best thing I ever did. He was a wonderful old bloke who worked hard, provided humour and he'd do anything.

Eventually we got cracking and our little convoy began to move up the east coast heading for Cairns. Our first assignment was at Noosa Heads because a transport company had been issued with the amphibious DUKWs and we were to help them along.

There are worse places to be than Noosa Heads. It was all open country in those days. As I remember it there was a great deal of open space on sand dunes behind a great beautiful beach with a roaring surf on it. Incidentally, we could see the whales which used to go up and down the coast. The CO of the transport company we were attatched to was a nice bloke, and my off-siders Peter Milne and Allan Ray were pleasant fellows. We found an old life-savers hut, pretty derelict, right on the beach at the back of the dunes and we moved into it. It was a fair distance from the camp, but we didn't mind the slight inconvenience. We made ourselves very comfortable there, going to sleep with the roar of the surf in our ears.

We did what we were supposed to do, teach people how to run DUKWs but in the process we used to do all sorts of silly things. It became the form that however big the surf it was never too big to take a DUKW out. A DUKW was only a truck with a hull built around it, but its centre of gravity was dead low. DUKWs had a tremendous capacity for letting the seas wash over them and around them, and they didn't seem to capsize. The engines kept going, generally speaking. It was quite exciting. Actually, I used to shit myself a bit, but you didn't dare let anyone know that's how you felt. You had to say, 'How good this is. Pity the waves aren't a bit bigger.'

I can remember sitting at the wheel and watching a big swell build up with a bit of foam on top until all you could see through your windscreen was a great wall of water with streaks down it. Then there'd be a crunch, and it would break over the cabin onto the truck part behind, which would almost fill with water. But they had tremendous pumps on them which used to whip the water out pretty smartly, which was just as well. And so you headed out to sea.

Coming back in was even worse. I dared not look in the rear vision mirror but just aimed for the beach and hoped for the best as the old DUKW glissaded down a great green mountain of water. But it worked out all right. On one occasion when we were doing this sort of thing a bunch of infantrymen on leave walked along the beach and stopped to watch. They asked me if they could go out. One of my sergeants was just about to head out, and I said, 'Why not? Get aboard.' They said, 'Thanks mate, sir', or whatever you said in those days. I sat on the beach watching as they left. The first big wave they hit burst the bonnet open, which lifted. The next wave came in and killed the engine.

I said to myself, 'Oh Jesus, what do I say at the Court of Inquiry? You know, six infantrymen with no business to be there, drowned.' Somehow they managed to get the bloody DUKW going, and got her in.

While I was at Noosa Heads the routine orders came out listing the promotions and demotions and there was that beautiful printed line—I can see it now—'To be Major: Lieutenant, Temporary Captain, Temporary Major Bowden'. There it was. And I thought they had forgotten all about me. I required a Court Martial after that to lose the rank, which I might have had if the DUKW had drowned those six infantrymen.

We slowly worked our way up to Cairns, doing the same kind of work, but it was much more pleasant there. We wintered there and the work was not hazardous, but even though I liked the Cairns experience so much, I could see the writing on the wall that this unit which I loved and had helped to establish—and we did do some useful work—had a limited life. I discussed this with certain senior officers I met from time to time and they were of the same opinion because the need for the intensive training of troops was running down. Also, I was thinking more and more about my beautiful young wife at home and my young son, and I made a mental note that I would leave the army as soon as I could do so with a clear conscience.

From Cairns we moved up on to the Atherton Tablelands and carried on there with workshop and training work. Winter on the Tablelands is reminiscent of Tasmania, a bit cold and bleak although not quite as extreme. It was there that old Jimmy excelled

Relaxing at Noosa

himself as a Tasmanian bushman. After I had set the unit up, with all the marquees, training tents, workshop, orderly room, truck park and so on, I noticed, brilliant soldier that I was, after getting it all laid out, that there was a big tree in the centre of it that didn't look too bloody safe.

As I had an ex-champion Tasmanian axeman in old Jimmy I called him over and explained the problem.

'Oh', he said, 'I can put that down all right. No problem.'

I said, 'You wouldn't do any damage would you, you old bugger?'

'Oh no, I can put it down anywhere.'

He did, too—smack bang across the workshop truck. That caused certain administrative problems but I managed to sort it out in the end.

At about that time I had a signal that I was to be inspected by a colonel from corps headquarters. As usual in such circumstances we tidied the place up, organised a bit of spit and polish where it would be noticed and I went out to meet him at the beginning of my lines.

Throwing a smart salute, I said, 'What would you care to do sir? Would you care to come to the orderly room first before inspecting the unit?'

He said, 'That would be a very good idea'. Stiff as a bloody old poker.

So we went and sat down and, to ease the tension a little, I put my hand in my pocket and produced a cigarette case and said, 'Would you care for a smoke sir?'

He said, 'Thank you', and took one but I noticed with dismay that he put it in his mouth reversed, with the cork filter poking out at me. I didn't know what to do but, in some embarrassment, said as I leaned forward with my lighter: 'Excuse me sir, but it's the wrong way round'.

'I always smoke them that way,' he said icily, and he did! In this 'relaxed' atmosphere he allowed me to light it as it was, and smoked it through the bloody cork. I was told later he wasn't a bad sort of a bloke, but he wasn't going to be corrected in any way by the officer of a unit he was inspecting. Surprisingly, we actually got through the inspection all right.

While I was on the Atherton Tablelands towards the end of 1944, I had a signal to report to Land Headquarters in Melbourne forthwith so I went to Movements and said, 'Why can't I take my staff car?' The very inexperienced young subaltern running the show said, 'Oh I don't see why not,' and gave me a movement order from the Atherton Tablelands to Melbourne. I got my driver, packed my toothbrush and with great joy off we went.

To do it on schedule we had to do 300 miles a day and after ten days that became a bit irksome. However, I made some discoveries on the way, and one was that coffee throughout Australia at that stage was completely standard. Every coffee shop in every town, big or small, had on its counter a tall nickel-chrome cylinder with a brass tap on it. When you asked for a cup of coffee, this tap would be turned on, and usually nothing would happen. So they would stick the handle of a fork or something up the tap, and she'd go 'glonk' and a concoction of what looked like caramel milk would come slurping out, with black stuff floating on top of the cup. We drank it because there was no Nescafe or the equivalent in those days. I think it was made from something called coffee essence. One of the brands was called Turban, and it featured an Arab in a turban on the front of the bottle. I think the advertisement of the time was, 'It's most disturbin' if there ain't no Turban'.

When I reached Melbourne I had the same experience as Dick Durance, my former CO who had flown south from Darwin on the cabbage plane. 'Hello Bowden, what are you here for?'

While they were sorting it out I applied for a week's leave in Tasmania and on the way over I developed an infected eye. At least I got some extra leave out of it, and during that time met Len Nettlefold who ran a motor business in Tasmania. He was considering setting up an engine reconditioning outfit to cope with the post-war situation, as it was believed there couldn't be any new cars for some time. He realised there would be lots of old cars which would need their engines re-bored and crankshafts and bearings ground. Would I be interested in taking it on? Well, would I what!

Len started action from the civilian side to apply for me and I got busy pissing in my Brigadier's ear and the combined approach was successful. I think I spoke to Len Nettlefold in December 1944 and things moved quickly, so much so that I did not return to my unit in Queensland. The engine re-conditioning concern was called TASCO—Tasmanian Automotive Service Company.

When the documentation came through, ending one's army career was very quick and a fairly down to earth sort of business. Matters of pay and records had to be gone through and so on, and eventually on February 2, 1945, I found myself walking into a transit depot in north Melbourne called Camp Pell. There was a sentry on guard, and as Major Bowden walked in he received his last present arms. Full hook it was, clock, click, bang! I duly returned the salute.

My visit was short. I signed some papers, was given a ticket to Tasmania and eventually I had to be transported away. I remember climbing into the back of a three-ton truck with a number of other friendly, pleasant troops who were also going somewhere, and off we took. I went in with a present arms, and out in the back of a truck—which I suppose is fair enough. My army life was over, thank Christ.

I won't dwell on the delights of coming home to my beautiful young wife and young son, but it was quite superb. We had been effectively separated for nearly six years.

Our DUKWs about to invade the Pacific. Mercifully, they behaved well in heavy surf.

I presented myself for work at Nettlefolds Pty Ltd where my salary was to be £500 a year—£10 a week—and I thought this was pretty good. I remembered my father used to get £10 a week in his senior job as Manager of Telephones and Telegraphs: that seemed an awful lot of money, but I had forgotten my father lived a long while before. It was Len Nettlefold who actually engaged me. I dealt with him entirely and he was a friendly bloke—naturally very guarded, careful and perhaps a little suspicious. He didn't know me personally, only by reputation. His right hand man was a bloke called Murray Philp whom I had known as a boy growing up in Hobart. Murray never liked me very much and we hadn't got on well as kids. He was overseas on a trip while all this was taking place and how he managed to have an overseas trip during the war I don't know.

I had grown up in the motor business in another firm and Murray was always very condescending as far as I was concerned. He was surprised, and I know disappointed, to know that I had been appointed to this job when he got back because he came to me when he returned from overseas and said that he was surprised Len Nettlefold had appointed me to the job. I said, 'Were you Murray?'

'Yes, very surprised. I thought he'd have paid more money and got a really good man.'

I said, 'Who would you have liked to have had the job?'

He named the head of the engineering school at the Trades Course at the Hobart Technical College and I said, 'Fair enough, my dear chap, but I've got the position and I'm going to try and make a job of it'. And there the matter ended. That was Murray's approach to these things. It was a curious atmosphere to be in for a while. After all, he was the assistant manager of the company.

The other 'dear kindly fellow' I had visited upon me was a man called Freddie Staples who was appointed as my clerk. I was warned about him and went to the accountant and said I didn't want him, that he had the reputation of being an obstructive old bastard. The accountant said it had to be, that was the company's direction and there was no way of altering it. In fact, when I got back from that interview Freddie was already there and had ensconced himself in the manager's office—my office! We began our relationship with me saying, 'Goodday Fred. You're in my office. Yours is that one over there . . ., pointing to a miserable little cubicle at the back. Anyway, he went.

Then we had a period of time when nobody spoke to anybody and he was just an incredibly difficult, rude old bastard. Finally I went to him and said, 'Look Fred, I didn't ask for you and I have it on pretty good record that you didn't want to come. But I've got you, and you're here. You've got me, and I think we should try and make a fist of it between us.'

Freddie, a little gnarled old man, looked up from his desk and said, 'I don't give a bugger what you think!' And that was how I began the job of building up TASCO from scratch.

Fortunately there were other more reasonable personalities around. The engineering foreman of the shop, a bloke called Eric Hyndes, was a good chap, but he had the most appalling stammer. It was one of those dreadful ones where people actually go into contortions trying to get their words out, but he was competent and he had a good sense of humour. He was responsible for the mechanical side of getting the workshop together, actually installing the machinery I managed to scrounge from various places.

A man called Eric Scaife was El Supremo of all workshops at Nettlefolds—including TASCO—and was the service manager of Motors Pty Ltd (the subsidiary company formed to run the General Motors side of the business). But at that time he was still in the army in the process of being released to industry. He was an extremely nice bloke but there was some delay in his getting out and any number of decisions had to be made about whether we bought this or that, or had the authority to buy and so on, but we were doing pretty well. However, as Eric's arrival got nearer, everybody ducked for cover and when I asked for an authority to do something, I was invariably told, 'Oh, wait till Eric Scaife comes'. Then I'd have to go to poor old Eric Hyndes who had made the request and tell him we couldn't do anything until Eric Scaife did come. This went on for some time.

Finally Eric came to my office carrying an emery wheel which had broken in half. It was a wonder it hadn't killed somebody, but it hadn't. And he said, 'Cccccccan I bbbbbuy a nnnew one? Or do I hhhave to wwwait till the fffffucking Mmmmessiah comes?'

We eventually got TASCO off the ground, started to recondition engines and continued to do so for several years. I think we made a few bob for the company and we certainly reconditioned a lot of engines. I had the marine side to deal with which was quite interesting as well as General Motors diesels. That meant mucking about in fishing boats a bit which was not without its business worries, but which, when things worked out, was very pleasant and a change from the claustrophobic confines of TASCO and the brooding sullen presence of the lovely Freddie Staples. He used to keep a little black notebook, by the way, and every time I would get upset about something and tell the old bugger what I thought of him, out would come this little black book and it would all be written down, doubtless to be relayed back to Len Nettlefold or Murray Philp. I'd love to have seen it. He kept it in a locked drawer and I was never able to get my hands on it. In general, though, my managership of TASCO was a pleasant period.

I left TASCO because Murray Philp died suddenly of a heart attack. He was Assistant Manager of the company but he also looked after the sales side, which of course didn't really exist during the war as there were no new vehicles to sell. However he died just at the time General Motors were starting up in Australia making

Tim and our first family dog, Bill

the Holden car, and Nettlefolds were confident of getting the agency for Tasmania although they couldn't be sure. Murray's death meant some quick re-organisation.

I was taken from TASCO and made Sales Manager for Southern Tasmania for Holdens. The overall Sales Manager was Len Nettlefold's cousin, Doug; a man named John Potter ran the Vauxhall side of the business. When General Motors started producing the Series 48 Holden we started to get them at the rate of about thirty a month. Such was the demand that we had a waiting list of at least three years!

To cope with this situation—and I think he was pretty wily here really—Len Nettlefold set up an allocation committee of three. It consisted of Doug Nettlefold, me and—guess who—dear old Freddie Staples. His job was to keep the records of what went on and I'm sure he also had a secret commission to report any skulduggery back to Len if someone wasn't playing it straight by the company. Freddie loved that part of it, of course, and out would come that little black notebook. So we would meet and allocate our thirty vehicles each month. It was a very difficult job. Although there was no skulduggery that I could spot, the cars were not always allotted on the first-come-first-served basis. There were some personal priorities to be considered, as well as company policy.

It was a very worrying time, although in a way not a bad break for me because I didn't have to cope with a market or selling immediately. It was a case of learning the job by being abused. Everybody who didn't get a vehicle would come and abuse the Sales Manager Holden. Oh God, I took some abuse over that period. I was accused of taking bribes—accused so much that perhaps I should have taken some.

If you bought a motor car and paid your £600 or £700 for it, it was worth £1500 as you drove it out the door. That was another aspect. We had to be careful that we didn't sell to someone who might just flog the car for a quick profit—although, thinking back on that, what the hell it had to do with us I don't know. This caused a lot of bitterness. People used to bring children in on crutches and wives who couldn't walk and parade them in front of me and say, 'You understand this is the hardship you are continuing by not letting me have a car' and so on. And I was only one of three because dear Freddie had the casting vote. Awful days, really, but they did not go on for ever, of course.

Eventually we would ring people up, trying not to say 'You're lucky you've got a motor car' but, rather, 'There's a motor car here, sir, you ordered it two years ago'. The reply was likely to be: 'I've been looking forward to this moment for the last eighteen months. You can stick it!' Suddenly our three-year waiting list became a potential six months' stock of unsold Holdens. I had to get off my arse, become a real sales manager and appoint and train a sales staff. Although we undoubtedly made mistakes in this learning process, we did get it by the throat eventually and maintained our share of the market, which was a bit better than the ratio of Holden to other makes in Tasmania in the early 1950s, and better than that achieved by the combined effort of the Holden dealers in Victoria. I found I could sleep fairly easily in my bed at night when that had been achieved.

We would slip back occasionally, and these periods were accompanied by a considerable cooling in Len Nettlefold's normally very friendly attitude towards me. Fair enough, I suppose.

Chapter Twenty

PEG

One extremely important part of the post-war reconstruction period I haven't dealt with was the arrival of those splendid people, Nick, Philip and Lisa. I think Peg and I thought we were going to conceive in the first five minutes after we got back together again after I got out of the army. I remember her saying, 'I think the desert sands have burned you out', referring to my capacity to make her pregnant, I presume, because I don't think my virility was in question after six years away.

Nicholas John Bowden was born in January 1946 and it was a period of great joy. The pregnancy and birth went very smoothly as I remember it. Of course, Tim was nearly nine years old by then, and had been brought up as an only child. He was tremendously excited about the prospect of a brother or sister and when Nick was born he counted the hours till Peg and the new baby brother came home from hospital.

'When are you going to feed him?' he asked Peg eagerly.

'At 10 o'clock.'

'Where are you going to sit?'

'Over here on the sofa.' Peg was a modern mother.

At 9.55 am Tim dragged over a stool and positioned himself strategically while Peg began to breastfeed Nick. After inspecting this activity from every available angle, he asked: 'What happens if he blows instead of sucks?' He set my mind wondering what indeed would happen.

The Bowden family, circa 1949. Post-war reconstruction has begun with the production of Nicholas and Philip.

Some eighteen months later, in August 1947, Philip Mark Bowden joined the party, and there we were with two little boys pretty close together and life was a bit hectic. When Peg became pregnant with her fourth child, after a break of three years, we hoped for a girl. After all, there were three boys around the place and we were very anxious indeed for a daughter. It was a fifty-fifty chance, of course, and there was some tenseness as the birth approached. By then I was forty-four and Peg was forty and I remember I was rather foolishly worried that maybe she shouldn't have any more children. I went to see Bill Wilson, our gynaecologist, and he examined Peg, confirmed that she was pregnant and said he saw no reason at all why she couldn't have another baby. Finally, Lisa Clair Bowden made her triumphant arrival on February 4, 1950.

It was not the fashion then for husbands to be present at the birth and I heard the news at home. I don't think they were technically as good in those days at the birth business, and a certain number of stitches was required when Nick and Philip were born. These made Peg very uncomfortable afterwards and there was a certain amount of family debate when Peg was going off to have Lisa and said, 'I hope to goodness I don't have any stitches this time'. When they phoned from the hospital and told me we had a daughter, I said, 'Well, that's wonderful news—how are they both?'

'They're fine.'

'Could you tell me—were there any stitches?'

'No.'

I turned to Peg's sister, Dot Lovett, who was helping us out at the time—she was also a mothercraft nurse—and said, 'It's a girl, seven pounds and no stitches.' Well, fourteen-year-old Tim took off down the street proclaiming like the town crier to the neighbours and anyone who wanted to hear: 'It's a girl, it's a girl. Seven pounds and no stitches!' So the whole district knew all the intimate details very early in the piece.

Unlike Tim, Nick and Philip had the advantages—and disadvantages—of growing up together. There were the usual competitions and squabbles between children of about the same age in any family, but they really got on very well. When they were old enough, they sailed a small Yachting World Cadet on the Derwent together. It was not a great success and there were vigorous debates on the right tactics to be sailed in races. Nick was the helmsman and somewhat pig-headed about what he intended to do, while Philip was rather . . . excitable, I think, is the word. Their arguments could be heard on a calm day echoing across the water. Eventually they decided to sail with different partners and all was well.

Lisa added great satisfaction and joy to the family through those delightful baby years. As time went on she grew more and more like Peg—not only cosmetically but in temperament. The 'irresistible force and the immovable object' situation inevitably arose with regularity, mainly over silly bloody things that didn't really matter like what clothes should be bought or worn, and I can remember being called on to provide the wisdom of Solomon act from time to time during Lisa's schooldays.

Later Lisa qualified as a secretary and then took up nursing before heading overseas to experience the wider world. Through all this a very strong bond evolved between Peg and Lisa, perhaps a bond beyond the ordinary.

Shortly after the war ended I was asked to join Legacy, which is an association created to try and make life better for the widows and children of servicemen who were killed or who had died as a result of the war. You had to be asked to join and I considered it somewhat of an honour. Occasionally it seemed less of an honour on a Friday afternoon when, after a high pressure week selling motor cars, I would remember I was on Roster at Legacy House at 6.30 pm. The Legacy children would be there and we would help amuse them, play games and then deliver them to their homes. I have to confess that many's the Friday night when I thought, now it's time to go home and have a gin and tonic with the woman I love and my family around me and have a nice meal, and so on, then came the realisation—God Almighty, it's my night at Legacy!

But the kids were delightful and the Friday night meetings were a good idea because many of the children were denied the adult male in their life. It was difficult to walk across the room at Legacy House without finding yourself hung all over with young children. It was rather beautiful, really. I have never had any interest in the RSL style of ex-service activity, but I found Legacy very worthwhile. I remember on one occasion one of the little girls I was delivering home said to me, 'Oh, goodness, I've lost me jumper'. Then she was silent as we drove towards the government housing estate suburb of Warrane on the eastern shore of the city where her mother lived. She would have been no more than six years old. As we pulled up at the front gate, she said with some urgency, 'Will you come in and tell Mum I've lost me jumper?' Well I did. Mum was pretty good about it, really, because I've no doubt she was having a battle to feed and clothe all her kids.

The side of Legacy I did not care for much was the ritual of the weekly lunch, with an address by a visiting speaker, sometimes good, sometimes not. Then we used to stand up, face a large picture of the Queen, sing God Save The Queen, say 'Lest We Forget', and then we would all leave. It's not much to ask a bloke to do, I suppose, and I could have done without it, but that is the sort of thing that Legacy is about. I did, however, regard it as a privilege to belong and to meet and work with the blokes that were members of it. I really enjoyed the part that involved the kids.

When Tim was about ten years old, he used to help our milkman, Mr Livingstone, with his deliveries. Even in the late 1940s the

Lisa—first day at school

milkman was still using a horse and cart for his morning round. There were some nice elements to this. The horse knew the round as well as Mr Livingstone and without being asked would amble up the street concerned to meet him at the appropriate spot. Another more pressing reason was the shortage of motor vehicles and petrol for many years after the war.

Mr Livingstone used to run his cows on the slopes of Mount Nelson behind our suburb of Sandy Bay, probably on the land once owned by my First Fleet convict ancestor, Edward Garth. There was no pasteurisation or any health controls on milk at all. It was transported on the cart in big churns and dippered with a pint measure by Mr Livingstone and sometimes Tim when he was helping on the round into saucepans and billies left outside people's front doors with the money. I remember that Mr Livingstone was an anxious kind of bloke. He always looked worried about something, almost as though he was about to burst into tears.

People usually scalded the milk and skimmed off the cream but one day Peg said that she didn't like the look of a sediment that always seemed to be in the bottom of the milk jug. 'It doesn't look nice at all.'

'Oh, don't be so bloody fussy, it's nothing to worry about.'

She held her peace for a while and then kept at me again about it. 'Look, John, we do have a Health Department. Why not take a sample in and get it analysed?'

I did this, feeling somewhat apologetic. 'Look, I'm sorry about this. My wife seems to think there's something wrong with the milk we're getting. It has a sediment in it which might only be a bit of honest cow dung or whatever, but she's worried about it. Will you investigate it?'

This was one of Peg's great triumphs. A letter came back from the Health Department saying that the sediment we took in was not just dust or dirt, it was dead pus cells, created by mastitis in cows! I was not allowed to forget that for a while. The Health Department didn't come charging around with the police or anything, but I went up the slopes of Mount Nelson to see Mr Livingstone armed with this letter and said: 'Look, I know this is something which will upset you as much as it troubled us, but something's got to be done about it. Will you please get this problem fixed, and then produce the evidence that the cows are healthy; that's all that needs to be done.'

He looked as though he really was going to burst into tears, but within a very short space of time he produced a certificate which gave his cows a clean bill of health.

Even though I had a very exacting job in the highly competitive motor business, this was a very happy and busy period just after the war, with a young family. We continued the tradition of camping holidays, with our tents and gear in a home-made wooden trailer, towed behind one of the early Series 48 Holdens. Then, in 1949, some friends said we could stay in their weekend cottage on the east coast of Tasmania, just south of Orford. The area is quite superb, overlooking sandstone cliffs and small dazzlingly white beaches out towards Maria Island, one of the early penal settlements in Tasmania. We just fell in love with the area and borrowed our friends' cottage whenever we could—perhaps rather ruthlessly I think, looking back. Then another couple we knew bought a weekend cottage overlooking Spring Beach, the next bay along to the north. The house was called *Arpies* after a damaged road sign that used to say 'Quarries', leading to an old sandstone quarry spectacularly situated on the foreshore cliffs. *Arpies* was an old farmhouse, said to have been shipped over from Maria Island after the cement works there failed in the 1920s.

I remember sitting on the verandah late one afternoon with Peg and some friends, gazing out over the Mediterranean blue of the stretch of water between Spring Beach and Maria Island and discussing how we could possibly get our own place there. The land at Spring Beach was owned by a bloke called Leo Ryan who was not anxious to sell, and wouldn't sell unless it was to someone he had some regard for, which was fair enough. But I did approach him and he sold me two blocks for a couple of hundred pounds, which I didn't have at that stage. But Peg's aunt, Dot Crick, suggested—I suspect strongly—to her husband Roy that he lend me the money, and we began to build a weekend cottage I eventually called *Askelon* because the location reminded me so much of the coast of the Mediterranean where I had seen the old Roman pillars and statues half buried in the sand during my war service in Palestine.

Unfortunately we had no sooner started to build *Askelon* when

How that little wooden trailer carted all that gear I'll never know. Askelon, 1949

Dotty Crick died. I managed to persuade the bank to lend me £200 so I could return Roy's loan, and kept going. Peg's contribution to the situation was to become pregnant with Lisa and to try and survive financially I gave up smoking. So did Peg, but it was somewhat easier for her as she generally knew she was pregnant because she found she couldn't bear the cigarettes or, indeed, cigarette smoke. In those days most people smoked and I was a heavy smoker. You always opened your cigarette packet and passed it to somebody when you stopped to talk to them, or at any social gathering. I'd tried to give it up many times before and failed, so this time I gave it the cold turkey treatment. I had cigarettes in the house, cigarettes in my pocket and so on, and just stopped. I didn't even tell Peggy I'd given it up.

I can remember it now. I think there's a medical term for it, Cheyne-Stokes breathing. I used to get attacks of that from time to time. For two weeks I did it the cold turkey method and had these terrible bouts of deep breathing and hitting my head against the wall. I'm quite sure there were times when the nicotine used to drip out of the roof of my mouth on to my tongue. And Peggy, busy with the preparation of garments for the new baby, sat in her chair knitting busily away and didn't appear to notice this was going on. Finally I couldn't hold back any longer, and I said, 'Have you noticed anything?'

'No' (knit, knit, knit).

'Well, I haven't had a cigarette for a fortnight.'

'Oh, haven't you? (knit, knit) That's very good.' (Knit, knit, knit.)

I haven't smoked since, thank God. I think it's a disgusting habit and have to stop myself asking people not to smoke in my house today. But it did enable me to buy batches of timber, nails, window frames and other essentials to keep *Askelon* taking shape. We decided to make it habitable, or at least able to be camped in, by Christmas of 1951. There was no power and the cooking was done on the fire or a primus stove. Lighting was by Tilley pressure lamp. We'd drive down on Friday night with a heavily loaded trailer towed by the Holden Series 48 with me feeling absolutely rooted after a week's hectic work, and Peg coping with all the kids—including baby Lisa—with saucepans or casseroles under her feet. Somehow there was also room for our little black mongrel dog Bill who, under the stress of the situation, would emit unspeakably foul doggy farts—the ones that seem actually to burn the insides of your nostrils.

The road from Hobart to Orford and the east coast was only sealed for the first twenty or so miles of the fifty mile journey in those days, and there were some quite steep hills to negotiate. The names were related to the old coaching days, Black Charlie's Opening, Break Me Neck, and Bust Me Gall. One Friday evening I was ploughing up towards Black Charlie's Opening with the usually overloaded trailer full of building materials, a dinghy topping the load, and the car crammed with kids, babies and the farting dog, when I ran over a flat piece of wood on the gravel road. I simply couldn't avoid it, but it did a most curious thing. It cocked up on its end and with fiendish accuracy chopped through the main hydraulic line to the brakes. I don't know what made me do it, but I had a feeling something queer had happened and I put my foot on the brake while the car still had forward way. There was nothing there! My foot just went flat to the floor. Without wishing to be rude about the Series 48 Holden, she was not noted for having the greatest hand brake in the motor business and, as the car came to a halt going up a quite steep hill, I slipped it into reverse gear and dragged on the umbrella-type brake handle near the steering wheel. I could *just* hold her, and I asked Tim, then about thirteen, to get out and find 'the biggest rock you can see and put it under the back wheel', which he did. Then I could take a breather and work out what I was going to do.

I crawled under the car to assess what had happened and using a rock, I managed to bend over the copper pipe which had been cut through, and beat it flat to block it off. That meant I had the front brakes only and we were able to proceed, as they say, with caution.

We'd pull up at the front door of *Askelon*, unload sleeping kids into their sleeping bags onto camp stretchers and beds, and unpack. Our Christmas holiday in 1951 was a working one but we still had time to go fishing in a little cockleshell wooden dinghy that we had, handlining flathead or setting a grab-all net and pulling in beautiful silvery trumpeter. They were good days! Peg's cousin Sheila and her husband Walter Loney and their young family had a great appreciation of outdoor life and camping. They fell in love with the Spring Beach situation and used to pitch their tents at the back of the *Askelon* block each Christmas and Easter holidays.

During one of those early Christmas holidays it never bloody well stopped raining for the entire time they were there. The east coast of Tasmania has quite a low rainfall usually, but occasionally a low pressure system approaches Tasmania and passes across from the west, but instead of moving off towards New Zealand it decides to circle the island. This time, that's what it did, and it just rained and rained for two weeks. The weather forecasting in those days was rather limited and Walter and I used to tap the barometer, look at the horizon and become our own weather predicters. Being outdoor types, we'd say: 'She'll be right tomorrow, mate, there's a slight change to the west in the wind, the moon looks different and there's no cloud on Maria Island'. But poor Walter kept digging ditches to stop the water running through his tents until one morning it dawned bright and clear and Walter and I, the great forecasters, met and said: 'Look at it, it's all over.

Peg particularly liked this photograph of the two of us.

The sun's out, the westerly has set in, and it's going to be fine.' So Walter's family pulled all their bedding out of the sodden tents and hung it on tent poles and the branches of trees and lifted the sides of the tents to dry everything out.

Both families set off with the boat and trailer to go for a picnic and some fishing at Rheban, about ten kilometres away to the south. Walter and I were out in the dinghy when we looked back towards the Spring Beach area and there was one of those big black clouds, rough at the edges and with bits hanging out of it so you can see the rain pouring down. It was pouring all over the bedding the Loney family had put out to dry. We hauled in our nets and hurried back and they moved into *Askelon* that night which was all very cosy in front of the open fire and very pleasant.

Building materials were hard to get for a long time after the war, and there were shortages and restrictions on the use of galvanised iron. You had to get a permit to use it and you weren't allowed to use it on weekenders. I was forced into putting on an asbestos roof. The asbestos came in big heavy sheets, about 4 feet by 8 feet. I planned to put them on myself but was advised to get the services of a man who laid them professionally, so we took off from Hobart one Saturday morning and arrived at Spring Beach about half past nine. It started to blow hard from the west and some of the gusts seemed close to fifty miles per hour. The chap was a tall, rather gaunt, fellow and not very communicative, but he did say: 'You're not supposed to lay this stuff when the wind's blowing more than fifteen miles per hour'. Then he added, 'But it's a bit different down here, isn't it'.

I asked what I could do to help and he said, 'Just keep out of the road, mate'.

The asbestos sheets were stacked in piles at the rear of the building so he put a ladder up against the lower part of the roof and put a little woolly cap, padded at the top, on his head. With the wind blowing in savage gale force gusts he'd walk up to the heap of corrugated asbestos sheets, wait for a slight lull, pick one up, balance it on his head and start running down towards the ladder. Still at a gallop and with this heavy sheet balanced on his head, he'd spring up the ladder and across the wooden purlins—the strips of wood on the roof to nail these things on to—and with a kind of swing of his shoulders, plomp it down in the exact position. It was really quite incredible. He even nailed them down as he went.

Finally I asked him if he'd like a cup of tea.

'No thanks mate.'

He went on doing this while we gazed in wonderment. After some hours he came down the ladder and said, 'Right. I can finish it now, I'll have a cup of tea'. And he laid the whole roof under those appalling conditions in one day.

Building *Askelon* was a wonderful thing for all our lives. It faces due east, out to sea towards Maria Island which is now, happily, a national park for all time. On sunny days the sea takes on the kind of irridescent blues and greens that reminded me of the Mediterranean. The sand on the beach is so white that you can't look directly at it in full sun without dark glasses. I still go down there whenever I can, in all seasons. The family manage it now, and share school holidays and weekends on a roster system.

Peg loved it there, too. Even after she became really too ill to travel, we would make a special effort to get down to *Askelon*. In the early 1960s, Peg became ill with chronic rheumatoid arthritis, and it is extraordinary how she handled this dreadful situation which she never made dreadful for other people. She managed to survive twenty years of this fearfully painful illness with its attendant side effects, and the way she put up with it all showed just what sort of a woman she was.

In the early days of her arthritis they put her in a thing called a spica, which is solid plaster from waist to ankles. She couldn't move the lower part of her body and this was because her hips were getting very painful. Now, a lot of people simply can't take that—they go crazy with the claustrophobia of it. Peg stayed in the thing for three months and handled it with her customary cheerfulness and optimism. She never lost that optimism, which made it so easy to do things for her, and inspired me to make devices to try and make life easier for her. There was never any feeling that it was a waste of time, because she undertook everything we did as though it was going to be a new lease of life. But, oh God, she had a time. The heavy doses of pain-killing drugs—like cortisone—caused all manner of ghastly side effects. She had fourteen major operations in those twenty years including a gall bladder operation, a temporary colostomy, both hips replaced with artificial joints, and it just went on and on.

And, of course, life went on. In the early stages I was still working as Sales Manager for Motors Pty Ltd, and was responsible for the sales of Holden cars throughout southern Tasmania. Despite the pressures of the job, I must say the firm were very good about the time I spent looking after Peg until I retired at the age of sixty-seven. The firm did not have any adequate superannuation policies for people of my vintage. The old rather feudal policy of Nettlefolds Pty Ltd (the parent firm) was to let people go on working for as long as they wanted to in lieu of a pension. This was not an attractive option, particularly because of the constant care and support Peg needed from me, and although I went straight on to the old age pension in the absence of an adequate superannuation scheme, I have no feelings of bitterness towards the firm because of the understanding they showed during the course of Peg's long illness.

Living at home was terribly important to her. She made it very clear that she had no interest in battling on if she had to live in a hospital or nursing home. Fortunately, I have some practical skills and was able to construct some of the aids she needed. Having warm baths is terribly important to a completely arthritic person, and it got to the stage where she simply could not get in or out of the bath. I considered the situation and, with the aid of a boat winch given to me by a nice bloke called Jim Bamford, I fixed a pulley to the bathroom ceiling, and this connected to a canvas seat rather like the one crew members use to paint a mast. I had it made at a sail-maker's, actually. Peg would sit back in the seat and I'd turn the winch and wind her up into the air. I would gently push her over the bath and lower her down into the warm comfortable water. The seat just stayed under her for the duration of the bath. Then I'd winch her into a standing position and help her out. I installed various rails in the bathroom to help her while she was in there. They were all ordinary things, really, but I was able to do them for her.

She loved reading but found it difficult to read in bed. I made her a book-holding gadget that swung over on an arm, with two little clips so that the pages didn't keep on flipping back, and I fixed a little concealed light on it that threw light on the book. That was a great comfort to her. She could rest her poor old arms and hands on the bed and the only time she had to move them was to turn over the page. That was most successful. I made various gadgets around the house for her and never at any time did I feel I was wasting my time. She used them all to the full.

We were invited out quite a lot to dine with friends. This was very important to us both, but it always entailed a lot of kind people fussing around with chair and cushions, and Peg would never admit that she was uncomfortable. So I converted a canvas folding chair to suit her particular requirements, with a padded back and arms and a footrest. It could be folded into the boot of the car. This meant that she could also sit up to another dinner table in relative comfort.

Then the matter of *Askelon* came up, which was very dear to us both. There wasn't a bath there, only a shower bay, so I managed to construct a canvas bath affair which was quite successful, and built a similar pulley and canvas sling arrangement—the same one actually. I just unhooked it from the winch and took it down as luggage, so the bathing was fixed. But then the lavatory became a

Peg and I, with her eldest sister, Mary Maslin

problem because it was too far from our bedroom and there was a step involved. Fortunately, the built-in wardrobe in our bedroom was large enough to accommodate a little toilet, and I built a kind of mini-bathroom there with a little handbasin and that worked well, too. I'm enjoying its benefits now. I only wish to God she was still using it.

When she went to hospital for her various operations she had problems getting out of bed, because hospital beds are pretty high, so I built a bed ramp thing that she could step out onto. The hospital seemed very pleased to let her use it. But it was so easy to do things for her.

Despite the pain and immobility caused by rheumatoid arthritis—which literally affects every moving joint in the body—Peg maintained any activity she possibly could. Eventually she had to give up cooking, not only because of the weight of the utensils, but because it was not possible to remain standing for more than a few minutes. But while she could, she taught me a great deal about the basics of cooking and preparing meals. She had always been keen on handicrafts and used to sew with a particular brand of machine she hated with a deep and bitter hatred. Peggy had normal attitudes to most things in life despite all, but she would sit down to this machine and blaspheme and curse at it—until she changed to a Bernina. The people who sold it to her were very kind and steered her in the right direction, and peace set in. She loved her Bernina.

When she could no longer sew, she began crocheting woollen ties which she made for friends, and which used to be sold at various handicraft outlets. I can see them now, those twisted painful hands with the crochet needle, working away. It was an example of the way Peggy never gave up until such time as the relentless progress of her disease made a particular activity impossible.

She had many friends who came often to the house to visit her. Because she maintained a cheerful, outgoing interest in other people and their doings and did not brood on her own situation, people just liked to come and talk to her. The house became something of a railway station at times, with a ring on the doorbell and a 'Yoo-hoo' as the next visitor came in. But it was wonderful for Peg, and the people who came did so because they enjoyed her company and not because they felt they had to.

We always did get on very well, in fact we were deeply in love and the fact that we were separated for the best part of six years during the war did nothing to diminish this appreciation and love of one another. But I think Peg's dependence on me and the fact that I was able to help her built something between us which is rather hard to describe, but it was very powerful. Similar situations are sometimes supposed to break up a home. In our case, Peg's long and difficult illness had quite the reverse effect. It simply reinforced a very great love indeed.

In 1984 Peg and I went to *Askelon* for Easter, and stayed on for a

The best crop ever of Johnny Bowden tomatoes!

few more weeks as we generally did at that time of the year. Peg became ill. It wasn't just her dreadful arthritis; she was extremely ill, and it became obvious that she would have to go to hospital. The

All the Bowdens—at Askelon, January 1987. Peg is the only family member missing. From left Back: *Nick, David Roberts (Lisa's husband), Philip, Tim's son Barnaby and Tim;* Middle: *Nick's wife Fran holding Amelia, Philip's wife Angie, Tim's younger son Guy, me with Philip's daughter Gina on my knee, Lisa holding Claire, and Tim's wife Ros;* Front: *Nick's son Tim, Philip's daughter Jane, Nick's second son Angus and daughter Anna, Lisa's son Martin and Philip's daughter Kate.*

ambulance came, and I went with her, of course, to the Royal Hobart Hospital. We waited in Casualty for some time to be admitted which is always—and of necessity—a long process. Now this was the beginning of the end for Peg, and I think she knew it. The hospital staff were tremendous, they really were. At first they had everyone see her, including nice little physiotherapy girls who said, 'Now, Mrs Bowden, we'll soon have you out to a convalescent home with a lovely warm pool where you'll have hot baths, and it'll be wonderful for you'. And while she was talking, this nice girl, with such genuine optimism, I could see a tear running down Peg's cheek. She removed her hand from the rail beside the bed—that poor old hand with all its bent fingers—and she reached out and sort of touched me, pushed me in the chest, and just said very quietly, 'Don't let them'.

Lisa was working as a Sister at the hospital at the time and she came in while I was sitting beside Peg's bed. As she sat on the corner of the bed I became aware that she was quietly weeping. I don't think it dawned on me till then that Peg was going to die. I think the fact that Lisa was dressed in her white Sister's rig somehow added poignancy.

Not long afterwards they moved Peg to another ward in the hospital, and I thought she was sinking. A very nice young doctor came in and said that they were going to try this and try that, and I said, 'Well couldn't you just let her die?'

He was a very nice young man and he said, 'Is that what you want?'

'I implore it—we have nothing to offer her.'

He said he would discuss the matter with his superiors. Lisa and I both made our attitudes clear. And, bless them, they did not continue with any drastic supporting treatment and I just got a ring at home to say that she had died. I don't know what happened, but I shall never cease to be grateful to those understanding doctors.

I talked to the medical people concerned as well as an old friend who knew her well, and was aware of the situation. I put it to him directly: 'What did actually kill Peg? What did she die of?'

'Peg died', he replied, 'of rheumatoid arthritis and its cures'. I think the official report on her death said septicaemia, which I suppose is another way of saying the same thing. Peg was seventy when she died. Shortly afterwards I wrote to the Australian Medical Association just stating that Peg had died after a long illness and that I could not express sufficiently my gratitude to the profession for the way she had been looked after through that illness. I listed the doctors—it was quite a long list—making the point that apart from the skilled treatment she received, she had the sort of advice that kept her buoyed up. It was always friendly and optimistic. The AMA wrote and thanked me for the letter and they published it in their journal.

There was no funeral. Peg and I had an understanding—in fact my whole family shares my feelings on this—that we don't have funerals and we don't go to funerals. I think it started in my mind back when my father died and had an enormous funeral. I remember the horse-drawn cabs with men wearing top hats and with black bows on their whips, and the procession that seemed to go on for miles. I can remember thinking to myself, 'Tomorrow, this isn't going to mean anything. It's not going to help the situation at all. Father will be dead and this will all be over.' Anyway, we Bowdens don't have funerals.

It was arranged that Peg would be cremated and they would let us know when it was over, which they did. And the death notice that was published in the paper was in the past tense, which removed the obligation of other people to attend her funeral.

In 1989, at the age of 82, I still live in my house at 37 Maning Avenue, Sandy Bay, Hobart. It is a beautiful house and most of its charm is due to Peggy. Her taste was impeccable and she had a yen for antique furniture and Persian rugs. We didn't have much money but we used to buy a bit here and there from second-hand places and antique shops. Peg also left me a legacy of domestic competence in the best possible way. While she could she showed me how to prepare good, decent food, and how to look after the house, and her help and training has helped make life worthwhile without her. I grow tomatoes and vegetables in my garden and greenhouse, I am surrounded by the most superbly supportive family and grandchildren, not only on my side—my own family—but Peggy's side. They are all tremendous people and they have been an absolute tower of strength, and this includes not only my own family, but the extraordinarily sensitive and understanding people they married.

I find that in my present life I have, I think, rather unmercifully depended on Lisa in particular to take over Peg's role in matters of advice and opinion. If it is irksome to her, she has never shown it. I get the same combination of sensitivity and directness. I don't quite know how life would be without her.

I live on in my house and I hope I can continue to live in my house until such time as they lead me or carry me away.